Praise for
SOLDIERS AND KINGS

Winner of the National Book Award for
Nonfiction • Longlisted for the PEN America/Jean Stein
Award • A *Time* 10 Best Nonfiction Books of the Year • An
NPR Book We Love • A *New York Times* Notable Book •
A *Boston Globe* Best Book of the Year

"This anthropological deep dive with an unmistakably human (and humane) voice is the result of seven years embedded with smugglers moving migrants across Mexico. Without fear, favor, or judgment, De León honors his subject's complexity, neither sentimentalizing nor condemning."
—*The Boston Globe* (Best Books of the Year)

"For seven years, De León tracked the lives of both migrants crossing the border and the *coyotes* who shepherded them. He unveils a profoundly intimate account of their world—of the work, the terror, and the human connections made on their treacherous journeys.... *Soldiers and Kings* seeks to buck the dangerous stereotypes that are often associated with migrants and smugglers, and instead shows their fully nuanced stories."
—*Time* (100 Must-Read Books of the Year)

"A unique read that emerges from seven years of research and firsthand experiences lived by the author amidst smugglers, or *guías*, on the U.S.-Mexico border.... De León offers a glimpse into a world rarely seen or understood."
—*Los Angeles Times*

"A rare inside look at human smuggling on the border ... Smuggling, [De León] says, 'is not the problem.' But as his own book memorably recounts, in a world with no shortage of problems, it's nevertheless one of them."
—*The New York Times*

"The author has an extraordinary talent for offering vignettes of these characters, teasing out their histories and inner lives . . . then drawing smart and sweeping conclusions. . . . *Soldiers and Kings* is a brilliant work of both journalistic reportage and engaged anthropology." —*London Review of Books*

"The book's great virtue is in its close attention to the individual lives of its small group of central characters. . . . Toggling between the macro and the micro: the globe-spanning, incomprehensibly vast forces that have brought these smugglers' lives into being, as well as their own individual struggles to make something of what the world has made of them." —*The New Republic*

"UCLA anthropology professor De León embedded with a group of *coyotes*, or migrant guides, over the course of several years to study the people behind the industry of human smuggling. His book seeks to dispel stereotypes about those involved with moving migrants across Mexico." —*Orange County Register*

"This is a real one. A work of extraordinary reportage and compassion, *Soldiers and Kings* takes us deep inside the lives of smugglers guiding desperate migrants across Latin America. One breathtaking scene follows another, rendered in vibrant, unsparing prose documenting grinding poverty and violence, but also young love and redemption. It will shock you, move you, and leave you changed." —Matthew Desmond, Pulitzer Prize–winning and *New York Times* bestselling author of *Evicted* and *Poverty, by America*

"A terrifying journey alongside men who have given up being men and are transformed into 'ghosts or demons or dust.' De León, our *guía*, documents their intergenerational tragedies with full complexity. This book ultimately leads one to question what it means to be human, and, as such, to examine what one's own responsibility is to this global issue. An enlightening, frightening, unforgettable read." —Sandra Cisneros, bestselling author of *The House on Mango Street*

"Rigorously researched and deeply felt, this book is for everyone who wants to understand the despair, sorrow, and violence that migrants and their guides experience each and every day while trying not to lose their humanity. Eloquent and urgent, it calls out to all of us to imagine what a better world might be."

—Ruth Behar, author of *The Vulnerable Observer: Anthropology That Breaks Your Heart*

"*Soldiers and Kings* is utterly captivating from page one. Jason De León's groundbreaking access to the lives of *coyotes*, or *guías*, offers a rare and intimate glimpse into their humanity. *Soldiers and Kings* is a powerful, immersive experience that will challenge readers' preconceptions and leave a lasting impression. Beautifully written, surprising, deeply informative, and intellectually provocative, this is a must read for anyone seeking a deep understanding of the human experience in the face of adversity."

—Laurence Ralph, author of *Sito: An American Teenager and the City that Failed Him*

"The stories of the guides made me cry at their immense suffering, laugh at their playful jokes, rage at the injustice they face, and feel inspired by their will to survive. . . . *Soldiers and Kings* [is] holy work." —*The Christian Century*

"Anthropologist and MacArthur Fellow De León offers a staggering view of the people who help move asylum seekers. His conversations with participants in a vast migration put human faces to a shadowy concept, and his story is illuminating and often heartrending in its telling." —*Booklist*

"A harrowing account of the work of human smugglers in bringing aspirational immigrants to America's southern border . . . [and] an exemplary ethnography of central importance to any discussion of immigration policy or reform."

—*Kirkus Reviews* (starred review)

ABOUT THE AUTHOR

||||||||||

Jason De León is Lloyd E. Cotsen Endowed Chair of Archaeology, professor of Anthropology and Chicana/o Studies, and director of the Cotsen Institute of Archaeology at the University of California, Los Angeles. He is also executive director of the Undocumented Migration Project, a 501(c)(3) research, arts, and education collective that seeks to raise awareness about migration issues globally. He is a 2017 MacArthur Foundation Fellow and author of the award-winning book *The Land of Open Graves: Living and Dying on the Migrant Trail.*

SOLDIERS AND KINGS

Survival and Hope in the World of Human Smuggling

Jason De León

PENGUIN BOOKS

PENGUIN BOOKS
An imprint of Penguin Random House LLC
1745 Broadway, New York, NY 10019
penguinrandomhouse.com

Copyright © 2024 by The Bigham De León Trust

Penguin Random House values and supports copyright. Copyright fuels creativity,
encourages diverse voices, promotes free speech, and creates a vibrant culture.
Thank you for buying an authorized edition of this book and for complying
with copyright laws by not reproducing, scanning, or distributing any part of it
in any form without permission. You are supporting writers and allowing
Penguin Random House to continue to publish books for every reader.
Please note that no part of this book may be used or reproduced in any manner
for the purpose of training artificial intelligence technologies or systems.

Interior photographs by Jason De León

Designed by Alexis Farabaugh
Map by Haeden Stewart

ISBN 9780593298602 (paperback)

THE LIBRARY OF CONGRESS HAS CATALOGED THE HARDCOVER EDITION AS FOLLOWS:
Names: De León, Jason, 1977– author.
Title: Soldiers and kings : survival and hope in the
world of human smuggling / Jason De León.
Description: [New York] : Viking, [2024] |
Includes bibliographical references and index.
Identifiers: LCCN 2023017436 (print) | LCCN 2023017437 (ebook) |
ISBN 9780593298589 (hardcover) | ISBN 9780593298596 (ebook)
Subjects: LCSH: Human smuggling—Latin America—History. |
Latin America—Emigration and immigration—History.
Classification: LCC HQ281 .D45 2024 (print) |
LCC HQ281 (ebook) | DDC 364.1/372098—dc23/eng/20230518
LC record available at https://lccn.loc.gov/2023017436
LC ebook record available at https://lccn.loc.gov/2023017437

First published in the United States of America by
Viking, an imprint of Penguin Random House LLC, 2024
Published in Penguin Books 2025

Printed in the United States of America
1st Printing

Some names and identifying characteristics have been changed
to protect the privacy of the individuals involved.

The authorized representative in the EU for product safety and compliance is
Penguin Random House Ireland, Morrison Chambers, 32 Nassau Street,
Dublin D02 YH68, Ireland, https://eu-contact.penguin.ie.

FOR LORENZO

Are you living the life you chose?

Are you living the life that chose you?

⸺

JASON ISBELL

Contents

Introduction	*1*
ONE. Honor y Patria	*17*

I. Soldiers

TWO. In the House of Pakal	*41*
THREE. Charismatic and Reckless	*58*
FOUR. La Reina del Sur	*80*
FIVE. Foot Soldiers	*95*
SIX. Papo and Alma	*110*

II. Kings of Pain

SEVEN. Duke of Earl	*131*
EIGHT. Kingston	*151*
NINE. Genesis	*172*
TEN. Apocalipsis	*186*
ELEVEN. Dinero, Dinero	*193*
TWELVE. Robin Hood	*206*

III. Exodus

THIRTEEN. Resurrection 221

FOURTEEN. Escape 228

FIFTEEN. Things Fall Apart 237

SIXTEEN. Liberty without Tricks or False Promises 250

SEVENTEEN. Suerte 257

EIGHTEEN. Xibalba 267

NINETEEN. "We Aren't Playing" 280

TWENTY. Temptation 290

TWENTY-ONE. The Future Belongs
to Those Who Dream 300

TWENTY-TWO. The Soldier Who Would Be King 311

TWENTY-THREE. Epilogue 326

Acknowledgments 331

Appendix: Soundtrack 339

Notes 345

Index 355

Chiapas, Mexico

Esperando

Chiapas, Mexico

Pakal-Ná

"Decent people shouldn't live here." Lechería, Mexico

Dreamer. Tapachula, Chiapas, Mexico

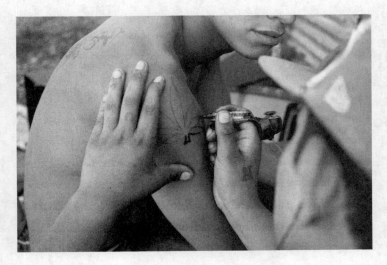

Las vías

Lechería, Mexico

Mormon in training. Pakal-Ná

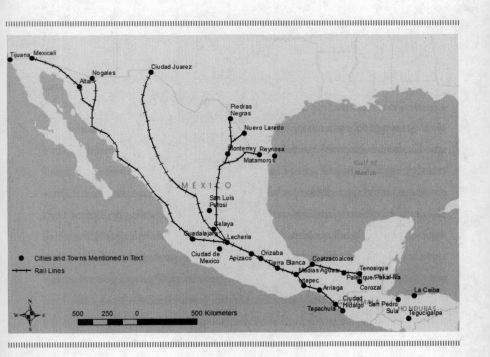

The Migrant Trail through Mexico

MAP BY HAEDEN STEWART

SOLDIERS
AND
KINGS

Introduction

Roberto's murder doesn't warrant much attention. This is not surprising in a place like Honduras, where homicide has become woven into the fabric of daily life.* Still, a local newspaper in San Pedro Sula manages to give him three sentences, although it gets his first name wrong:

> José [*sic*] Roberto Paredes died Friday night at Mario Rivas Hospital. Family members reported that he had tried to travel *mojado* [illegally] to the United States but in Chiapas, Mexico, was stabbed during an assault and admitted to a hospital. After his discharge, he returned to Honduras and a few days later his condition worsened and he was brought to Rivas Hospital, where he died after several days.

The story gets most of the basic details right. Roberto was in Mexico illegally when he was stabbed. He later died in Honduras from his wounds. But he wasn't a migrant headed to the United States, at least not anymore. He'd given up that fantasy a while ago. For the past few years, he'd lived as

---

* Honduras has consistently been a leader in homicide globally. Igarape Institute, "Homicide Monitor," January 29, 2023, https://homicide.igarape.org.br.

a street urchin making a little money guiding fellow Hondurans on the Mexican train tracks as they made their way north toward the American dream. What he did for a modest living goes by many names in English and Spanish: smuggler, *coyote*, *pollero*, *pasador*. Interchangeable terms that refer to a person who is paid to help someone get across a geopolitical boundary while avoiding detection by immigration agents. Roberto, like many others in his situation in Mexico, preferred to call himself a *guía*, a guide: a designation with potentially less negative semantic baggage and one that more directly reflects the work. He is the one you follow, the one who can potentially lead you through danger. The one thing you can't call Roberto is a human trafficker. People who are trafficked have that happen against their will, usually through force, fraud, or coercion. Those Roberto smuggled were willing participants who actively sought him out and paid for his services. I repeat, human smuggler and trafficker are very different things, a concept that popular media and the general public often fail to grasp.

One only needs to turn on the news to get the simple point that we are living in a worldwide migration crisis where poverty, violence, political instability, and climate change are forcing millions each year to leave their homes in search of a better existence. Given the rate that global inequality is growing, coupled with rising sea levels, increased drought, and the appearance of environmental monsters like super hurricanes, you don't need to be a soothsayer to predict that things are about to get a lot worse for all of humanity. The response of the Global North has increasingly been to harden its borders and pour money into migrant detention and deportation-industrial complexes. Build barricades. Fire tear gas and rubber bullets at mothers holding their babies. Put children in cages. Deny due process to asylum seekers. But history has shown us that border walls are no match for human determination and the will to live. Our species' survival has long been reliant on our ability to move across the landscape in search of resources and new habitats. Human mobility cannot be stopped. The human spirit cannot be broken.

Introduction | 3

As countries like the United States (and now places like Mexico) attempt to beat back migrants from their front door as if in a scene from P. D. James's *The Children of Men*, the human smuggling industry has ballooned. Sneaking people past border guards has grown from a mom-and-pop business into a billion-dollar global industry that will only become more important as parts of our planet grow to be less and less livable. Roberto, the *guía*, was a tiny cog in the behemoth economy of human smuggling. The media often portrays people like him as "bad guys" who prey on the innocent. But the story is not so simple. As countries make it harder to cross their borders, migrants find it necessary to contract the services of someone like Roberto who can provide protection and safe passage. Arrest and deportation by law enforcement, robbery, kidnapping, extortion, and murder at the hands of transnational criminal organizations: these are the dangers migrants increasingly face. Many have come to see the labor of people like Roberto as necessary and sometimes lifesaving.

This isn't to say that *guías* can't also be thieves, traffickers, murderers, and/or rapists. They can potentially be all those things and then some, which will become apparent as this story unfolds. But people contract smugglers because they give them the benefit of the doubt that no matter what happens, they will eventually get to their final destination, even if it involves hardship and shelling out more cash than was initially agreed upon. All migrants have heard stories of evil smugglers who abuse clients, and a significant number of them have had their own terrible firsthand experiences. But still, migrants make social contracts in good faith with guides in the hope that they will be protectors and not rob them, sell them into slavery, or abandon them in the jungle, desert, or the back of a semitruck. There are just enough "good" smugglers in the world for the economy of clandestine movement to function, even with the constant risk of things taking a bad turn at some point on the journey.

In Western popular media, smugglers are often portrayed as potbellied

Latinos with silver-capped teeth and slick hair. They reek of cologne and drive shiny trucks bought with the hard-earned (or borrowed) money of desperate people trying to get to *la USA*. Roberto defied these stereotypes. He was a skinny, banged-up Honduran kid who was often homeless and living hand to mouth. He rarely had more than $20* to his name and was often more desperate than his clients. He knew how to guide people along the train tracks and through the jungle because he came of age in those dreadful places. But he never saw huge piles of money. He never got to drive a car. He was not a kingpin or someone who called the shots. There was nothing glamorous about his lifestyle or his brutally short existence.

Roberto's modest grave is marked by a wrought iron plaque that bears his name, birthday, and date of death. Somehow the engraver managed to get his last day on earth incorrect. But many would say that the details don't matter. To most, Roberto is a nobody. Just another young man from Honduras with a history of substance abuse and violent behavior. He was someone destined for an early grave, and cemeteries across Central America are full of the skeletons of people just like him: children born into generational poverty whose bleak futures are predetermined before they can even speak; kids who live fast and die fast because those are often the only choices they are given. Roberto is one of those kids. But he is not a nobody. He is a young person with dreams and aspirations who carries hope with him until the very end. Roberto is important enough that people will wail at his funeral and pray for his soul. Someone will scratch "I love you" in the wet concrete that is poured over the top of his tomb.

I will come to know Roberto as a soldier trying to survive on the train tracks in Mexico. He confides in me that he wants out of the smuggling game. It's gotten out of control. Death is breathing down his neck. He wants to run far away and reinvent a life for himself that doesn't include guns or

---

* All money is in U.S. dollars unless noted otherwise.

knives or desperate people doing desperate things. Roberto asks me for help to escape his nightmare. I will have my chance to save him, but I will fail and he will die. The train tracks will take his life, and I will forever carry guilt for the things I didn't do.

As I sit on Roberto's grave in rural Honduras, I ponder the surrounding lush countryside. It's an awe-inspiring landscape that holds no future for so many people who must head north and roll the dice: migrants who will follow the train tracks across Mexico and pray that whatever is waiting for them at the end of the line is better than the cruel hardships and early death that they are running from in Honduras. This book is about Roberto and others like him who get caught up in the smuggling game. People on the train tracks who go by a thousand nicknames: Kingston, Flaco, Alma, Papo, Chino, Santos. People whose birth names are often mysteries until the end, when they are inscribed onto tombstones. In this book you will learn about the lives of smugglers and their intimate relationships with death. Destitute men and women who find themselves trapped in a world of violence and fast money while in search of hope; a world of *guías* who have no one to lead them to safety except maybe themselves. This is a journey down those train tracks.

Oral Histories of Violence

I am looking in the rearview mirror at the many gang tattoos etched across Flaco's bare arms and chest. His big frame takes up the middle seat as he tries to get comfortable between his two soldiers who flank him. Flaco sees me looking at him. He flashes a devious smile as we pull onto the Mexican highway and head toward a nearby market to buy coconut milk, a key ingredient needed to add flavor to a pot of iguanas we left simmering back at the safe house.

6 | SOLDIERS AND KINGS

Flaco: Hey, bro, thank you.

Jason: For what?

Flaco: For giving us a ride to the *tienda*. For letting us ride in your car and not being afraid.

Jason: What's to be afraid of?

Flaco: Well, you know. We could steal your car.

Jason: It's a rental. Feel free to steal it; it's insured.

Flaco: *Jajajaja.* No, but *en serio.* Thank you, bro, for not being afraid of us, for letting us sit in the car and not worrying about us doing something. A lot of gringos who come down here are afraid of migrants. They hold their bag tight as if we are going to steal it. It's cool that you trust us enough to give us a ride.

Jason: Well, if I can't trust you, how do I expect you to trust me? How can I expect you to be comfortable with me asking lots of questions and taking photos of everything? I'm going to be here awhile. You're going to get sick of me asking stupid questions and taking pictures of everything. You'll get sick of me recording all of our conversations. The only way that I can start to understand your job is if I trust you and you trust me.

I am often asked how I have gotten access to guides like Flaco. How have I persuaded him and others who are involved in a range of illegal and often

Introduction | 7

violent activities to let me follow them around, take their pictures, and record their voices? The answer is simple. I've committed many years of my life to driving people to the grocery store, to eating roasted iguana on the train tracks, to dancing to reggaeton coming out of a janky boom box in some bleak safe house in a forgotten part of Mexico. I've given a lot of my time and energy to being with smugglers as they go about living their lives. While doing all this, I've tried to be as nonjudgmental as possible. We have long been taught that smugglers are the villains in the global migration story and that no sane or ethical person would spend time with those who rob and assault migrants in the name of the almighty dollar. But the story is never black-and-white, and to understand smuggling in all its complexity requires a lot of work.

Participant Observation

This project would not have been possible without the benefit of time on my side. I'm not a journalist who has a fast-approaching deadline. There is no editor back at the office telling me I need a sound bite for tomorrow's paper. I'm an anthropologist who has the luxury of dedicating years to a single project at my own pace. It helps that I am married to an anthropologist who understands the realities of fieldwork and who shares the burden with me.*

Anthropologists often play the long game, which means I can spend days or weeks or months with people, seemingly doing nothing, while in reality I'm soaking in all the important minutiae before something "interesting" or

---

* Over the years, my wife and I have developed a parenting strategy that allows one of us to be absent for extended periods of time. In other moments, we have had to relocate our entire household to a foreign country for months while one of us pursues research, which is what happened during this project. For good or for bad, fieldwork is a family affair.

out of the ordinary happens. I observe and sometimes participate in people's daily lives for extended periods of time, although with smugglers (for legal reasons) I tend to just do a lot of watching and listening. Many refer to this approach as "deep hanging out," although it is more widely known as an anthropological method called *participant observation*. Regardless of what you label it, the goal is to spend a significant amount of time in a community in order to produce a detailed and nuanced ethnographic description of people, their environment, and the sociopolitical, economic, and historical forces that shape their existence. My long-term commitment to studying human smuggling has helped me build trust and rapport with marginalized people who are at best ignored and at worst demonized.

Some might compare what anthropologists do to a form of slow journalism, of which there are some excellent examples. While there are a few parallels to journalists who use participant observation, I would argue that anthropology in its current (and increasingly critical and decolonizing) form is generally more self-aware and more concerned about positionality, representation, and the repercussions our work can have on people's lives. I like to think of anthropology as a deeply intense and engaged form of representing the experiences of others that comes with the neurotic hang-up of constantly questioning why we are doing the work, how we are doing the work, and if we should be doing the work in the first place. We are plagued with being the Larry Davids of the social sciences, researchers who aren't afraid to openly confront the many socially awkward and emotionally challenging moments that happen both in the field and later, when we have to put pen to paper to describe the lives of others.

For close to seven years, I followed smugglers as they moved from the jungles of southern Chiapas to the deserts of northern Mexico. I spent endless hours with Flaco and many other guides in safe houses. I partied with them on the train tracks and in shitty bars. I watched as they tried to survive while maintaining their self-respect in a world full of indignities. I listened in Mexico, Honduras, and the United States as they explained their dreams, aspirations, and worries. However, for as much access as I was given, there were certain things I didn't do. I didn't ride on the tops of freight trains or accompany people as they tried to sneak past immigration agents, as others have done. I am a firm believer in the limits of participant observation, and I know that my presence during certain parts of the smuggling process would have been illegal and problematic for me and potentially dangerous for those I work with. Therefore, I spent most of my time with smugglers either when they were stationary and waiting to make a next move north or when they were between jobs.* I also made it clear from the beginning that I wanted to understand and observe how smuggling works, but I didn't want to put migrants who were being moved in danger or compromising positions. This meant that I mostly avoided interviewing those who were being smuggled because of worries that they would say something that could anger their guide and put their trip at risk. This isn't to say that I don't directly address abuses carried out by smugglers in this book. I tackle that issue head-on in many chapters. However, this discussion of abuses tends to come directly from the mouths of guides themselves.

Trust

I could easily write a book about the evil things that smugglers do without ever having to leave the comfort of my office, but that is not my intention here. When I began this project many years ago, I told myself that I had no business writing about *guías* unless I could find something human and

---

* I tracked smugglers' progress across Mexico and met them at different stages of the journey, but never physically traveled with them when they had clients in tow.

relatable about their existence. It's easy to dehumanize people, especially those caught up in the illicit economies of clandestine movement. But reproducing the trope of the evil smuggler is lazy and does nothing to help us understand why the system exists in the first place, nor does it provide any useful insight into its inner workings. Admittedly, understanding this furtive and vicious process requires some suspension of judgment. It also necessitates becoming close to people who are often doing things that I find problematic, if not reprehensible. This does not mean that I condone the various forms of violence that I discuss in this book. Anthropologists use the concept of *cultural relativism* to describe our attempts to avoid evaluating members of a different sociocultural group by our own morals, laws, and practices. However, cultural relativism has its limits, and there were many moments during fieldwork when I had to speak up and express my discomfort about things I heard or observed, even if it potentially put me in danger. I was never a fly on the wall, nor was I ever a wholly "objective" observer. I have my own ethics and morals that I brought with me into the field, and I had to grapple with them throughout this project. Because of this, I tended to gravitate toward smugglers I felt some level of comfort with, and I avoided those who gave off a bad vibe. This meant keeping a distance from people who scared me, especially those I suspected of being involved in the direct assault of migrants.

As part of their job, smugglers have to be good judges of character and of difficult situations. In what was often just a few hours, they sized me up pretty quickly and decided whether I could be trusted. In all my initial meetings with *guías*, I fully disclosed who I was and what I was doing. People then had to evaluate my character and determine if they believed me enough to be sure I wouldn't screw them over later. Obviously, not everyone I met on the migrant trail wanted an anthropologist following them around and documenting their lives. But those who did gave me a surprising amount of access. Over the years, I recorded countless hours of oral histories and interviews in Spanish and Spanglish, with a significant amount of American slang mixed in, thanks to the fact that many people I interviewed had spent time in the United States.* Through handwritten notes, photography, audio recordings, and video, I also captured hundreds of everyday moments across a wide range of contexts, primarily in Mexico and Honduras.† In great detail and through various means, smugglers described their troubled and difficult lives, which often implicated them in illegal acts. Those whose lives I've followed have faith that I won't use their words‡ to get them in legal trouble or that I will publicly out them.§

The *guías* in this book trusted me to tell their stories, but this relationship was a two-way street. I had to trust people to guide me through the many potentially dangerous situations I found myself in. Thankfully, the mostly male smugglers¶ I came to know well treated me like a student or a little

---

* Dialogue in this book includes words like "foo" (short for "fool") and "nigga" that were often used by smugglers who had lived and been incarcerated in the United States.

† I also collected and analyzed copious text messages, voice messages, cell phone videos, and photographs that people sent me.

‡ Interview excerpts and dialogue come from either transcribed audio or video recordings or notes I made during and after a conversation. Most conversations presented in this book were in Spanish and have been translated to English, with some words left untranslated for effect. Many of the smugglers I worked with spoke some English, and parts of our conversations were often conducted in Spanglish.

§ I have taken several steps to protect people's privacy in this book, including using pseudonyms for all smugglers who are still alive, and changing or omitting certain details from backstories to prevent their identification. Consent from research participants was verbal, and there is no paper trail connecting their identity to any of the data.

¶ Although women were often present in migrant safe houses, the majority of guides moving people on the train tracks were men, and those were the people I often had the most access to. To date, little attention has been paid to the important role that women play in the smuggling business, although see Gabriella E. Sanchez, *Women in Migrant Smuggling: A Case-law Analysis* (Vienna: United Nations Office on Drugs and Crime, 2019); Howard Campbell, "Female Drug Smugglers on the U.S.-Mexico Border: Gender, Crime, and Empowerment," *Anthropological Quarterly* 81, no. 1 (2008): 233–67; Gabriella Sanchez, "Women's Participation in the Facilitation of Human Smuggling: The Case of the US Southwest," in "Irregular Migration and Brokerage," ed. Cetta Manwaring and Noelle Brigden, special issue, *Geopolitics* 21, no. 2 (2016): 387–406.

brother they vouched for, guarded, and instructed in the ways of the train tracks and their hypermasculine world. They taught me whom to speak to and how to speak to them. They showed me whom to avoid and advised me when to keep my mouth shut. They invited me into many intimate moments but were also clear as day when they wanted me to leave. This project would not have succeeded without the kindness of strangers. But before I take you on a winding journey down the train tracks, perhaps it's important to know a little about me (your anthropological guide) and how I got here.

Among Strangers

There are many things from my childhood that suggest I was destined to become an anthropologist. As an Army brat, I spent the first decade of my life bouncing between military bases in California, Germany, Pennsylvania, Missouri, and Texas. I grew accustomed to being the new kid in school who had to make friends on the fly. I got used to being one of the few brown students in the room and definitely the only Mexican-Filipino within a hundred miles of most places. I grew up a stranger in many foreign lands.

My journey as a child constantly navigating new cultural spaces made me curious about the world and instilled in me an outgoing nature that was partially a defense mechanism. I made and lost a lot of friends in different places over the years and thus tried never to take relationships for granted. This became especially true after my parents' divorce, when I was eight years old, which led to spending three traumatizing years with my father in South Texas, just a few miles north of the U.S.-Mexico border. My father worked evenings as a security guard at a trailer park, which meant that I became a third-grade latchkey kid who spent a lot of time alone, watching

Introduction | 13

1950s sitcoms on Nickelodeon and fending for myself. This was a period when I tried to fill my solitary days and nights with hours of being outside with my friends. I never wanted to go home. I couldn't stand being alone.

For as long as I can remember, I've gravitated toward strangers because of my genuine interest in understanding how the other half lives. But I also think that I seek people out because of a loneliness I carry inside myself. I'm not saying that I live a miserable or isolated life; I have a wonderful family and good friends who constantly remind me that I am a very lucky person. But there is something about meeting strangers and connecting with them that brings me back to my childhood and my need to find comfort and inspiration in a seemingly isolating world. It wasn't until I discovered anthropology that I was able to put a name to this eternal quest I've been on.

My undergraduate career in anthropology was a long and winding road trip with many detours and crashes. I dropped out of UCLA in the first quarter of my freshman year. At the time, I felt like higher education was unwelcoming to a brown first-generation student like me. I also believed that there was life outside the classroom that I needed to experience. After moving back home following a grand total of five weeks in college, I discovered a student loan check waiting for me in my mom's mailbox. I took that money and bought a 1982 Ford cargo van so that I could tour with a punk band I had started in high school. For forty days, seven other dirtbags and I piled into our cramped and malodorous vehicle and meandered from Long Beach, California, to the East Coast and back. Along the way we disappointed microscopic audiences in places like Mobile, Alabama; Little Rock, Arkansas; and New Haven, Connecticut, while surviving on a steady diet of St. Ides, Newports, and Taco Bell. That journey across the United States opened my eyes to many new worlds I would soon find mesmerizing: Drinking cases of shitty beer and making gasoline bonfires with skinheads in Lake Charles, Louisiana. Drinking coffee with our teenage host's dad in a tiny trailer in D'Iberville, Mississippi, while talking about the shared experiences of the poor. Driving around rural Cable, Wisconsin, with a bunch of redneck teenagers listening to Hüsker Dü and being irresponsible with someone's grandma's hunting rifle. It was a time of exotic wildness that confirmed to me that all over the country there were interesting people who liked to tell stories and have a good time, and I wanted to be right there alongside them. It was during this trip that I figured out I was a pretty good listener and that people seemed to enjoy telling me about their lives.

The band thing never worked out, but the touring experiences I accumulated instilled in me a love of travel and a love of being with and learning from strangers with backgrounds different from my own. I didn't know it at the time, but I was doing what anthropologists call *ethnography*. I was immersing myself in the culture of others. I was learning about people by observing and participating in their lives.

After a few years of trying to make music a full-time job, I found myself living in my mom's garage and facing two choices: (1) move in with my grandmother, whom I would kindly describe as an elderly Filipina gangster with a gambling addiction and a propensity for fake heart attacks (à la Redd Foxx saying, "I think this is the big one!"); or (2) go back to UCLA with my tail between my legs and beg them to let me re-enroll. I chose the latter and soon found myself back in school and back to accruing student loan debt.

As a kid, I had always wanted to be Indiana Jones. As soon as I returned to UCLA, I started slogging my way through a bunch of anthropology courses that quickly dispelled my dreams of finding golden monkey skulls while being chased by a runaway boulder. It was during this rude awakening to the realities of archaeological research that I discovered ethnography via a course called Deviance and Abnormality, taught by anthropologist Conerly Casey. That class helped me understand a couple of key things that would profoundly influence my later career. First, I learned that my conceptions of deviant behavior were culturally constructed and often ethnocentric. Instead of judging others by my own cultural standards, I began to

Introduction | 15

examine the world with a more open mind and an eye toward seeing how violent behavior is often not random, nor does it happen in a political or economic vacuum. Professor Casey taught me that violence needs to be contextualized and understood as part of larger sociocultural environments. Second, I started reading ethnographies and became fascinated by the fact that anthropologists made careers out of hanging out with strangers, one of the few things I thought I was actually good at. I eventually completed a PhD in anthropology and went on to start the Undocumented Migration Project (UMP), a nonprofit research, arts, and education collective that seeks to raise awareness about clandestine migration while also helping families locate their loved ones who have died or gone missing in the process.

The first major ethnographic project conducted by the UMP was a multi-year study of the experiences of people crossing the U.S.-Mexico border that culminated in my book *The Land of Open Graves: Living and Dying on the Migrant Trail* (with photographs by my longtime collaborator Michael Wells). That book focused on the 1994 Border Patrol policy known as Prevention Through Deterrence, a security paradigm that for decades has been purposefully funneling people toward places like the Sonoran Desert of Arizona where the rugged natural environment is intended to act as a weapon against migrants. In that harsh environment, border crossers have to traverse hundreds of square miles of desert and deal with extreme temperatures, a scarcity of water, and many other "natural" obstacles. For five years, I hung out in humanitarian shelters in northern Mexico and interviewed people who had just been deported or who were planning to enter the desert. I hiked hundreds of miles of trails to document the harsh landscape that people have been trying to get across since the mid-1990s. Along the way, I collected thousands of backpacks, water bottles, and other artifacts that had been left behind. I also worked closely with families of those who had died or gone missing en route. By the end of the project, it was clear to me that the U.S. Border Patrol had outsourced nature to brutalize millions of people and that thousands had died or disappeared as a result of Prevention Through Deterrence.

After many years of working with and writing about migrants, I knew I was missing part of the story. Smugglers had been present throughout my fieldwork in Arizona and Mexico, but always on the periphery. Migrants talked about them as a necessary evil needed to help one avoid detection by law enforcement. Border Patrol blamed them for the thousands of deaths that happened in the Sonoran Desert, which were actually the direct result of immigration policies. I knew that the story was much more complicated than the simplistic dichotomy that was being proposed. Smugglers weren't walking people through the desert because they liked hiking. They were in the desert because border policies had forced people there, and migrants needed guides to get across that "hostile terrain."

Unfortunately, when people put faith in illicit economies, there is no guarantee that things will work out or that those you pay for protection won't betray you. I soon began to ask a series of questions: Who are smugglers? How does someone get started in that occupation? What does their daily life look like? How does it feel to be responsible for providing lifesaving passage while also being implicated in (or directly responsible for) the many forms of violence that migrants experience? This book is an attempt to answer those questions. It's also an attempt to walk in the shoes of those who are the most despised in the migration process. Some critics will undoubtedly say that I am doing the Devil's work by trying to "humanize" smugglers. Let's be clear. That is not my goal here. I am not trying to "humanize" anyone. Instead, I begin this book with the seemingly radical proposition that those who try to make a living guiding people across hardening geopolitical boundaries are themselves human.

CHAPTER ONE

Honor y Patria

I push around an overpriced cup of coffee while my reflection stares back at me from a polished marble table. Everything in this restaurant is clean and bright and perfumed with that pungent disinfectant smell characteristic to Latin America. CNN in Spanish plays loudly on a television mounted above the bar. Talking heads drown out the traffic sounds of Tegucigalpa, Honduras, outside. I am seated among lawyers, diplomats, and other fancy people who consume their continental breakfasts in a country with some of the highest poverty and murder rates in the world.

The landscape beyond the walls of this restaurant is overrun with Honduran criminals, some with face tattoos and some in three-piece suits. These are people who prey on rural and urban communities alike while exploiting the country's geography to capitalize on the Western Hemisphere's drug trade. Juan Orlando Hernández, the outgoing president of Honduras whose own brother is a politician turned convicted narcotrafficker, has long been suspected of having deep ties to the Central American drug trade. Hondurans jokingly refer to cocaine by his name. *Oye, perro, let me get some of that good Juan Orlando shit!* After decades of internal political corruption,

U.S. military and economic interventionist policies that disproportionately benefit Honduran elites, and a 2009 coup d'état, many citizens have lost faith in their government's ability to protect their rights or ensure a functioning democracy. Outside this café lies the real Anchuria.

I am here to interview members of the Grupo de Operaciones Especiales Tácticas (GOET), one of the Obama administration's secret weapons against undocumented migration in Honduras. I am here to learn why people are leaving the country and the international efforts to stop them. I first heard about GOET during a fortuitous conversation with a high-ranking official at Customs and Border Protection. That official miraculously granted me access to these agents in hopes I would write something to help the American public understand what is actually happening in Central America and in Mexico.

The GOET agents I meet in this restaurant sport Honduran flags on their uniforms, but they should be wearing stars and stripes given their affiliation with the American embassy and the significant amount of support they receive from the U.S. federal government. They are a Honduran police force that largely focuses on stopping their own people from leaving the country and heading toward the United States. GOET's stated primary mission is to identify, detain, and repatriate four classes of migrants: (1) unaccompanied Honduran minors, (2) Honduran citizens under the age of twenty-one who do not have written permission from both parents to travel out of the country, (3) single parents traveling with their children who do not have written permission from their spouse or a judge, and (4) undocumented people coming from countries as close as Nicaragua and as far away as China and Somalia. Little is publicly known about the origins and organization of GOET, but it is clear that they are the brainchild of the Obama administration and that their enforcement work ramped up following the 2014 spike in unaccompanied minors arriving at the U.S.-Mexico border. I am in Tegucigalpa because I want to know more about these agents who are protecting Honduras by preventing young people from leaving a place they can no longer call home.

The men who sit across the table from me all look the same. Stiffly ironed khakis and gelled flattops that you can bounce a quarter off of. They wear polo shirts with arm patches with the words *Honor and Homeland* stitched above an image of a scorpion ready to strike. My U.S. Border Patrol handlers in Arizona and Honduras (yes, Honduras) who facilitated this meeting speak in awe of these federal police officers. They tell me these men have integrity and are tough as nails. They tout GOET's integrity because these agents are regularly polygraphed to prove they aren't taking bribes from organized crime networks. My U.S. handlers know these men are tough because they have put them through the ringer during training sessions at military bases on American soil and on the ground in Honduras. The Border Patrol agents I speak to don't seem to be concerned that training and arming Central American soldiers has repeatedly led to U.S.-supported bloodbaths in places like El Salvador and Guatemala.*

My interviews with these agents are long, but the men all basically say the same things. They uniformly speak of the hell that many Hondurans cannot escape, partly thanks to the work of GOET catching people at the border.† I don't know how to approach these officers, so I am blunt.

---

* You can draw a straight line from the School of the Americas, an elite U.S. government military training center at Fort Benning, Georgia, to events like the 1981 massacre at El Mozote, El Salvador, when U.S.-trained soldiers on a mission to root out left-wing guerillas killed close to a thousand children, women, and men and turned an entire village into a charnel house. See Mark Danner, *The Massacre at El Mozote* (New York: Vintage, 1994); Harsha Walia, *Border & Rule: Global Migration, Capitalism, and the Rise of Racist Nationalism* (Chicago: Haymarket Books, 2021), 45.

† Here I have compiled five interviews into one.

Jason: I've had a lot of people tell me that they would rather die on the train tracks in Mexico than be murdered on a street corner in San Pedro Sula.

GOET Agent: It's true. Many migrants that I've interviewed have also told me they would prefer to die *en el camino* than stay home and wait to die from gang violence or hunger. That's why people decide to leave for the United States. Their job is to try and give their family a better life. That is what all Central Americans are looking for.

This revelation is striking given that it comes from someone who is literally charged with catching his fellow citizens as they try to escape their "home" country. The agent continues.

GOET Agent: If you visit the *colonias* you will see the poverty of [Honduras]. There are mothers and fathers with small kids and babies, and they want to give them a better future. But there is no work. There is no support to help them take care of their kids. There is no other option but to migrate to the United States to find what we call "the American dream."

It is not my intention here to lay out the economic and political history of Honduras. However, it is important to note that this is the setting where O. Henry famously coined the term "banana republic," a foreshadowing of the government corruption and U.S. political and economic intervention that would shape the country's history for over a century. These factors would help create an enormous prosperity gap between the tiny elite class and the rest of the population and mirror a larger pattern seen across Central America.

Honor y Patria | 21

After decades in which the government disenfranchised the working class through neoliberal reforms while simultaneously using the U.S.-backed military to crush attempts by the marginalized to politically mobilize, Honduras has earned the distinction of being the second-poorest country in Latin America (right behind Haiti) and one that often appears to be teetering on the verge of political collapse. The World Bank has estimated that almost half of the country's population (4.8 million people) lives on less than $5.50 per day. Before the impact of COVID-19 and the back-to-back category 4 hurricanes Eta and Iota that devastated the country in 2020, close to 15 percent of Hondurans were living on less than $1.90 a day. Keep in mind that the country is still reeling from the destruction caused by Hurricane Mitch in 1998. The impacts of these more recent disasters have only made things worse and will likely be felt for decades to come. In a nutshell, there is no economic prosperity in sight for the millions of poor Hondurans looking to make ends meet. But one of the GOET agents explains that it's not just hunger that makes Honduras unlivable.

> **GOET Agent:** We are a poor country and the *maras* [gangs], the *pandillas* [gangs], are a huge problem. The *colonias* are full of *mareros* [gang members] who start threatening kids. They tell them that they have to join, and if not, they will kill them. They even start threatening their families. So these kids get scared and leave the country because they are afraid that they will lose their lives. They leave because they don't want to end up like the *maras* who are taking drugs, robbing, assaulting, and killing people.

Mara Salvatrucha. MS-13. 18th Street. *Barrio 18*. Little Salvis. Santa María Salvatrucha. Cycos Locos. Hoover Tiny Locos. Central American gangs go by many names, but in the end these labels all refer to the same basic type of group: poor and disenfranchised young people who exert control over territories and neighborhoods through threats and ruthless violence. With origins in East Los Angeles, gangs like MS-13 and *Barrio 18* engage in warfare with rivals while extorting locals for protection money (*la renta*). They also spend a lot of time and energy forcing young people to join their ranks or face death. For Hondurans, the *maras* have become an unfortunate part of daily life that people must navigate or run from. For many Americans (and the anti-immigrant politicians they support), MS-13 and other transnational gangs have come to play an important role as the tattooed, machete-wielding bogeymen whose supposed threat to suburbia makes a strong case for tougher immigration security measures. What many fail to realize is that it's not MS-13 trying to climb over a border wall or trudge through the desert. Those seeking refuge from Honduras tend to be the youngest and poorest people whose lives are at risk from gang violence.

What interests me most about the GOET agents I speak to is the cognitive dissonance they must experience when trying to stop people (including a lot of unaccompanied minors) who are literally running for their lives.

> **Jason:** After all that you've said about Honduras, do you find it hard arresting kids trying to leave when you know you are sending them back to someplace dangerous?

> **GOET Agent:** Look, immigration is very complex and we have to uphold the law. But when you catch someone and get to know their story about why they are migrating, it makes your heart hurt. It really impacts you. But I have to block out those thoughts because this is my job, and with pain in my soul I have to do it. Yes, it's difficult because you detain people at the border and they say, "I can't go home. The

mareros will kill me if I go back. I have to leave." It's difficult because people will start crying in front of you. You are human like them so you feel their pain. It impacts you. But the law requires that I stop them. The majority of people we catch tell us that they are going to get killed if they return. You really feel for them, but it doesn't matter. We are the law. We have to do our job. If we don't do it, the system won't work.

Jason: That has to be hard.

GOET Agent: It hurts me that people have to migrate, but they have no options. They live in cardboard houses in extreme poverty. They have to migrate because they have nothing. They can't live in our country. They have to leave for the United States because there is no other road for them. There is no other way out.

Jason: And this probably means a rise in smuggling, which also makes your job harder.

GOET Agent: Yes, those in the smuggling business are organized in many different forms and are constantly changing their work routines. They keep getting better at it. That makes our job harder, but as they get better, so do we. They improve and we improve. We are working hard to slow them down and reduce their numbers.

Jason: And the U.S. government helps you do this?

GOET Agent: Yes. We take courses in Honduras given by the Border Patrol where they teach us tactics. We have also received a lot of support from [the Border Patrol], including new technologies. Your government has helped us a lot so that we can reduce the flow of people trying to get to the United States.

Programa Frontera Sur

GOET is by no means an anomaly. It is part of a larger constellation of security initiatives co-sponsored by the U.S. federal government that have been taking place across Latin America for decades. One of the primary goals of all of these projects is to stop the flow of migrants from Honduras, El Salvador, and Guatemala to the United States. This issue gained massive public attention in the summer of 2014 when thousands of unaccompanied minors from Central America (primarily Honduras) showed up at the U.S.-Mexico border. These children ended up on the nightly news as they huddled in overcrowded detention centers in Texas and Arizona. President Obama recognized that this was not a problem to be addressed at our country's southern geopolitical boundary. Instead, his administration began to exert pressure on Mexico to stop Central American migrants before they got within sight of the United States. This pressure resulted in the launch of Programa Frontera Sur, a 2014 Mexican immigration enforcement project that was supposed to help Central American migrants en route by ensuring there was enough infrastructure to protect their rights.

In reality, this binational initiative was less about protecting migrants from abuses and more about ramping up the number of Mexican immigration checkpoints, raids, and deportations. Taking cues from the American handbook, Mexico started to deport more Central American migrants than their northern neighbor. In essence, Programa Frontera Sur is an extension of Prevention Through Deterrence. Instead of relying only on the Sonoran Desert of Arizona to stop migrants, Mexico's vast geography and bolstered immigration security forces now also act as an impediment to movement. More important, the United States is absolved of any responsibility for human rights violations that may happen on Mexican soil (even if they are partially footing the bill).

"File a Report with Our Office"

Escobar's wiry frame makes a surprisingly loud thud when the immigration officer slams him into the side of the van.

"I bet you wouldn't try this shit if I wasn't in handcuffs!" he growls.

"Shut your mouth," the agent responds.

"I'll shut my mouth if you go fuck your mother."

"Goddamnit, Escobar," I say under my breath. I look at him and put my index finger to my mouth in hopes that he will keep quiet and not make things worse than they already are. While he is pinned to the side of the van, I sit on the sidewalk and bake in the unforgiving afternoon sun of southern Chiapas, Mexico. A tall Mexican immigration agent with thick jowls hovers over me as if I am a misbehaving child.

"You shouldn't be hanging out with these Hondurans," he says, pointing at Escobar. "Your friends are very bad people."

"I am sorry," I say. "I don't want any trouble. Will you please let him go? He didn't do anything."

"Your friend has no papers, so he is going back to his country."

Escobar hears this and starts softly bumping his head against the van in silent frustration. His hands are bound behind his back, so he tries to wipe away a tear with his shoulder.

The tall man with thick jowls continues to scold me. "This is what happens when you start poking around where you shouldn't be." He doesn't appreciate the fact that I have been talking to Central American migrants about run-ins they have recently had with corrupt Mexican immigration agents. Run-ins that usually involve beatings, robbery, kidnapping, and extortion. Those extracurricular activities are lucrative, and a nosy anthropologist like me is bad for business. He also doesn't like the fact that I'm friends with Escobar, a low-level smuggler who makes a living by helping migrants avoid people like the tall man with thick jowls.

"I am so sorry," I say as I begin to cry. "Please just let my friend go and I'll do whatever you want. I'll leave town. I promise."

"It's too late for that," he says with a smirk. "Your friend is going back to Honduras."

Escobar sees me crying and tries to reassure me with a smile and head nod.

"*Oye, papi*," he coolly says to the agent, "you think I really care about this? You think I am afraid to go back to Honduras? You can't do anything to me. Send me back. I don't give a fuck. You can't stop me. I'll be back soon, but next time I won't have handcuffs on. I'll see you in five days on the train tracks, you son of a bitch!"

As the van pulls away, Escobar grins at me through a barred window.

"Have a good night," the tall man with thick jowls says as he leaves me standing on the sidewalk crying.

A few days later Escobar calls from the train tracks: "I told you I'd be back."

Six weeks before this encounter, I meet the man with thick jowls for the first time.

THE JUNGLE HUMIDITY of southern Mexico is crushing us. I stare up at a sputtering ceiling fan that offers false hope. From the audience, I watch as dark stains form in real time under the armpits and around the neck of our guest speaker, who stands next to the tall man with thick jowls. I fight drowsiness as the stocky black-haired agent at the front of the room reads aloud dense paragraphs of text off his digital slides.

> We are from the office of the Fiscalía Especializada en Delitos Cometidos en Contra Inmigrantes [Special Prosecutor for Crimes Committed Against Immigrants] (FEDCCI) that was started in 2008 with the intention of protecting migrants here in Chiapas because this is a primary crossing place for people coming from El Salvador, Guatemala, Honduras, Nicaragua, and Cuba. Our office was created to protect migrants because our constitution considers them to have rights and be protected as soon as they enter Mexico.

FEDCCI (also simply referred to as the Fiscalía) has graciously offered to give this presentation so that my research team can hear about their work and the impact that Programa Frontera Sur has recently had on migration. It seemed like a helpful gesture. I later realized this was an opportunity for them to learn our faces and spy on our activities. The speaker passes a cloth over his wet face and continues.

> Here in the Palenque region, the crime we most often see is human smuggling. When we detect a person who is transporting people,

what they call a *guía*, we detain them and transfer them to the federal police . . . We have been especially focused on *anti-mara* [anti-gang] activities in the region. *Maras* have been intimidating local inhabitants and migrants passing through the area, creating insecurity and fear. As a result of our recent operations carried out in Pakal-Ná, a municipality of Palenque, we have dismantled the criminal gang known as the Hollywood Locos of MS-13. They were extorting migrants and requiring them to pay a *cuota* [fee] of $100 to be able to continue their journey north. Those who cannot pay are threatened and often thrown off the train. They are then kidnapped by another group who holds them hostage until they can pay the *cuota*. These assailants typically use knives, machetes, and handguns to threaten their victims.

What this federal agent fails to mention are two key points. First, for many, paying the *cuota* to the gangs and cartels has long been part of the process. Migrants expect to hand over cash at various points in their journey to ensure safe passage. However, they often rely on their *guía* to make sure fees are paid to the right people and that no harm comes to them after payment. This is because guides these days tend to have a gang affiliation, which helps facilitate this economic exchange. Without a go-between, migrants may pay the *cuota* and still end up being thrown off the top of a train or in a shallow grave. If your *guía* is homies with the gangs who are collecting money, it makes everything run much smoother. Government officials say that arresting smugglers protects migrants, but in reality this just makes them more vulnerable and their journeys more difficult.*

---

* Arresting smugglers and separating them from their clients is a tactic that the U.S. government has used along its southern border, and one that they falsely describe as being a protective measure. This practice actually increases the risks that migrants face; see Jason De León, "The

The other thing the Fiscalía fails to acknowledge is that the rise in criminal activity targeting migrants is the direct result of initiatives carried out by them and others as part of Programa Frontera Sur. Heightened security measures make travel more difficult, leading border crossers to take remote routes. Criminals, who were targeting migrants before the launch of Programa Frontera Sur, now find it even easier to tax and assault people. In response to this rise in violence, gangs like MS-13 have become involved in smuggling, and people now pay them for protection against others. Increased security leads to more danger and higher costs, all of which means more business for smugglers.

Before advancing to the next slide, the agent turns to get approval from the tall man with thick jowls, who solemnly nods. Someone in the audience asks about the rumor that the Fiscalía is conducting illegal raids on trains in search of migrants. Another person asks if the Fiscalía ever hands migrants over to immigration officials for deportation, a direct violation of their office's mandate. You don't have to be in Chiapas very long before you start hearing stories that Mexican federal agents are just as bad as the gangs when it comes to extorting people. Our guest speaker seems to be allergic to these questions. He deflects and redirects.

A few weeks after the presentation, I see the tall man with thick jowls at the local migrant shelter run by a group of nuns.* He is there to give a presentation about how the Fiscalía is committed to protecting human rights. He stands up in front of dozens of weary and exhausted people who are

---

Efficacy and Impact of the Alien Transfer Exit Program: Migrant Perspectives from Nogales, Sonora, Mexico," *International Migration* 51, no. 2 (2013): 10–23.

* Migrant shelters in Mexico are often run by religious organizations or nonprofits that are funded by private donations, churches, and support from international NGOs and the Mexican government. For a discussion of migrant shelters in Mexico, see John Doering-White, "In the Shadow of the Beast: Violence and Dignity along the Central American Migrant Trail" (PhD diss., University of Michigan, Ann Arbor, 2019).

mostly from Honduras and asks, "How many of you have experienced an assault while traveling through Mexico?" Almost every woman and man in the crowded room raises their hand. "If that is the case, we recommend that you file a report with our office and with the police," he says.

A scrawny kid in the back stands up and asks, "What if it *was* the police that robbed you?" The entire room erupts in knowing laughter, a cacophony of voices confirming this migrant universal truth.

The tall man with thick jowls tries to take control of the crowd. "Sir, please come see us after the meeting so that we can make a report. We are here to help."

After the agent leaves, a Honduran man whispers to me, "I've already been to the Fiscalía's office. That's where they tied me to a chair. That's where they tortured me until my family sent money."

From Point A to Point Z

For many decades, the standard profile of an undocumented migrant attempting to enter the United States was someone who was young, male, and leaving Mexico for largely economic reasons. This made the system of clandestine border crossing relatively easy to follow. Mexican migrants would contract a *coyote* who was well known in their home community, usually someone operating at a mom-and-pop level. It was good to hire a local smuggler so that if things went bad on the trail, you knew whose door to bang on with pitchforks and torches. The *coyote* who was hired would either be the one to physically guide the client to the United States, or they would pass them off to colleagues who would be entrusted to fulfill the contract for a fee ranging between $3,500 and $7,500. Half of the money would be provided up front to the *coyote*, who would be tasked with paying various expenses associated with the journey.* Upon arrival in the United States, the other half of the fee would be wired and the client would be released.

In recent years, the demographics of border crossers have changed. The majority of those attempting to enter the United States are now from Central America. This has made the migration process more complicated and convoluted. One of the major differences between Mexican migrants and those coming from places like Honduras is that the latter have longer and more difficult journeys that require crossing numerous geopolitical boundaries and avoiding law enforcement in multiple countries. This means that Central Americans often have to contract smugglers for different parts of the trip well before arriving at the U.S.-Mexico border. They also pay thousands of dollars more per journey. Another distinction between these two groups is that, unlike Mexicans, who are likely to have relatives in the United States who arrived during previous waves of migration, Hondurans often have smaller social networks (and fewer prospects) on the other side of the border. This is especially true for the many young people who leave Honduras in the middle of the night because of threats of gang violence. They often start their journeys with no real game plan for what to do next other than to stay alive. People may find themselves in perpetual motion on the migrant trail in search of something better or at least safer than what they are leaving behind. Some will make it all the way north and try their luck crossing the border. Some will stay in Mexico and try to make ends meet as undocumented workers or asylum seekers. Others will find easy money through the wild and seemingly attractive world of smuggling.

In previous generations, those fleeing Central America were able to get

---

* This includes hotel rooms and food, a per-person head tax paid to the local cartel that controls entry across the border, supplies for a desert or river crossing, and payment to the *levantador* (driver) who picks people up on the U.S. side and provides transportation to a safe house.

across Mexico relatively quickly by latching on to *la bestia* (the beast), the freight trains known for devouring people's arms, legs, and lives. *La bestia* was dangerous, but at least it moved fast and didn't require a ticket. Programa Frontera Sur added new levels of security on the train tracks that made this route harder to access. In record time, migration became orders of magnitude more difficult. People leaving Central America suddenly found themselves needing help to cross Mexico, which inevitably led to a rise in the role of human smugglers.

Those who engage in smuggling seem to fall into it. They often start off as migrants themselves riding *la bestia* in search of opportunities. Along the way they learn the routes and the tricks needed to avoid detection. They then end up meeting new migrants who know very little about Mexican geography. Nascent smugglers realize they can turn a small profit helping people safely cross the country and serving as liaisons with the gangs and cartels charging fees on the trail. However, employment for these guides is unpredictable and often low-paying. This is because those fleeing Central America typically don't have the upward of $10,000 that is now needed to cover the cost of a trip that doesn't involve hiking through jungles, riding on the tops of freight trains, or spending weeks in ramshackle safe houses. The impoverished and desperate people fleeing the Northern Triangle often start their trip broke and without a *coyote*. They end up cobbling together small amounts of money to contract low-budget *guías* for various parts of the journey.* The people these destitute migrants end up relying on to get across Mexico are often as broke as they are. Instead of the *coyote* with the fat wallet, these days *guías* tend to be active gang members, fellow migrants headed north who have previous crossing experience, or random drifters

---

* The difference between a *guía* and a *coyote* is that the former does the physical work involved in migration and often works for or operates at a smaller, mom-and-pop scale than the latter, although the terms may be used interchangeably for simplicity's sake.

going where the day takes them. As I will detail throughout this book, one of the biggest ironies for Central Americans is that they are leaving home because of gang violence, only to run into the same gangsters on the migrant trail where they are now offering their guide services.

CRACKING DOWN on human smuggling is largely impossible for the simple fact that it is a beast with many heads. Granted, there are certain individuals who sit at the top of unstable criminal hierarchies, but their positions are fleeting and they are easily replaced following arrest or death. The same is true of the grunts who do the bulk of the dirty work involved in getting migrants from point A to point Z. Arresting low-level smugglers simply guarantees work for their underlings or the next batch of kids looking to make quick cash. Over the years, I've spent a lot of time listening to U.S., Mexican, and Honduran immigration agents explain to me how smuggling works and their various minor successes at slowing it down. These presentations usually include color-coordinated PowerPoint slides of apprehension and deportation statistics along with the occasional somber mug shot. The speakers will usually spice up the conversations with stories about child assassins, people getting dissolved in acid, and other salacious tales that are used to justify bloated federal budgets and heavy-handed tactics. These federal agencies are hunting for the Pablo Escobar of human smuggling. They are looking for the next Sister Ping.* But these searches are a fool's errand. You will not meet any crime kingpins on the train tracks in Mexico. What you will find are desperate people living complicated, ambiguous, and often violent lives.

---

* Cheng Chui Ping (aka "Sister Ping") ran a large-scale human smuggling operation between China and the United States for close to two decades and earned upward of $40 million in the process. See Patrick Radden Keefe, *The Snakehead: An Epic Tale of the Chinatown Underworld and the American Dream* (New York: Anchor, 2010).

Part I

SOLDIERS

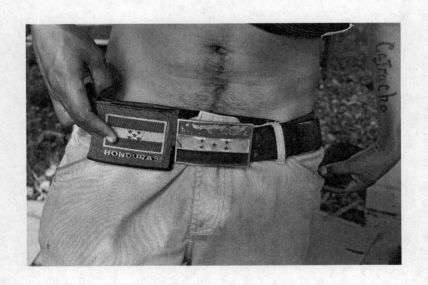

In the sudden silence that fell after the workers had departed,

Chan-Bahlum could hear the scuffling descent of more people, this time from the

temple above. He turned and saw five captives being dragged down the stairs by the

honored kinsmen of the dead king. A woman and four men would go to Xibalba this

day to accompany Pacal on his journey. Some of them moaned in terror, but one young

man trod forward to meet his fate with insolent pride. He was an ahau taken in battle

and chosen to go with Pacal because of his arrogant courage and reckless bravado.

LINDA SCHELE AND DAVID FREIDEL,

A FOREST OF KINGS

CHAPTER TWO

In the House of Pakal

Pakal-Ná* in Chiapas in Mexico is a poem, a bloodletting, a roadside memorial, a wish.

Laughter echoing from inside a dark place. Blinding heat. Clothes wet with jungle. Railroad ties shiny and smooth from a million frantic footsteps. It is the sun reflected off sharpened metal. A rooster screaming. A man screaming. Hope and hopelessness. Desire and greed. Pakal-Ná in Chiapas in Mexico is the center of migrant worlds that disappear only to remake themselves in new outlines and shadows.

"LOOK, KID, YOU'RE MEXICAN," Papo says. "You're from here and we're not. When you're older you'll have the privilege of leaving Pakal-Ná and crossing up to the border without worrying about getting deported before you even get there. So, for now, fuck off."

The boy, who is probably six or seven, stands firm. He doesn't want to leave.

---

* Pronounced pa-call-NA.

"Get the fuck out of here!" Papo yells.

The kid is a statue, naked except for threadbare dress pants whose frayed cuffs barely reach his ankles. A miniature Robinson Crusoe shipwrecked on these train tracks. He is poor even by migrant standards. He is immovable.

Papo's jaw tenses and his scrawny, tattooed arms flex in anger. He pushes the boy to the ground. I flinch.

The boy's four-year-old brother looks at Papo with great concern.

"We told you to get the fuck out of here," someone says.

"Just go," Santos implores them.

The boy stands back up and is now crying, but he holds firm. His little brother tugs at his arm.

"These fucking children have no fear!" Chino jokes.

I try to intervene. "*Mira, papi*, it's only because we're talking about adult stuff. It's better that kids aren't around."

He gives me a blank look. Tears begin to fall. I awkwardly put my arm around his shoulder. He keeps crying. He starts to hyperventilate.

Alma shakes her head. "Just give him five pesos so he will leave." She is cradling her four-year-old daughter Dulce and tries to shoo the boy away. "*¡Vaya! ¡Vaya!*"

I put a thick Mexican coin into the kid's dirty hand.

Papo takes a few aggressive steps toward the children.

The boys turn and start heading south down the tracks. In unison they step over scattered piles of garbage that decorate the ground, as if following some unspoken choreography. The older boy puts his arm around his little brother as they disappear into the distance. How many years will pass before they turn around and start heading in the other direction like so many children before them?

"Jason, don't worry about it. Let him go," Alma tells me as she puts her bleached-blond hair into a tight ponytail. "These kids in Pakal-Ná are too much. They are always here. They are always stealing food from us. Every time we are drinking and smoking that older kid is here. He even drinks *caña* [cane liquor]. That's why I keep my daughter close and don't let her play with him."

"That fucking kid stole a bottle of tequila from us the other night!" Papo yells.

"*¡Oye!* You better be nice to those children," Chino jokingly admonishes us, "because in a few years they will be the new ones robbing us on the train tracks."*

We all laugh knowing full well that it's true.

Pakal-Ná

Unless you are a migrant, there are few reasons to have ever heard of Pakal-Ná, Mexico. You may, however, have heard of its nearby neighbor Palenque, home to one of the most famous Maya archaeological sites in the world. Buried deep in the lush jungles of southern Chiapas, Palenque is renowned for the lavish tomb of its most famous king, Pakal the Great,† and the site's many inscription-laden monuments that have been crucial to deciphering ancient Maya writing. This city of shimmering white temples has captivated the Western imagination since the earliest explorer reports from the eighteenth and nineteenth centuries. Hundreds of thousands of tourists flock to it annually. Lonely Planet calls Palenque a "national treasure."

After seeing the Temple of the Inscriptions and Pakal's sarcophagus, many high school— and college-aged visitors end their day at one of the

---

* "The train tracks" (in Spanish *las vías*) usually refers to the sections of the migrant trail where the train passes.

† Pakal ruled between 615 and 683 CE.

budget resorts on the edge of the archaeological park, where they consume copious amounts of booze, marijuana, magic mushrooms, and whatever else young backpackers from Mexico City and Berlin are into these days. Surrounded by dense jungle and clouded by the misguided romanticism of what many think the ancient Maya world was like, hippies dance with fire sticks nightly, creating swirls of pulsating white light and heat. Dreadlocked Mexicans in hemp chokers and *Subcomandante Marcos* T-shirts pound out hallucinogenic rhythms. Come for the archaeology, stay for the bacchanalia.

I first visited Palenque in 2006, when I was a graduate student conducting archaeological research in nearby Veracruz. My memories of that trip are hazy but include drinking late into the night with expats and local hippies, falling into a creek on the walk back to my cabana, and nursing a debilitating hangover the following day that was not in the least bit helped by the intense tropical humidity. It was during this initial trip that I first heard reference to a hardscrabble *colonia* eleven kilometers from Palenque called Pakal-Ná. The town, which centers around a small freight train depot, is infamous for high rates of crime related to drug smuggling and violent attacks against the thousands of Central American migrants passing through every year. Home to around seven thousand people densely packed into modest cinder-block homes and wooden shanties, Pakal-Ná means "House of Pakal" in Maya, although it is unlikely that the famous king himself would have ever spent much time in the ancient hamlet underlying the modern community. Nowadays a tourist would visit (with a local escort who is in the know) only because they are looking to buy cocaine (more than a local Palenque bartender can provide) or are just trying to find some trouble on a Saturday night. Within spitting distance of one of the largest tourist attractions in Mexico, Pakal-Ná is a hidden national scandal just on the other side of the tracks.*

---

* The current president of Mexico, Andrés Manuel López Obrador, maintains a large ranch and walled compound near Pakal-Ná that has been the subject of recent scrutiny because of the

In the House of Pakal | 45

There are two primary ways that migrants currently enter Mexico from Guatemala (see map on page xxix). They take the southern Chiapas trail that passes through the city of Tapachula and head toward Oaxaca, or they try their luck on the northern passage that runs through Pakal-Ná and on to coastal Veracruz. Both follow the path of Mexican freight train lines that eventually lead to Mexico City and then to the border. Travel on either one of these routes has grown increasingly complicated in the era of Programa Frontera Sur. If migrants are lucky, they'll be able to hitch a ride on *la bestia* for parts of the journey.* The rest of the trip will have to be undertaken by walking, running, hitchhiking, or taking some form of public transportation where they will likely be overcharged because they are undocumented.

The road to Tapachula is densely populated and has a long history of migration compared with the one that runs through Pakal-Ná, which means there is a greater security presence and a higher likelihood of arrest, deportation, and robbery. The path through Pakal-Ná is often chosen because of its remoteness. However, it also has its share of dangers, including a growing immigration enforcement presence, gangs that target migrants, and locals who aren't altogether thrilled about having Central Americans in their towns.

I ended up in Pakal-Ná partly out of convenience. In 2015, I ran an anthropological field school focused on the experiences of Central American migrants who were just starting to feel the brunt of Programa Frontera Sur. Having been to Palenque previously as a tourist, I knew that it had

---

proposed use of federal funds to remodel areas surrounding his property. Staff Writer, "Las fotos de cómo quedará la remodelación de Pakal-Ná, la zona donde está el rancho de AMLO," *Infobae*, January 22, 2021, https://www.infobae.com/america/mexico/2021/01/22/las-fotos-de-como-quedara-la-remodelacion-de-pakal-na-la-zona-donde-esta-el-rancho-de-amlo/.

* In recent years, companies have hired private security guards to prevent migrants from boarding their trains. For a discussion of the criminal activities of these security guards, see John Doering-White, "In the Shadow of the Beast: Violence and Dignity along the Central American Trail" (PhD diss., University of Michigan, Ann Arbor, 2019).

sufficient gringo-friendly amenities to house, feed, and entertain my project's more than two dozen students and staff. I also knew that nearby Pakal-Ná was an important stop on the migrant trail and had a humanitarian shelter for border crossers.

When fieldwork began in June of 2015, I hadn't planned on working with smugglers. My research team and I spent our first few days in Pakal-Ná interviewing migrants. After being warned repeatedly by staff at the local shelter to be wary of the *delincuentes* lurking just outside, I went for a walk to satiate my curiosity. Poking around on the train tracks, I encountered a group of rough-looking young men sitting around talking shit to one another through a thick haze of marijuana smoke. I invited myself into their circle and tried to explain what anthropologists do and why I was there. I mentioned a book I had just completed on migrants crossing the Sonoran Desert, and my new companions came to the conclusion that I was some sort of journalist or chronicler and relatively harmless. More important, I was able to reassure them that I wasn't a cop and that I had no qualms about buying food. I soon found myself spending all of my free time with Chino, Santos, Papo, Alma, and the rest of their crew. The social network that I would develop from this initial encounter in Pakal-Ná would end up sending me across Latin America and the United States in search of insight into the lives of smugglers. "Everyone says that we are all bad," Chino laments to me on the first day we meet, "but that's not true. It's just that no one ever listens to our stories."

Cómo Me Duele

A bifurcated water bottle is held against the speaker of a cell phone. Valentín Elizalde's song "Cómo me duele" (How it hurts) rings out. Flip-flops kick up dust to a loping rhythm on a godforsaken street corner. *Cómo me duele*. People sleep on beds of newspaper and dirt, a purgatory until a $60 wire transfer magically appears. Clarinets whine, a tuba thumps. Feet keep moving, feet keep moving. *Pobre Valentín** knows that it hurts so good. *Cómo me duele*.

The tattoo gun's sad little motor keeps puttering out as the needle is dragged across Chino's brown flesh. Every time it dies, Santos rattles it to bring it back from the dead. The shaking motion sprays blood and computer printer ink onto the piece of cardboard serving as a communal rug on this street corner that people have taken to calling the Pleasure Palace, one of the many ephemeral places in Pakal-Ná to eat, drink, gossip, and get in trouble. Chino buries his face in his shoulder in an attempt to block out the pain. Santos is only on the third letter of the word "*catracho*," and given the rate at which the gun keeps jamming, it's going to be a while. His grimy fingers clean the muck obstructing the needle's movement. The motor reluctantly resumes its slow whirl and digs back into the letter *t*. Chino winces. *Cómo me duele*. We tease him about not being able to take the pain inflicted on his left arm. His right arm has a grisly collection of machete scars.

"No wonder Immigration keeps catching you," I say, laughing. "You have 'Honduras' tattooed on your leg and now you're getting '*catracho*' on your arm. *No mames*, Chino, how are you ever gonna pass for Mexican?"

He laughs his kid laugh. So goofy and juvenile, with a baby face that makes him look younger than he is. He makes a measuring motion with his thumb and index finger.

"Well, everyone knows, especially the ladies, that *hondureños* have a little bit extra compared to Mexicans," Chino jokes. "You know what I mean? This tattoo is so that the ladies will know what to expect."

---

* Elizalde was gunned down in Tamaulipas, Mexico, in 2006, most likely by the Mexican drug cartel Los Zetas.

48 | SOLDIERS AND KINGS

We laugh and shake our heads at him.

In the 1850s, Honduran soldiers fought William Walker, an American asshole who tried to colonize Central America. The Honduran resistance was led by General Florencio Xatruch, whose followers soon came to be called Xatruches. The general and his army eventually caught up with Walker in 1860 in Trujillo, Honduras, and ceremoniously filled his body with lead. The Xatruches were hailed as heroes, but many found their name too damn difficult to pronounce. "Xatruches" linguistically evolved into "*catrachos*" and subsequently became a nickname proudly worn by *hondureños* into the present.

Today, a small army of *catrachos* occupies Pakal-Ná, waging battle against both Mexican immigration agents seeking to deport them and criminals (including fellow countrymen) who see migrants as a source of income. There are so many *catrachos* here that the running joke is that they should rename this place Pakal-Ná, Honduras.

Papo, Alma, and their four-year-old kid Dulce huddle in the shade of a nearby tree and watch Chino get tattooed with great amusement. Hovering over a bag of Mexican dirt weed, Papo carefully removes seeds and stems while occasionally shaking his long black *rockero* hair out of his face. Someone passes him a paper tortilla wrapper that magically becomes a tightly rolled joint. Bin Laden and the Breadman perch on overturned paint buckets, watching Papo with great interest. Both men wait to go under Santos's needle. He will etch the names of their children into flesh. "I always carry my kids in my heart," the Breadman tells me, "and soon I will also carry them on my arms."

Bin Laden, a sinewy twentysomething with a scraggly beard and olive-colored skin, inhales twice and passes the joint to the Breadman, who is shirtless. The Breadman's dark skin shows off a series of fresh cuts on his chest, the result of recently getting tangled up in barbed wire while running from immigration agents. He takes several long pulls and then stares at the smoke leaking from his nose and mouth. He is at the start of a convoluted story when Santos gives him a hard look that signals to hurry up and pass the joint. No one seems to trust Bin Laden or the Breadman, which is noticeable even in this milieu, where suspicion is king. They are tolerated mostly because they are fellow smugglers and it serves everyone's best interests to avoid unnecessary conflict while working. Plus, you need permission from higher-ups if you want to start trouble with someone, and it's usually not worth it. That doesn't mean you have to like it that these two always seem to crawl out of the woodwork with open hands when someone else has food or weed. The Breadman finally lets go of the joint. He picks up two thick aluminum needles and begins to push and pull at the yarn dangling from the unfinished handbag sitting in his lap. Over the years I will grow wary of men on the migrant trail who knit.

"Cómo me duele" keeps playing as a group of nervous migrants quietly passes us on their way to the shelter directly across the street. They try to avoid eye contact with the ragtag people smoking weed, dancing, and getting tattooed on the corner. Someone in the Pleasure Palace crew hands the stereo over to Bin Laden and then runs up to the passing group. "*Oye*," they say to a startled teenage couple, "go inside the shelter. The door is right there. They are going to serve lunch in a little bit." The couple naively gives thanks for the information. Alma and a few others watch as the teens walk away. They give each other a knowing look.

The Road

In order to understand the inner workings of smuggling, you need to understand the basic process. It goes something like this.

Zero, a gangster and mid-level smuggler, texts the pickup location and the head count. *Seis personas en Corozal. Ya están listos.* The guides have never met Zero and never will. It doesn't matter as long as they have their marching orders. Zero is just a voice on the other end of the line that serves up clients for a particular segment of the journey, in this case from the Mexico-Guatemala border up through Veracruz. As an individual, Zero will come and go. Arrested. Deported. Retired. Murdered. It's not important. He's not your friend. He (or sometimes she) will often be replaced at the drop of a hat by some upstart with ice in their veins and a desire to take a turn at controlling this portion of the migrant trail. Rest assured, though, that when Zero's phone stops working, there is always some new number to call, a new voice to give orders. This machine stops for no one.

Six people need to be picked up in Corozal, a border town 170 kilometers south of Pakal-Ná. The guides don't ask Zero too many questions. They never ask what he is making off a trip. It's better not to know. They tell themselves it doesn't matter as long as the information is good and their money gets transferred. Zero offers $400 to cover all expenses and guide fees. Every day young men like Chino and Santos willingly accept these types of jobs and make the trek down to the Guatemala border from the interior of Mexico. Heading south is easy. It's coming back that's a bitch.

The rendezvous in Corozal is simple. The men from Honduras have been eagerly awaiting safe passage to Pakal-Ná. So much restless energy. So much laughter to keep spirits up. So much desire to keep that forward momentum. To stay still is to die.

Everyone in the group is under twenty-five and close in age to their guides. The clients ask few questions because they know that *guías* are full of shit. Everyone knows that guides lie. That's their job. The only truth among these young men is that they are all running from the same monsters that have made home unlivable for years.

Zero puts $200 into a burner bank account that can be accessed from a chain convenience store. The other half is to be paid upon safe delivery to Pakal-Ná. Two hundred dollars to cover food, water, bribes, marijuana, phone calls, and any other expenses. For the price they are paying, the nightly accommodations will be rustic. If you want to sleep in hotels, brother, you gotta come with more cash.

If the guides are good, the trip will be uneventful, with no surprises and no unexpected costs. If the guides are bad, that $200 will soon be in the hands of an immigration agent whom the group can wave to as the detention van drives them back to the Guatemala border. Zero assures the clients that his guys are good and that the money is worth it. Low-level guides like Chino and Santos often have years of experience riding the rails across Mexico and tend to specialize in certain segments of the journey. This is why they are hired by third-party smugglers who can't keep up with the ever-changing Mexican geographies of clandestine movement. Low-level guides know specific routes well and how to move through them undetected. More important, they can be paid a fraction of what those who brokered the deal are making. It's migrant capitalism at its best.

As soon as they are on the road, the guides tell the group that each person will have to cover their own food, which is not what Zero promised when they first made the arrangement. *If you don't like the deal, then you call Zero to renegotiate, but I'll tell you right now he doesn't give a shit what happens out here as long as we get to where we are going.* For the entire trip, the guides will continue to nickel-and-dime their clients as a way to maximize their own meager profits.

In the wake of crackdowns on Central Americans riding freight trains across Mexico, the journey has increasingly become one undertaken on foot. To get from a place like Corozal to Pakal-Ná now often means walking almost 200 kilometers. This means sometimes cutting through dense jungle to evade immigration checkpoints, and other times taking to the highway to circumvent choke points in the woods where bandits are lying in wait. All along the way the group will forage for food and shelter like hunter-gatherers in Converse sneakers and soccer jerseys.

They march through blistering days and humid nights. They memorize the backs of their companions' heads, and their gaits. They watch their shoes disintegrate in real time. When sleep comes, it's restless and in roadside ditches and behind chicken coops. So much stopping and hiding and waiting for unseen villains to pass. They tell dick jokes and talk about the money and babies they are going to make in the near future. Some in the group wonder what drove their guides to leave home and end up on the tracks. Did they kill someone, or is someone trying to kill them? Maybe it's both.

A prune-faced old lady in tired-looking sandals sells them beans and tortillas from her plywood shanty a few hundred feet from the highway. For ten pesos they wash up at her *pila* out back. The guides eat for free (of course) and charge their cell phones inside her house before they move on.

Later, they are dying of thirst when a greasy kid emerges from the jungle like a fairy from a fever dream—an angel carrying a bucket of cold bottles of water and warm *baleadas* that his grandma learned to make after so many requests from road-weary Hondurans looking for a taste of home. Tired and bored, they send the kid on a mission to find some *mota*.

The following night they shelter in a factory long abandoned, its walls covered in graffiti of the damned. Rock art in spray paint, shoe polish, and smoke. Petroglyphs scratched by the dull tips of pocketknives and rusty nails. *Jesús loves María. Jesús loves me. I love Jesús.* Skeletal hands with clawed fingernails make the sign of the devil. *Hollywood Locos Forever. Only God can judge me.* A giant phallus with fuzzy testicles greets a smiley face. The men get high and look for hidden messages in this cave of broken dreams.

The next morning, they use fistfuls of rocks to terrorize the local iguana population. They tie the legs of their stunned captives with shoelaces and carry them back to camp dangling from whittled tree branches. They smoke the last of the marijuana and jokingly taunt each other with the lizards like children playing with reptilian action figures. Their bloodshot eyes watch in awe as green skin turns black over an open flame fueled by twigs and scavenged pieces of plastic garbage. Cell phone cameras snap photos of them laughing and ripping flesh from charred iguana bodies like cavemen.

The laughter stops after two straight days of trudging through heavy rainfall and black mud that sucks their shoes off. There is little humor in feet that don't seem to dry and blistered skin that peels off in sheets. They huddle under a ragged tarp at night for warmth and complain about the lack of weed.

The sun finally breaks through the clouds as they come upon a tiny cottage hidden in the jungle. It is cobbled together from warped plywood and sheets of plastic. The gnome's house is surrounded by rusted-out skeletons of machines from a bygone era. A corpse of a dog sits in the yard, licking its groin raw and looking unimpressed by the approaching squadron of dragging men. A stubby Maya farmer in rubber muck boots and a Peterbilt hat breaks the frame of the door. He holds a machete bowed from years of sharpening like some archaic Persian warrior wielding a scimitar.

The clients spend the night in a corn shed out back that drips with water and spiders. Creatures shuffle under foot and under their makeshift beds. In the quiet dark they can hear the guides laughing and banging their drinks on their host's kitchen table until well after midnight. At dawn they are driven twenty kilometers north and again left to meander through the darkness of the jungle.

Hunger pain builds and the men grow tired of hiding like scared animals. They start to question those in charge. Concern is expressed about the money they have shelled out for a trip that was supposed to be three days and is now turning into a week.

How much farther?

We are almost there.

You told us that two days ago.

How much farther?

We are almost there.

A few kilometers outside Chancalá, a coked-up cholo puts a revolver to one guide's head.

¿Quién es el bueno?

The perpetual question.

They breathe a collective sigh of relief when Zero picks up the phone. To survive these types of encounters you have to know whom to call. You have to have someone who can vouch for you and confirm that you have paid. Zero smooths everything over and they are soon on their way again. A few of the men joke about what they would have done if that call had gone unanswered. They fantasize about what they are going to do when they get to where they are going. They no longer question any decisions their guides make. The brotherhood is restored. Just west of Tenosique they spot *la bestia* making her way toward them. She hums and rattles and belches black smoke up into the sapphire sky. The rosary is whispered. A hand grabs on for dear life.

FROM THE TRAIN they can see Pakal-Ná on the horizon. It's an oasis. An internet café, an indoor bathroom, and a place to charge a cell phone are waiting for them. So is MS-13.

They call him Payaso, the Clown, but there is nothing funny about him except for the fact that he is an avid knitter. But no one in their right mind would laugh about his hobby, which he picked up after a prison stint. Shaved head. Demon tattoos. Quiksilver board shorts and dirty flip-flops. Eyes

In the House of Pakal | 55

glassy and opaque like a dead fish. Payaso is the guardian at the gate, Pakal-Ná's troll under the bridge. He is part of Zero's network of enforcers who make sure that no guides or migrants sneak in under the radar without paying what is due. It is impossible to avoid him. It is unhealthy to run from him.

The *guías* check in. *We got six. They are Zero's.* The men are given a pass. Zero has already paid the local taxes for his clients. Payaso relays this information to Pato, a friendly thirtysomething and father of two who runs a tiny grocery store. Pato marks this information in a ledger where he keeps track of who is coming and going, who has paid and who owes. A toddler takes a few steps in front of his store and falls. He picks up the crying child and tries to calm her. No one walks into Pakal-Ná without Pato knowing about it.

Some guides try to sneak past Payaso without checking in. Some guides try to avoid paying any money to Pato. Those are not smart moves. Payaso has eyes everywhere. Papo's and Alma's eyes are Payaso's eyes. That old lady who rents rooms in her house by the Pleasure Palace is Payaso's eyes. Those half-naked little kids who are always huffing glue by the train tracks are Payaso's eyes. If you are hiding in the jungle, he will find you. If you are hiding in a rented room, he will find you. *Which one of you is the guide? Who do you know? Where is my money?* Payaso has no patience or sense of humor. Some killers can smile and joke. Payaso does not do those things.

The six men shake hands with their guides before entering the migrant shelter run by nuns. A new person will come for them in a few days and once again lead them north. They will wire Zero money to pay for the next round of expenses, including the *cuotas*, that will be collected by MS-13 and the Zetas farther up the road: Coatzacoalcos, Medias Aguas, Tierra Blanca, Orizaba, D.F., and Huehuetoca. At least six locations where they will have to pay between $100 and $200 per person to get through. Two hundred dollars to prevent someone from shocking your balls with a car battery. Two hundred dollars to prevent someone from taking a few fingers as souvenirs.

Six stops where there will be new Payasos waiting. After this pricey gauntlet, it's another $3,000 to get from Mexico City to the border with Texas. That segment of the journey has (for the time being) fewer locations where someone like Payaso is waiting to collect money, but it is often more dangerous. Instead of run-ins with MS-13, north of Mexico City people have to deal with the cartels who have long cornered the market on kidnapping, extorting, recruiting, and murdering migrants.

If you get all the way to the border with Texas, your guide gives you three chances to cross before you have to pay another $3,000. If you make it across, you will spend some time in a miserably overcrowded Texas safe house before you are packed into a truck or van and delivered to your final destination. If you fail to cross the border you could either end up back in Mexico (if you are lucky) or be sent home to Honduras to start the whole trip over again.

Each of these clients will eventually pay out close to $7,000 for a trip up to the U.S.-Mexico border. But all that money still doesn't guarantee that they will soon be plucking chickens in Arkansas or washing cars in the Bronx.

But that's their problem.

The two guides head to a convenience store to collect their $200 from Zero. They count out their cash in the woods. Each will pocket around $120 for a week's worth of work. They put credit on their cell phones. One of them wires $40 to a baby's momma back in Honduras. They buy quarts of beer, some tortillas, and several cans of refried beans. There's a party tonight at the Pleasure Palace.

WE CAN PAINT ugly and tragic pictures of human smuggling, but it is impossible to fully grasp the structure or extent of the systems of clandestine movement. The diagrams we draw will always be missing pieces. The ragtag crew in the Pleasure Palace represents a blurry snapshot of a fragment of a complex and expansive international criminal network that is subject to rapid change and constant reorganization. Despite their deep involvement, members of this crew would be hard-pressed to explain to you how things function outside their small, individual orbits. The nebulousness of this system is further exacerbated by the numerous roles that people play over time and sometimes simultaneously. As anthropologist Noelle Brigden points out, "Violence and migration produce a fundamental ambiguity and uncertainty along the route. At various places, the roles of 'migrant,' 'smuggler,' 'gang member,' 'state official,' and 'kidnapper' overlap or become fluid." In the real world, categories such as "migrant" and "smuggler" often defy the tidiness of social science organization.

I have spent a lot of time with members of this loosely connected crew, both in groups and in one-on-one situations, in an attempt to better understand smuggling on the ground and at macro levels. I have followed people on the migrant trail. I have followed them to the United States and back to Honduras. I have watched them disappear and reappear. I have watched them collectively dance to "Cómo me duele" one day and be at each other's throats the next. It is through their lives that I hope to illuminate the fact that human smuggling is not a problem to be solved with fences or detention centers. It is a violent global process that can be addressed only if we understand why it exists, how it functions, and what the dirty work looks like.

CHAPTER THREE

Charismatic and Reckless

¡Ándale Chino! ¡Píquele a la calabaza hombre!

—VALENTÍN ELIZALDE

From the top of the train, the world seems infinite in all directions. A story yet to be written. Young people looking to feel in control of something for once in their lives. A saga overflowing with possibility and excitement and working-class glamour. The hero wins in the end, if only for a brief moment.

THE LEAD ENGINE lurches fifty feet forward, stops, and then reverses, slamming hard into the car behind it. Grinding metal and screeching engine brakes compete with roosters and tropical birds. The train heaves forward and once again reverses and slams backward. The process repeats, adding more railcars each time. Chino is fifteen feet above us, stoned and giggling as he leaps from one moving car to another. A Third World Peter Pan in knockoff Crocs dancing for an audience of locals, migrants, and me. He hams it up, waving and grinning and then sprinting across three moving cars in a matter of seconds. He stops just at the edge of the lead car and then doubles back, mimicking the rhythm of the moving train. A couple of times I think his forward momentum will be too much and will send him flying when he tries to put on the brakes. It's a dangerous, stupid, and entertainingly juvenile game that allows him to show off for the crowd and remind people he is crazy as hell and not to be fucked with. The rubber sandals he is wearing have shit for traction, so it's easy to envision him slipping and falling to the ground, his brains exploding onto the steel rails below. I wonder what they would do with his body if he died playing this game of freight train hopscotch. Maybe an unmarked grave in Palenque's potter's field. Maybe his family can miraculously come up with the several thousand dollars needed to ship his corpse back to Honduras. It's a macabre exercise in what-ifs.

I remember myself at his age doing equally dangerous and irresponsible things to entertain my friends. Dangling from a third-story roof, drunk and high on Vicodin. Putting a half stick of dynamite in my mouth and accidentally lighting the fuse while pretending it's a cigar. Pushing a 500-pound dumpster down a steep hill and then running in front of it to re-create a scene from *Raiders of the Lost Ark*. In college I never drunkenly ran across the top of a moving train, probably because I didn't have access to a train.

On the surface, my shenanigans were mischievous at best and irresponsibly dangerous at worst. I thought of my behavior as simply the kind of jackass things young people did for kicks, shit to make people laugh (which they often did). Deep down, though, I was also trying to fill a hollowness that lived inside me: a darkness that manifested itself in bouts of crippling depression, intense feelings of isolation and rage, and a playful death wish that loomed over my teenage years and early twenties.

People have asked me how I can spend so much time with smugglers whose lives are dominated by risk and creeping demise. It's partly because it feels strangely familiar. I don't know what it's like to rob or kill someone,

60 | SOLDIERS AND KINGS

but I know what it's like to want to live fast and die. For many years, it felt like hints of death were the only things that could make me feel alive. This is probably one of the reasons I get along so well with Chino. We are long-lost kin bonded by childhood trauma and long histories of dangerous self-medicating and self-harm. I see something of my adolescent self in his youthful recklessness, in his embrace of a life where death is something to be taunted and almost welcomed. The death wish that I had to overcome and my lifelong struggles with complex PTSD seem to give me some privileged insight into Chino's worldview as well as that of many other men involved in smuggling.

As I watch him foolishly play on top of a moving train, I think about a cynical line from Faulkner's *As I Lay Dying*: Addie, the matriarch of the Bundren family, says, "The reason for living was to get ready to stay dead a long time." What if the reason for dying is to know that you were once alive?

It takes some coaxing, but Chino finally comes down from the top of the train. He is laughing and winded. I give him shit for acting so stupidly, but he flashes his boyish smile and starts cracking jokes, which makes it hard to stay mad at him. "When that train is really moving, you better watch out," he warns me. "You can get hit in the head by a tree branch, or if you are standing near the edge and they brake, you can get thrown off."

"I imagine it's worse if you are tired or drunk. Do people ever ride the train fucked up?" I ask.

"Chino does sometimes," he says, laughing. His use of the third person somehow makes this troubling statement funnier than it should be.

We shelter under a *palapa* someone has erected next to the tracks and pretend that the heat isn't smothering us. He grabs a stick and starts scratching out a map of train routes in the dirt. Names of towns are rattled off like a poem: Tapachula, Benemérito, Palenque, Corozal, Ixtepec, Tierra Blanca, Tenosique, Lechería, Salto de Agua, Coatzacoalcos. This uneducated young man has an advanced degree in Mexican geography. Places to avoid, places

Charismatic and Reckless | 61

where a church might open its doors, places where teenagers with machetes and no patience collect $100 head taxes. Survival here is a knowledge game with a steep learning curve. Chino speaks of a violent world of cycles with no viable end in sight.

Chino: Man, I've spent a lot of time on the train coming and going. Sometimes they grab you at a checkpoint [*he points to the dirt map*] and then they send you back. You try again and they catch you again. Then you know that they'll grab you in that place, so you don't go through there anymore. You try a different route. Then they catch you farther ahead the next time and they send you back to Honduras. You come back and now you know where they caught you the first and second time and you go around those places. It's simple. Immigration gets tougher and we invent new routes.

Jason: How many times have you tried to cross Mexico?

Chino: Maybe five times. I got as far as Laredo, Texas.

Jason: Did Immigration catch you while you were crossing the border?

Chino: No, I got across. It was incredible. I ended up living in a tree. I found some plywood and climbed up into a tree with it. I made a bed and tied it to some branches with rope so that I wouldn't fall out. I tied my water bottle, bag of food, and backpack up there. I was up there in my little house with my cigarettes. I stayed there at night. I spent like eight days sleeping in a fucking tree [*laughing*]. Immigration would show up looking for me, but they couldn't see me. Chino was up there smoking his cigarettes. It was easy. Then they caught me coming out of a 7-Eleven. They were watching me as I left the store and stopped and asked where I was from. I told them I was headed to my house, but they knew I was undocumented because of how I talked.

Jason: How long were you in the U.S. for?

Chino: Like a month, but the problem is that you get there and then what? Where are you going to go? You just end up on the streets.

Jason: How old were you when you first came to Mexico?

Chino: I was sixteen at the time. On that first trip I got as far as Arriaga [in Chiapas] before getting caught by Immigration. I told them I was Guatemalan, so they deported me there.

Jason: Why did you leave in the first place?

Chino: I couldn't really go to school or stay with my family because of economic problems. There were so many of us in our house and only my mom worked. I had to work too. I finally had to say, "*Mamá*, you brought me into this world, so thank you. But I don't want to be another headache for you because you have enough of those." So, I left . . . I had a friend who was like, "It's pretty good over there in Mexico. Let's do it. Let's go." But in reality, it's really fucking hard here. There's Immigration looking for you, and being un-

Charismatic and Reckless | 63

documented means you can't get a job. You go and look for work here [in Mexico], but people don't want to give you a job because you're Honduran.

Jason: When was the last time you were in Honduras?

Chino: I left seven months ago. I've been thinking about returning, but it's dangerous there because of the *maras* and all that stuff.

He continues sketching out a map in the dirt. It shows the border with Guatemala to the south and Mexico City and Laredo to the north. His map covers thousands of square miles. Chino knows dozens of cities, towns, and villages, but his view of them is tethered to the tracks. He never sees all that these places have to offer. It's like he's looking at the world through storefront windows.

Origin Stories

The driver turns around and looks at me. "Are we okay to enter this street?"

"I think so," I nervously reply. A battered red Toyota flies past us down the hill, as if trying to escape this working-class Honduran neighborhood. We inhale its trail of dust. The sun is also making its exit on the horizon. Armed kids will soon take positions on street corners and rooftops. Walkie-talkies will chirp. Nervous drivers will put on their emergency lights as a signal that they mean no harm. Aggressive little heads will poke through car windows. *Where are you from? Who do you know?*

Marina sighs and catches a tear with the palm of her hand. "My brother has known suffering his entire life," she says. "He's known suffering since he was child." Chino's older sister tells me this as we sit on her couch in a tidy one-room cinder-block house in Villanueva, Honduras. Mexican pop music softly plays from a stereo nestled in the corner. Chino and other relatives smile at us from framed photos decorating the walls and tables. "You need to know that our family has suffered," she continues. As we sit in her little house on an unpaved street, a narrative of struggle and loss begins to unspool—a story that she hopes will help me better understand her brother's troubled life.

CHINO'S TEENAGE MOTHER, Celia, steps onto the mud-floor patio of her parents' dilapidated house and takes a seat in a plastic chair. Although the place isn't much to look at, the view of the lush green valley of Concepción del Norte is stunning. San Pedro Sula is only two hours away, but this place feels like a different planet. Celia is exhausted. Six-month-old Chino squirms in her arms as mother and child bathe in the unrelenting heat. He screams for attention that she is unwilling or unable to give him. The words feel unreal when they come out of her mouth: "You either take this child or I'm going to give him away." Chino's grandmother Luz takes a seat and then asks for the baby. Her deformed arthritic hands aren't strong enough to hold him, so she rests the child in her lap. The baby she looks down at kicks and claws the air.

She barely has enough energy to feed the six children living under her roof, but Luz welcomes her grandson into her home. Chino quickly proves to be a sickly child who suffers from asthma attacks and a near-fatal bout of pneumonia. "When he was a baby, my mom had to hitch a ride on the back of a trailer just to get him to the hospital," Marina remembers. "He turned purple and everyone thought he was dead. They pumped him with fluids for three days and he survived." The baby is a fighter.

Charismatic and Reckless | 65

Chino's grandparents assume the role of mother and father to him as they collectively struggle to make it in a dirt-floor house with no indoor plumbing. Luz irons and washes clothes for the neighbors when her arthritis isn't flaring up. Her hard-drinking husband, Inocente, farms a small plot of land and rules the house with an iron fist typical of men of his era. Times always seem to be tough, with too many days of empty cupboards, grumbling stomachs, and the impossible math of how to feed a half dozen kids with a couple of eggs. When they are truly desperate, Luz goes door to door, begging the neighbors for rice or a little credit to buy tortillas. Still, Marina reflects fondly on those years: "The house we grew up in is very humble and falling apart, but it is the place where all my favorite memories of my family and brother were made."

As he ages, it becomes obvious that Chino is hyperactive and hates to sit still. His grandparents sporadically enroll him in school, but there is often little money for books or supplies, and he hates being cooped up inside. As he becomes more aware of his family situation, bitterness and hatred begin to develop, due to the fact that he rarely sees his drug-addicted birth mother and never comes to know his biological father. Luz and Marina shower him with love, but he can't escape the fear of abandonment that makes him restless and unmoored. Chino leaves school for good at age twelve to work the land with Inocente. He proves to be bad at farming and grows to resent the work. Farming can only reproduce the inescapable hardships that surround him. Farming means a future of plywood houses with mud floors and no money for medicine. You can theoretically survive off the land, but surviving doesn't always mean living.

Chino lucks out and finds a youth job program with the Honduran government building low-income housing. He learns rudimentary construction skills while traveling across the countryside building homes in impoverished neighborhoods for $5 a day. The work is underpaid, but he feels like he actually has some purpose in life. He also loves the new freedom of movement it affords him. It speaks to his restlessness. Chino wants to stick with the program, but it's hard to imagine how $5 a day will ever allow him to build the dream home his grandmother deserves after all her suffering and the many sacrifices she has made for him. But before he can decide whether to pursue the career of a vagabond construction worker, tragedy upends his young life.

"There Is No God"

Chino's grandmother has spent her entire adult life trying to make a happy home for her children and grandchildren. Even when her gnarled fingers and toes make it almost impossible to do the simplest of household chores, she still fights to put food in bellies and keep the kids laughing and smiling. "She is a warrior. She is my warrior," Marina boasts. But sometimes hope, love, and a fighting spirit are no match for the curse of crushing poverty and its handmaid violence. By the time Chino turns thirteen, Luz has already known an incomprehensible amount of loss.

> **Marina:** My mother gave birth to seven kids and only three of us are still alive. Our first brother to die was killed at a dance. He had gotten into a drunken fight with a guy who beat him to death. My mom then lost a little girl who got sick and died when she was young. Her death happened during a barbaric time when the economy was bad and we had no money for doctors or medicine. The third child died while my mom was giving birth to her in our house. There wasn't money to go to a hospital, so the baby died of complications at home. The fourth, my older brother [Miguel], was twenty-eight years old when he died. He was cutting down a tree

Charismatic and Reckless | 67

near a power line and got electrocuted. That just left Chino,* my two other sisters, and me. When my oldest brother died, his kids were very small. The girl was only nine months old and the boy wasn't even born yet. My brother's wife stayed at our house and gave birth to the baby in January. Four months later she decided to go with another man and left the two children with me and Chino.

Miguel's death has devastating consequences for the entire family. Inocente falls into a deep depression and barely has enough energy to get dressed daily. He abandons his tiny agricultural field and rarely leaves the house. Luz finds herself the primary caretaker for two small kids, a four-month-old boy and a seventeen-month-old girl. She tries to feed the family with what little cash she earns cleaning clothes for the neighbors. Marina soon leaves to take a low-paying factory job in nearby Comayagua. She sends much of her meager paycheck home to keep her dead brother's children fed and in clean diapers.

While the family tries to figure out how to survive with two new babies in the house, thirteen-year-old Chino struggles with the debilitating loss of an older brother who was both a father figure and his best friend. At Miguel's wake Chino becomes intimate with *guaro*, a distilled sugarcane liquor that can peel the paint off the side of a barn. The drinking is soon accompanied by marijuana and whatever else he can get his hands on. When he isn't solemn and refusing to speak to people, Chino is out partying with his friends well past his eight p.m. curfew. His grandparents plead with him to behave. Inocente resorts to old-school beatings and forces him to sleep outside. But nothing works. A darkness begins to take hold. The change in Chino is impossible to miss.

The cemetery on the side of the mountain gives all the ghosts a striking

---

* Here Marina discusses Chino as if he were one of her siblings; technically he is her nephew.

view of the green valley below. Sometimes the living sit here with their troubled thoughts. Sometimes a brother wails into the night, trying to wake the dead. Chino hurls bottles and screams into the darkness until he is exhausted. The crying goes on and on until there are no more tears to give. Someone will wake him in the morning and quietly help him home.

Chino's world is now one of rage, resentment, and instability. He has lived through abandonment, and now God has taken his best friend. Sadness consumes him. His faith is eroded. He tells Marina, "There is no God. But there is a Devil and he is powerful. The Devil is inside me."

Two Roads

Chino can't stand the claustrophobia of his grandparents' village. He also can't bear to be so close to his brother's grave. Angry and restless, he finds himself living with his birth mother, Celia, and his stepfather, Wilson, on the outskirts of San Pedro Sula in a *colonia* called Dos Caminos. It is here that his fourteen-year-old life will take a bad turn.

There is no warning. No questions asked. The kids descend on him. Kicks and punches blur his vision. Grins and laughter. Chino will recognize some of the young faces later when they are hanging out and partying. Soon he will be the one laughing when they do this to others. For now, he dusts himself off and staggers home. Welcome to the crossroads.

Chino needs someone to replace Miguel. Someone to teach him survival skills and how to be a man. His drug-abusing stepfather takes him under his wing and introduces him to the thrill of armed robbery. The fast cash that Wilson can access is a stark contrast to the $5 a day Chino had been earning laying bricks and pouring concrete for the government. The easy money is far more attractive than replicating his grandfather's hard life in the *milpas*,

Charismatic and Reckless | 69

where fourteen hours of daily labor doesn't guarantee your kids will eat that night. Fourteen grueling hours so that you can go home and work out your frustrations and feelings of impotence on the bodies of your loved ones. The only thing that can be harvested in the fields is sorrow.

Wilson teaches an enthusiastic Chino the ins and outs of assaulting and stealing. These new skills serve him well when he joins the local teenage gang. Gang life makes Chino feel powerful and protected. He learns how to be street smart. He figures out how to enter neighboring *colonias* undetected so that he can mug strangers. Chino begins to excel at violence. In less than a year of living in Dos Caminos, he has turned into a nightmare. Life revolves around robbing people and getting fucked up. He is out of control, and no one can tell him what to do. No one can stop him. Annihilation becomes a way of life.

CHINO DREAMS as his hammock swings to the rhythm of the afternoon heat. It's a trance that brings a brief quieting of fury. His little homie Casper sits in the courtyard waiting for the sun to go down. Chino's eyes are closed. He is someplace else. He thinks he hears footsteps. Are the footsteps a dream? No, they are real. The gunshots and the screams and the ghosts of smoke are also real. Chino looks up just in time to see a youthful shadow much like his own escape through the front door. He sees Casper lying on the ground. That kid will never dream again. When Marina asks Chino how he feels after witnessing his friend's murder, all he can say is, "I now feel death close to me."

Clavo

Understanding migration from Central America requires an up-close look at the monster that is chasing many out of their homes. It is a monster created by the familiar ingredients of the Third World: poverty, corruption, disenfranchisement, rage. This beast that stalks neighborhoods has many names, faces, and a never-ending arsenal of weapons. Its singular goal is to make people do its bidding. Those who refuse get nailed to a cross.

It can start a million different ways.

A family owns a *tienda* and is struggling to pay *la renta* to the neighborhood gang, which wants 40 percent of their monthly income to guarantee their "safety." Even during a profitable month, that percentage is ludicrous, unsustainable. They can barely keep the lights on as it is. They tell their extortionists that this request is unreasonable, an impossibility.

Fuck you. That's your problem.

After a missed payment, two people pull up on a motorcycle in broad daylight. They shoot the family matriarch in the head at point-blank range as she sweeps the entrance to the store. Six people saw it happen, but no witnesses come forward when the cops show up three hours later. The next day family members are on their hands and knees scrubbing blood and brain matter off the concrete when a kid from the neighborhood delivers a message: *Pay the rent or you are next.* They shutter the store, throw some clothes in a backpack, and run.

A fourteen-year-old lingers on a street corner with no place to go. School is too expensive and home is just a place to be hungry and reminded of how tough times are. A group of young men corners him. It's time to start putting in work for the gang. It doesn't matter if he isn't interested in that life. It doesn't matter that they've all known each other since they were in diapers. Those days don't count for shit now. Join them or leave town. Join them or the kid and everyone he loves will die. If the kid is lucky, his family scrapes together $500 to partially finance a trip north to connect with an uncle in Chicago. The cash will get him into Mexico, where they hope and pray someone can take out a loan to cover the remaining $6,500 needed to complete the journey. At least they won't be murdered walking to the store.

Charismatic and Reckless | 71

Maybe the kid's family has no money. There is no uncle in Chicago. There is no support network. The kid is already hanging out on the street and getting into trouble. He falls in with the *maras* because it's all he can do. He has no escape plan, and staying alive is better than getting dead. Besides, being with them means they won't be coming after him or his family (for now). It's even exhilarating at first. The kid likes the partying and the chaos. He likes the attention that girls in the neighborhood give him when he parades through the streets smoking blunts and carrying a pistol like he owns the place. He gets off on the fact that adults are now deathly afraid of him. He can take what he wants with no fear. It's the first time in his poverty-stricken young life that he feels powerful and unafraid. Soon it's him cornering kids, saying, "Join us or die." But how long can he keep this up? How long before he is in over his head? How long before gang life means a commitment to bringing death?

"Look, it's like this," Chino explains to me as he points to the train tracks in Pakal-Ná. "If you live on one side with your gang, you can't cross over because another gang is there. We are on this side and they are on that side. Then someone crosses the tracks looking for trouble. The two gangs start fighting and it turns into a clusterfuck. Soon everyone over there starts fighting with everyone over here. Sometimes they end up killing someone. It can start as a joke and then they kill someone. It's unbelievable, but you can get killed over some jokes. Then the next day it keeps going. That's how the war starts."

The monster that stalks neighborhoods in Honduras needs to perpetually reproduce itself. It offers money, drugs, and thrills as incentives for kids to give away a part of themselves in service of the mission. But the things it offers are not sustainable for most, and those that fully commit either end up dead or in prison. For many, the violence is invigorating until it's not. Drugs and alcohol are fun until people need them because it's increasingly difficult to stomach extorting one's friends and neighbors. Old people begging for their lives don't make young gangsters feel powerful anymore, just worthless. They begin to wonder what purpose is served by terrorizing a kid with a machete because he looked at them the wrong way. They watch petty robberies and petty squabbles turn into petty murders. Kids watch other kids die. They start to avoid eye contact with the neighbors who suspect them of killing one of their children. It wasn't them who did it, but it doesn't matter. People will always think it was, and they will never be able to outlive that here.

The monster that stalks the neighborhood becomes too much to live with. Kids who thought they were tough start making escape plans. Better to leave now before someone crosses the tracks looking for them or before they no longer recognize themselves in the mirror. Whatever is waiting in Mexico is hopefully safer and less soul crushing than staying in Honduras. But as soon as they leave, they can never come back. The gang does not forgive or forget. They leave town with a *clavo*, a nail, a problem that will follow them forever and make them deathly afraid of the place they once called home. It doesn't matter why they left, though, because on the migrant trail everyone is running from something.

Machetazo

"It's calmer here than in Honduras," Chino tells me one day while we sip cold sodas on the tracks and watch locals on their way to work and the market. "But it's still possible to make enemies and get into trouble. For example, if I offend some of these Mexicans, they are going to come after me. I could also end up offending some of the Hondurans around here. It's easy to offend Hondurans because we come from a country where people act foolish, people act crazy. It's dangerous over there. The gangs that are running around there are crazy. They will take everything from you. There are little kids on the street who will come after you. They don't care. It doesn't matter if they don't have guns. They'll make them. They make these famous *chimbas* that are just two metal tubes with a nail in one end. They put a twelve-gauge shell in the tube and the nail hits it and fires. They will go out and kill each other with those things. If you go out after eight p.m. in Honduras, you are going out looking for trouble. It's better to just not go out. I'm telling you all this because I was involved in that stuff in Honduras. That's how I got this." He twists his right arm to display a collage of scars that run from shoulder to wrist like engorged centipedes crawling across his flesh.

BY THE TIME Chino sees them coming, it's too late to get away from the raven-haired men with bulging eyes and hot breath. He turns to question his partner, who is no longer there. His friend is now a phantom running at the speed of someone who has just been recognized by the wrong people. *This is on him, not me*, Chino thinks. *I didn't do shit. This is on him, not me. There is nothing to be afraid of.* His hands go up. He offers a street corner surrender that is not accepted.

Metal cuts the air before breaking skin and touching bone. *Turn and run. You have to turn and run.* The machete burns across his back. Somehow his spine is not severed. Maybe God is protecting him. Hot metal. Alkaline smell. Muscle and tissue exposed to air. He crawls and swims in his own blood. An antique revolver slips out from his waistband. He fires several wild shots that break the afternoon sky. Smoke rises while men and boys who are high on violence retreat. Chino lies in the street, bleeding to death.

A man leaving a nearby factory spots him and attempts to intervene.

"You have to call my sister," Chino pleads. "Please call my sister."

On the phone the man tells Marina, "I have someone here who says he is your brother. He is really hurt."

"Please help him!" she cries. "Please help my brother!"

"Tell me the truth. Is your brother a good person? If he is a good person, I will help him."

"I will pay anything," she says. "Just help him."

Chino flatlines in the ambulance. "They took him to the hospital and by the time he got there he was dead," Marina remembers. "His heart had stopped. They injected him with adrenaline and gave him five bags of saline and several pints of blood. They somehow brought him back to life. He was sixteen at the time. It's a miracle that he lived. I think God was protecting him."

The severity of his injuries almost costs Chino his right arm. He spends weeks in a San Pedro Sula hospital recuperating and staring at the countless staples and screws embedded in his flesh. Fingers on his right hand now twitch uncontrollably from muscle damage. In Pakal-Ná he gets "*catracho*" tattooed on his left arm. Now both arms bear symbols of his nationality. Toward the end of his hospital stay, two things become clear. He has nowhere near the amount of money needed to cover his expenses (around $650), and he now has a *clavo* and can't go back to Dos Caminos. On the day of his scheduled discharge, Chino climbs out of his first-floor hospital window and vanishes in a taxi. A few days later, he starts heading north.

El Camino

Mexico is a dark fantasy for sixteen-year-old Chino. A world of restlessness and freedom, a time of exploration and violence that he navigates with an increasingly warped moral compass. The train is his playground. The tracks are his home. He traverses the country in search of something unnamable and, worse, uncontrollable. New levels of poverty and desperation become

Charismatic and Reckless | 75

familiar. Complicated scenes of violence and kindness unfold before him. On this inaugural voyage he learns how to survive and avoid deportation. He learns how to be a guide. He learns many things.

The two of us stand on top of a decommissioned freight train. The jungle meets the horizon in every direction. We can feel the heat emanating from the metal boxcar beneath our shoes. Chino has lessons he wants to teach me. He speaks directly. He speaks in metaphors. He speaks in a hushed third person. *Don't fall asleep sitting up. That's how you end up taking a tree branch to the head. Keep your mouth shut around the police. Mexicans say* chingada *and* no mames *a lot. You gotta talk like a Mexican to avoid getting deported.* I laugh because Chino's Honduran accent is too over-the-top to ever hide.

He tells me that some kid you meet from Tegucigalpa or Tela might have your back until they vanish. *Amigos del camino* they are called. But people let you down. People disappear. People always disappear.

An older Mexican woman might invite you into her home. Her bed will be warm. She will teach you many things. But you will run away addicted to crystal meth and worried that she has cursed you. Maybe you've been cursed your whole life. "Sometimes you can offer women protection on the tracks. In exchange, they have to do anything you tell them." Chino says this with a smirk. "There are Mexicans on the tracks who will pay you for sex. They prefer Hondurans because of the rumors about our manhood. Some fags will even give you 50 pesos just to show it to them." He nervously laughs and tries to gauge my reaction to this last line.

Chino spends a year in Mexico cutting his teeth swinging from freight trains and sleeping rough. He is filthy and laughing. Strangers drop pesos into his grubby hands. They give him more when he sings the Honduran national anthem on a street corner. People feel sorry for Hondurans. Their national anthem is a funeral dirge that elicits sympathy even from Mexicans, many of whom are screwed themselves. Chino runs from a *clavo* but also searches for adventures that can satiate his wanderlust. Reaching the United

States is now a fantasy to daydream about while embracing a lifestyle of movement, violence, and partying.

He misses his family but rarely makes contact. He is too embarrassed of how he is living. Months will go by with no word. Marina lights candles and prays for his safety. The few times he does call, he is drunk, like on Mother's Day when he promises Luz he is working hard to buy her a dream house. Marina begs him to come home. All he can say is, "There is nothing in Honduras for me but death."

But the Mexican adventure eventually runs its course. Chino returns home with empty pockets and a blanket he bought (or maybe stole) for Luz. He says the blanket will keep her warm when her arthritis flares up.

> **Marina**: When he finally came back, his hair was long and he was dirty and smelly and had gotten tattooed. It made me so sad because I had tried to take such good care of him when he was a kid. I kept him clean and always made sure he was wearing fresh clothes. I asked him, "Why are you like this now?" and he said, "Marina, you don't want to know what has happened to me. I'm just happy to be home."

It becomes clear, though, that he is not happy and that he has returned carrying hidden baggage.

> **Marina**: He came back angry. He was a different person. He was drinking like I had never seen before. Now he always had a beer in his hand and he drank *guaro* like water. He came back with all new vices like crystal meth and cocaine. During Semana Santa he got so angry at a party that he tried to kill my sister right in front of our father. He later tried to kill one of our cousins, and he completely destroyed my

Charismatic and Reckless | 77

house in a drunken rage. We had to call the police on him. He ran off and came back the next day and started tearing up my house again. It was like the Devil had gotten inside of him.

Chino terrorizes his family for almost a year with his drug- and alcohol-fueled rages. Finally, there is nothing left for him to do but leave again for Mexico. When we first meet in Chiapas, he is seven months into life on the streets a second time and cognizant of the fact that he is becoming a poster child for the damage that *el camino* can wreak on young lives.

Jason: How long have you been in Pakal-Ná on this trip?

Chino: Like twenty days.

Jason: Who did you come with?

Chino: I came up with Santos and this kid we met *en el camino* who we offered to help. The kid is sick and I'm worried about him . . . I sent him to the migrant shelter because he is underage and they can help him . . . I told him he should go there to take a bath and change his clothes. I also told him that I think he should go back to Honduras. I kept asking him, "What are you going to do?" I told him, "Look, I'm twenty years old and you are barely sixteen. You think that when I left home I wanted to end up running around like this? You don't think I'm sorry now? That I don't want to be with my family? To be in school studying?" . . . I have a kid brother at home who wants to join me here, but I don't want him to see how I am now, how I am suffering. I

don't want him to take on this life. That's what I keep telling this sixteen-year-old kid. I told him, "You're young and
really need to think because you don't want to end up here [in
Mexico] smoking and drinking and doing drugs. I'm not here
because I like it. Why do you think people come to Mexico?
We're trying to find something better. I'm not trying to get
mixed up in the same stuff I was doing at home."

It's not just the threat of death that keeps Chino away from Honduras.
His failure to get to the United States and earn money for his family is a
source of embarrassment that he speaks about in the third person.

Chino: It's like a bad joke sometimes. There are a lot of
people that go back to Honduras because they can't make it
work here in Mexico. It's humiliating going back. People
leave Honduras humiliated and fearful. And they come here
and get even more humiliated. Imagine how that person
feels. They come here to try their luck and can't find a job.
They fail and have to go back to Honduras broke. Then they
get back into what they were doing before, the bad stuff that
made them leave in the first place.

Jason: Do you think you could ever go back to Honduras?

Chino: I can go back, but what I am going to do there? Get
killed? The problem is that if I go back I will end up doing
the same things that the gangs are doing. I will go back to
what I was doing before. I mean, I would have power, guns,
money, women, everything. I would be living the life, but I'd

Charismatic and Reckless | 79

also be hurting my own people, and I just can't do that. I would have no choice but to join the *maras*. I would have to join them or they would kill me. I think it'd be better if they killed me.

Jason: So, what do you want to do?

Chino: Head north.

Jason: All the way to the border?

Chino: No, just to Mexico City. There's more freedom there than here. It's a place where you can get lost. It's *más tranquilo* than Pakal-Ná.

Jason: But Mexico City can be dangerous too, right?

Chino: Yeah, but Chino knows where to go and not to go [*laughing*]. You gotta be smart and stay alive out here. Like they say in Honduras, "A wise soldier doesn't die in war." You gotta know how to survive.

We spot the Breadman walking on the other side of the tracks. Chino whistles at him. A sputtering Volkswagen Beetle selling copies of the local newspaper drives past us. A rusted speaker mounted to the roof plays a scratchy recording of the day's headlines. All I can make out from the narrator's voice is "migrants were killed yesterday while riding *la bestia*."

CHAPTER FOUR

La Reina del Sur

A metallic groan signals an iron monster emerging from the forest. With an ancient machine gun across his chest, the guard glares down at us from the bow of the train like a figurehead trying to ward off evil spirits on the tracks. Bravado prevents the congregation of mostly young men from even acknowledging this passing metal behemoth or its sentry. Chino leans in and looks down the tracks toward Pakal-Ná, the train coming within just a few feet of his head. He turns and grins and then passes Jesmyn the blunt. She takes several deliberate hits and smirks as dagger-shaped smoke escapes from her mouth and disappears into the jungle air like a fleeing premonition.

In her pink *Heartbreaker* T-shirt and quiet way, Jesmyn seems out of place among this company of petty smugglers and low-budget hustlers. Barely twenty years old and barely five-two, she doesn't intimidate, but it's clear she holds her own. Her dark feline eyes coolly take stock of everyone and everything around her. These men with peach-fuzzed jawlines and bad attitudes do not impress her much. Their scarred and tattooed flesh is a dark-skinned road map marking pain, adventure, and dumb luck: a poorly repaired bullet wound peeks out from under a T-shirt collar; a bare arm shows off a crudely drawn pair of praying hands in blue-black ink asking for forgiveness; the ghosts of machete and knife blades walk across arms and legs. These birthmarks of violence speak a thousand truths about living through (and with) trauma, experiences that Jesmyn has come to know as quotidian.

These men talk too much for their own good. Jesmyn knows better. She understands the value of listening. She knows when to avert her eyes and when to run her mouth. Her mix of coolness, boldness, and camouflaged hyperawareness is something I will see in the more seasoned smugglers I later come to know. This attitude keeps you from painting yourself into a corner. It keeps you drawing a breath. Jesmyn is a migrant who has found herself mixed up with a bunch of male smugglers, but she clearly has the street smarts to join this crew should she choose to. She can hold her own in this hypermasculine world.

> **Jesmyn:** No one believed me when I told them that I hadn't crossed Mexico before. They said, "Tell us the truth, you've come through here." I kept saying, "It's my first time, I swear to God." People said, "This chick knows what's going on." But I didn't know anything about Mexico so I had to be wary of everyone, even the people I was traveling with. It was like I was going to school and learning. I had to listen to all the conversations happening around me, including the ones that the *guías* I was with were having.

A year after our first encounter, Jesmyn and I stand on a second-story balcony of a cheap motel room outside San Pedro Sula. The sound of us laughing our asses off and cracking open beers mixes with nighttime traffic and the screams of alley cats fighting it out below.

"Well, the impression that I got when we met in Pakal-Ná was that you had a lot of experience on the tracks," I tell her. "I thought, *She doesn't give a fuck. She's hanging out with these scary motherfuckers and seems fearless. I mean, it was obvious from the start when I first met you that you were chingona.*"

Jesmyn has been in Pakal-Ná only a few days when I meet her. She has worked her way up from Guatemala with a group of migrants and smugglers she ran into at the border with Mexico. The group includes Chino and Santos, who had gone south to help a man called Shadow transport several Honduran women. Jesmyn tags along after Chino promises her safe passage for at least a few hundred kilometers. It helps that she thinks he is good-looking.

Pakal-Ná is supposed to be a pit stop on her way to the United States. Instead, she finds herself stranded there for almost a month, trying to raise enough money to continue on. She falls in with Chino, Santos, and the rest of the Pleasure Palace crew, who are all waiting for the right moment to get moving again. Rather than pass the days in the jungle, Jesmyn quickly adapts to the situation and finds work at a restaurant in Palenque. She spends her nights in Pakal-Ná, where she enjoys her freedom being away from home. She also takes no shit from anyone.

> **Jesmyn:** I left work one afternoon and went to the park in Pakal-Ná where there were a bunch of Honduran guys that I knew. We were drinking with this Mexican and he started messing with this Honduran kid. We try not to get mixed up with Mexicans because we know that we are in their country and can't really protect ourselves. Still, this Mexican guy kept bothering this poor kid. He was grabbing him by his shirt and harassing him. No one I was with wanted to get involved. No one. Someone finally said, "Hey, *loco*, leave him alone. We don't want any trouble." But the Mexican just

La Reina del Sur | 83

ignored him and kept messing with the kid. Finally, I got pissed and stood up and told the kid to come sit with me and I offered him a beer. The Mexican came towards us and I started yelling at him like I was all big. I told that Mexican, "Get the hell out of here! Leave this kid alone! Go home and sleep it off because you are fucked up." Everybody got quiet. No one was saying anything. The Mexican didn't know who I was and got scared. I was screaming at him and he was like, "Who the hell is this chick? What the hell is her problem?" I got crazy on him and he took off and didn't come back. All the men I was with were like, "This woman has huge balls. We got the fucking Reina del Sur* [Queen of the South] here with us!" [*Both of us are laughing.*]

Jesmyn defies the simplistic stereotype of the vulnerable female migrant that has often captured the imagination of journalists and the popular media. She doesn't cower. She is not meek. However, she is also not naive. She understands that the migrant trail is an especially difficult place for women, who are subject to higher rates of assault, rape, kidnapping, sex trafficking, and murder compared with men. Rape at the hands of bandits, law enforcement, and smugglers is so pervasive during the migration process that some begin taking birth control pills before they start their journey. Given the higher risks that women face, many have developed gendered strategies for mitigating danger en route. This can include performing the role of an overly feminine or chaste woman in need of protection or overemphasizing personal toughness. One of the most common strategies is to travel with male companions who can ostensibly provide physical protection. This male protective role can be played by a relative, a stranger, or a smuggler. In some

---

* *La Reina del Sur* was a popular Mexican telenovela about a female drug kingpin.

instances, a female migrant and her male guide may even take on the temporary roles of husband and wife, which also provides a cover story that helps facilitate entry into migrant shelters that don't allow smugglers. However, these relationships of protective pairing are complicated and can lead to women being forced into sex for protection, something that Chino has hinted at. But as Wendy Vogt notes in her ethnography of Central American migration across Mexico, women are not voiceless in the process, and the realms of smuggling and personal intimacy are not so clear-cut: "The lines that separate smuggler, guide, companion, friend, lover, and family members can become blurred during a single journey. Migrants' agency and strategies for survival . . . [challenge] the often gendered constructions of migrants and human smugglers as either victims or criminals."

Jesmyn begins her friendship with Chino after he offers to escort her to Pakal-Ná. She decides to go with him mostly because of a physical attraction that soon blossoms into a relationship. She makes it clear that she was not someone actively seeking male protection.

Jason: Was there a time when you were scared?

Jesmyn: Me? The truth is no, because I wasn't in my country. I'm more scared here in Honduras . . . than I am in Mexico. I was in Mexico trying to get away from the bad people in [my country], and yet they were all there. I mean of course Mexicans can treat you badly on the journey, but thank God, I never experienced that. I ran into a lot of Mexicans who would ask how you were doing, if you were okay. These were people who tried to help you and sometimes even offered to hide you in their house. Because of that, I never had any fear in Mexico. Actually, I felt free because my mom wasn't around telling me what to do [*laughing*]. Nobody was bossing me around.

Jason: Do you think your way of being tough on the streets and always watching out is because you are from Honduras?

Jesmyn: I think so, because [here] you are always on guard. There are a lot of times in Honduras when something bad can happen to you, so you just get used to it.

Kinship

Five-year-old Jesmyn stares at her mother, Ramona, as the diminutive woman in a modest housedress kneels in the the street rocking back and forth. Ramona looks up at the blinding Honduran sun and pleads with God for mercy. Gravel cuts into her kneecaps. Her moaning and wailing cut through the murmurs of the growing crowd around her. Segregated in grief by yellow police tape, she pleads with the corpse on the ground to rise up. The primal tongue of sorrow, a language devoid of grammar or syntax, echoes off the boiling blacktop and is felt deep inside the chests of gawking strangers. Jesmyn knows that he is dead but doesn't yet understand what that means. It will take years to make sense of it all, years for the realization to set in that violence is both senseless and predictable, an inescapable part of life. For now, all she knows is that her mother is in pain, but she herself feels nothing. A child's innocence shields her from experiencing agony in this moment. She quietly watches as blood pools under the body of Oscar, the young man she believed to be her brother.

Jesmyn: I thought I had the perfect family. My mom, my dad, and my sister always doted on me, and I didn't really know why. My dad worked hard to take care of us. He showered me with gifts. My mom always took me with her to church. I was happy. Then when I was ten years old, my parents told me that I wasn't their kid. At first, I thought they were joking. My mom said, "You are not my child. I am your grandmother and your father is your grandfather. That is not your sister, that is your aunt. But it doesn't matter, we raised you and we are your parents."

It was then that Jesmyn understood that the lifeless body lying in the street five years earlier was not her older brother but her biological father.

Growing up in poverty often enculturates children to understand two interrelated issues. First, violence (in its many forms) is a fact of life that one grows accustomed to: domestic violence, interpersonal violence, structural violence. People die because they don't have health insurance or access to clean water or the meager funds needed to buy antibiotics. People die because there are too many hungry mouths to feed and a few dollars a day isn't enough to fight off malnutrition. People die because poverty breeds rage and that rage needs an outlet. Maybe it's violence toward your kids, your spouse, or that guy on the corner who looked at you funny. Second, growing up poor means that kinship is an ever-evolving survival strategy. A grandmother raises her children's children because there is no other option. A neighbor adopts a kid from down the street because not doing so would be a death sentence for the child. The man you call father is actually an older brother or an uncle. The households of the poor may not mimic the stereotypical American nuclear family, but they are not broken. Children being raised by siblings, grandparents, or nonbiological kin is a functional response to capitalistic systems that disenfranchise the poor, lower their life expectancies, and provide a constant source of familial disruption. Poverty forces migration. Poverty begets violence. Violence (and migration) rupture family structures. Families adjust to provide support, love, and stability against all odds. Jesmyn's kinship diagram is not an anomaly but rather the norm for much of the world. Before she ever understood what was happening around her, she was already learning that bad things can come to pass at any time, and you and your family must learn to live with it in order to thrive.

The Righteous and the Wicked

Jesmyn's father, Oscar, like Chino, is a wild child who matures quickly on the streets of Llanos de Sula, a rough-and-tumble *colonia* on the eastern edge of San Pedro Sula. The neighborhood is controlled by 18th Street, but Oscar avoids directly affiliating with the gang so that he can move freely across territories. He is outgoing and quick to fall in with anyone looking to have a good time, which means he parties with both 18th Street and MS-13. Street life is thrilling, but he doesn't want to choose sides.

By the time he is a teenager, Oscar occupies a man's body and is often assumed to be much older than he really is. When he hooks up with Jesmyn's mother, Julia, he is fifteen and she is twenty-two. Being tall and handsome and experienced with women and the streets makes it easy for him to convince her that he too is in his twenties. It's not until Julia becomes pregnant that she learns her boyfriend is a kid wholly unprepared for parenting or supporting a baby. Soon after her birth, Jesmyn comes to live with her grandparents, who assume the role of mother and father. Oscar plays the doting older sibling.

Jesmyn: I always thought of [Oscar] as my brother because we were raised together like that. Still, I could tell that he really loved me. I knew that because I could see the difference in the way he acted with me versus my sister. He was always closest to me. He was always buying me presents, but I didn't know why. If you look at pictures of him you can see that we are almost twins. We look the same. We talk the same. People would say that we were identical. I think that's why my parents and sister spoiled me later on, because I reminded them of him.

Oscar loves to party with his friends, but he can't escape the intense religious upbringing that his mother, Ramona, a devout Seventh-day Adventist, exposes him to. Church is the most important thing in the household. His mother doesn't want to have a conversation unless it circles back to the power and might of God and the difference between the righteous and the wicked. Oscar lives it up on the streets, but he is also committed to trying to do the right things, the godly things. If he sees goodness in you, he wants to help. If he sees you sinning, he can't look away.

When Jesmyn is five, Oscar takes a job in San Pedro Sula. He wants to give straight life a try. One day at work he learns that an employee is stealing from their boss. His Christian upbringing tells him he can't keep quiet if he sees someone being wronged. He confides in his boss, and his coworker is soon unemployed. This righteousness will come back to haunt him.

"My mom was making breakfast for me and my sister one morning when there was a knock at the door," Jesmyn remembers. "Someone came in and said, 'I have to tell you something, *señora*, but it's really difficult to say.'" A bottle of milk explodes on kitchen floor. *This is not real*, Ramona tells herself. *I will not cry, because this is not real. This is not happening.* Ramona does not believe the news. A kid soon rides up to the house on a bike and bangs on the door: "Come with me and I will show you where your son is." The teenage psychopomp leads her into the darkness. She soon returns for Jesmyn and her sister. Ramona is different now. She has seen it. She now believes. The two small children squeeze their mother's hands as they race to the crime scene.

The endings are horrific and life-shattering, but the plots are often simple. A former coworker holds a grudge. Oscar is out partying and unsuspecting. The knife comes from behind. It enters several times before the pain registers. His shirt becomes damp and a metallic smell fills the air. He staggers in the street, his hands grabbing at pierced flesh. A fountain of fluid that cannot be contained. Words escape his mouth, but that doesn't matter anymore. Nothing can be done.

Jesmyn stares long and hard at Oscar resting in his fabric-lined box. "It hurt to be at his funeral," she recalls, "but I didn't cry. He looked the same to me, and I didn't really know what was happening. In my mind I guess I knew that my brother had died, but I didn't feel tremendous pain. My parents did, though."

Five years later, Jesmyn would learn the truth about Oscar and cling to her few clear memories of him. A body lying in the street. A body lying in a casket. She and her father lying in a hammock together giggling like children.

Running Scared

Even before Oscar died, Jesmyn had already noticed them. It's hard not to. Young men roaming the neighborhood, scaring old people and showing off for girls.

Jesmyn: There are a lot of women who like attention from those types of people. They feel like big shots because their boyfriends are *pandilleros*. They think that no one can touch them or say something bad to them, and if they do, their boyfriends will respond. The majority of women who date *mareros* think that they are untouchable. I guess I really started paying attention to them when I was around eight years old. Their guns and the way that they talked got my attention. In the beginning those guys scared me, but I also got excited by them.

Smiley has grown accustomed to getting or taking whatever he wants, especially girls. He will fuck anything that moves but prefers the young ones—the virginal ones with timid hands and clean-smelling hair. As a high-ranking gang member, Smiley has lots of girlfriends across various neighborhoods. He also has a steadily increasing herd of baby Smileys running around. Still, there is always room for more, and he loves the hunt.

He's been watching Jesmyn for a long time. So precious in her schoolgirl uniform, hands covering her mouth every time he makes her laugh or blush or scamper away half scared. It's hard for a thirteen-year-old girl to process what it means to be the violent sexual obsession of a man more than ten years her senior. A powerful man. An obsessed man. A heavily armed man.

Jesmyn: I was thirteen or fourteen and he was like twenty-five. He was an adult, but he was in love with me. He would come walking down the street dressed like a cholo. He wore a bulletproof vest and Nike Cortez and baggy Dickies pants. He always had a lot of guns that he carried in his waistband. He would scare me because he would start following me and asking questions like, "Can I walk you home?" I would say, "No, thanks, I live really close by." But I would be shitting

La Reina del Sur | 91

my pants. I was so afraid, but I was also kind of in love. Not like in love for real, but it was like he was my first crush as a little kid.

He was always looking for ways to run into me. He would be waiting for me outside of school and would try to walk me home . . . This went on for two years. I was becoming increasingly more afraid of his attention. I started high school and he was still waiting outside of school, except now he was on a motorcycle. I would see him on that motorcycle and would take routes home that I knew he couldn't follow because they were too narrow for his bike. I would walk home as fast as I possibly could. Still, he would stop me and say, "Hop on, my love," or "Can I take you home?" I would say, "No, thanks, I'm in a hurry and have to take this shortcut." Other times he would catch me walking and try to put his arm around me. He would start asking me questions: "What's your name? How old are you? You are so beautiful. What's your phone number?" I was so afraid that I wouldn't even say anything to him. I would just start walking faster. People saw him coming after me, but everybody knew that I wasn't like that. They knew that I was a homebody, a schoolgirl. A girl who went to church and never went out. But he didn't care. He was in love with me and followed me on that motorcycle. He would drive around my house, but he wouldn't dare come to the door because he was afraid of my mom.

A meeting is called in the girls' bathroom at school. "I've got something for you," her friend says. Jesmyn takes the manila envelope, thinking it might be an early birthday present. She reaches inside and pulls out a cell phone. She puts her hand back in and extracts a photo of Smiley. Her heart stops. She looks at her friend in disbelief. She puts everything back into the envelope and returns it.

"I want nothing to do with this." Jesmyn starts thinking about an escape plan.

It is dark outside when she pulls off her blouse and tosses it onto the dresser. She pauses for a moment to inspect her naked torso. That's when she notices the outline of someone's head peering over her shoulder through her second-story window. Jesmyn turns to confirm it's him before quickly returning her eyes to the mirror. The metal security bars squeak as he adjusts his hands and tries to steady his dangling body for a better look. Their eyes lock in the mirror. He probably thinks she is posing for him. In reality, she is too scared to move. Jesmyn steadies herself. She turns around, walks to the window, and closes the curtains without saying a word.

> **Jesmyn:** After that, I had to tell my mom what had been happening. I couldn't deal with the fear anymore. It had been going on for years, and now that I was older I thought he might rape or kill me. Who knows what he could do to me when he was all drugged out? I told my mom what was happening and how long it had been going on. She was shocked because I had never said anything about it. I'd always told her I was okay. That was when she said I had to leave the house.

Running away can be a dangerous move. Smiley has contacts across Honduras. Jesmyn's sudden disappearance after spotting him in her bedroom window could make his pursuit of her even more aggressive and violent. So instead of escaping, she goes into hiding. For the next year, she never ventures out alone. Her life begins to revolve around going to school, church, and an occasional shopping trip, always with a chaperone, usually her Bible-thumping mother. Jesmyn passes a lot of time sitting on the front porch. For almost a year, she watches Smiley circling her house on his motorcycle, always flashing a grin. Then one day her mom comes home in tears.

Smiley has been arrested.

The worry now is that with Smiley in prison, he will have more time to fixate on Jesmyn and will start sending his soldiers to harass her (or do worse). Conversely, this could be a good time to disappear, since he is overwhelmed with court proceedings and adjusting to life behind bars. It breaks Ramona's heart to send Jesmyn away, but she knows that now is the time. It is the only way to protect her. The only way to keep her away from a violent man with a deadly fixation.

With tears running down her face, Ramona packs her teenage daughter's bags and puts her on a bus to a distant coastal town. "You can never come back here," she cries. Jesmyn's destination is the place where her birth mother lives, a woman she barely knows. No matter—it's easier to survive in a locale where she has family who can help her keep her story straight about why she left San Pedro Sula. Jesmyn will live in exile for almost a year.

IN ONE SCENARIO, it was an accident. Maybe faulty wiring or somebody fucking around with something that's not a toy. In another version, the one whispered into ears or spoken in low voices behind closed doors, it was a deadly surprise for Smiley that came gift wrapped. *You open it, homie. It's your birthday present.* Both versions end the same. An explosion of light and a hail of unforgiving metal rain. A cloud of smoke and dust. The sounds of screaming mixing with the percussion of debris falling from the ceiling of the prison cell. When the dust settles from the bomb, Smiley makes no noise at all.

"When we heard the news," Jesmyn remembers, "my mom said to me, 'God can liberate you from anything.' The only thing I was thinking about was that now I could go wherever I wanted." No longer afraid to return home and no longer forced to live among strangers, Jesmyn seeks liberation. She grabs the backpack that once carried her high school textbooks and fills it with clothes, some makeup, and a cell phone charger. She knows that her destiny is not in Honduras, so she boards a bus headed for the Guatemala border with the aspirations that many of her generation have.

Jesmyn: I want to be somebody. I want to shine. I don't need to be rich. I just want to have some money so that I can say to my parents, "You don't have to work. I will take care of both of you. I will go to work so that I can pay for everything." That's my dream. I don't know why, but I feel it in my heart that one day I'm going to be in the United States and I will be able to take care of my parents. I will give them the life they want and pay them back for all they have done for me, because life in Honduras is difficult.

CHAPTER FIVE

Foot Soldiers

The Sonoran Desert sun is disorienting and merciless. Santos can't make sense of north or south. He thinks they are headed in the right direction, but that is really only because he puts faith in the Mexican who is leading this train of drug mules. Days into this exhausting journey he is starting to question his decision to come. Still, carrying drugs on his back will cover his border-crossing fees all the way up to Phoenix. On his own, he could never come up with the $3,000 to $5,000 needed to pay a *coyote* for this trip. He puts one sluggish foot in front of the other and quietly prays for rain and a future job that doesn't involve doing this type of bullshit or working for these types of assholes. His daydream is shattered by the pathetic voice of a young kid, the only other Honduran in this crew of smugglers.

"Give me a chance, *loco*. *Cinco minutos*," the kid begs.

The guide barks back, "Fuck you! Hurry up."

"I can't."

"I'm not asking you. I'm telling you."

"*Cinco minutos*. Please, bro."

The knife he pulls out is chipped and rust-stained. It has craggy teeth like a child's drawing of a monster.

"Get up now or you're gonna get two *puñalazos*. Then I'm going to leave you here to die, motherfucker."

"*Cálmate, loco*. Don't say that shit," Santos pleads.

"Stay out of this. It's none of your business."

"Please, please, please. Don't let them kill me! Please!"

"Get the fuck up."

"Leave him alone," Santos commands.

"Why the fuck do you care?"

"He's a *catracho*, a *paisa*.* How's it gonna look if two *catrachos* enter the desert and only one of us comes out? I can't let that happen. If you're going to do this shit to him, how do I know you won't do it to me too?"

Santos unties the coarse ropes cinched around his shoulders and chest. Fifty-five pounds of hard-packed marijuana makes a dull thump as it hits the dirt. Above them the sun is an angry red eye looking down at the train of drug mules. The kid starts vomiting foam. The other men get restless.

"This is bullshit. Fuck them both. Let's go!" someone yells.

The guide sticks a SIM card into his cell phone and dials.

"*Jefe*, I'm gonna kill both of these motherfuckers right now because they won't move."

"Who?" his boss asks.

"The *catrachos*. They say they don't want to go on."

Santos shakes his head. "We want to go on, but we can't. Look at this guy. He can't even walk."

"But you can walk, *güey*. Fuck him. Let's move."

---

* In this instance, *paisa* is short for *paisano* ("fellow countryman") and not a reference to the Paisas, a Latino prison gang.

Foot Soldiers | 97

"This *vato* is a *paisa*, *loco*. How can I leave him?"

"Goddamnit! If I get caught because of you, I'll find you in Mexico and fucking kill you."

"Kill whoever you want, but I'm staying here."

"This is bullshit. We are wasting time. Fuck!" someone screams.

The kid groans and begs, "Please don't leave me here!"

The guide whispers something into the phone and hangs up. He tells everyone to hide their packs.

The men lie in the dirt beneath gnarled mesquite trees that offer little respite from the violent midday sun. The kid sips tepid water and tries to slow his pounding chest. His skin is pale and cold. He wonders how he can be freezing in this heat. Around him, men in camouflaged clothes are scattered about the desert in similar positions of uneasy repose. For hours they chase shade and pretend that an escape from the heat is possible.

The kid's voice breaks as he speaks to Santos. "You saved my life. I was going to die and you saved me. They were going to kill me. I could see it. The darkness. It was coming for me. I could feel it coming."

Santos thinks about his mother and imagines how she would feel if he never walked out of this desert. Time quietly passes. The sky blackens and night brings on a temporary sense of stillness.

The men have been walking for hours by the time rays from a piss-yellow sun warm the morning horizon. Santos synchronizes his steps with the kid and watches from behind for signs of fatigue. By midday, one of the Mexicans is weak-kneed and delirious. His staggering increases before his body finally admits that the weight on his back is too much. He falls to the ground, forcing the group to pause.

"Get the fuck up! We need to keep moving!" the guide yells.

Twenty minutes later he falls down again.

"Come on, *culero*! If those fucking *catrachos* can do it, so can you!"

The Mexican wobbles for a few hundred feet and collapses.

"The sun is too much. He's going to slow us down," the guide says. "We'll wait until dark to move again."

"Why aren't you yelling at him?" Santos asks. "Why don't you threaten to kill him and leave him out here? Why don't you talk to him like you talked to us? You think Hondurans are animals so you can treat us like shit? Answer my fucking question!"

"We are wasting time," the guide coolly responds. "Hide your packs and we will try again after dark."

Stars are beginning to emerge high above them when one of the Mexicans passes Santos a lit cigarette. The stranger looks away as he starts quietly speaking into the coming night. "You don't have what it takes to be a guide out here."

"Why is that?" Santos asks.

"You're too soft. This job requires that you do bad things. People die out here. If you don't threaten them, they won't keep going."

Santos opens his mouth and releases a cloud of dry smoke into the Sonoran Desert air. "Well, *loco*, I think you're right. I'm not built for this."

WE ARE ON THE TRAIN TRACKS in Pakal-Ná on one of those rare afternoons when a light breeze cuts the dense humidity. Reggaeton pumps out of someone's cell phone—"Fanática sensual" by the group Plan B. A robotic bass drum and snare pulsate, filling the jungle air with a sluggish rhythm. Santos's baby beer gut and tattoos are visible through a black mesh shirt. Santa Muerte grips a scythe as she dances on his chest. One of his hands clutches a plastic cup of beer while the other tugs on his belt buckle as he swings his hips to the music. Santos is encircled by laughing men, a jester entertaining a band of ruffians. His sensual movements make us blush and cackle.

Of all the guides I meet on the migrant trail, Santos is the one who seems to have the most earnest plan for getting out. He previously spent time in the United States working a straight job and now wants nothing more than to get back to those backbreaking (but honest) twelve-hour days framing houses and laying roof tiles. For him, life on the train tracks is only temporary. He yearns to save up enough money for a desert crossing and a return to an American life of semi-steady paychecks and a roof over his head. "I just want to work, Jason," he tells me one afternoon in Pakal-Ná early in our relationship. "I just want to get away from all of this." Over the years that I've come to know Santos, a few things have become clear. He is kind and gentle and ill-suited to making smuggling a long-term career goal. He wants nothing more than to find a job that will provide him with some safety and stability. He also can't seem to catch a damn break.

Papo passes a joint. Chino yells for the music to get louder. Bin Laden hurriedly refills our beers like a good host while Santos dances and we all laugh. The dembow repeats and repeats, but time doesn't move. I freeze this moment in my mind and then rewind it so that I can hear the rhythm again and again. I rewind it so that I can remember a time when this chaotic world was briefly still and none of these men were ghosts or demons or dust.

Soldados

In a tiny village two hours east of San Pedro Sula a child watches the body of his father being lowered into a void of dark soil. He's been legally dead only a few days, but everyone started to say goodbye after the stroke that left him in a vegetal state. The boy watched his father wither away for three months before his heart finally stopped beating. Santos doesn't know it yet, but that ringside seat to a slow death is a preview of sadness and loss he will come to know intimately as an adult. Two years later, that child, now barely thirteen, begins walking north out of the village. He never looks back.

Juvenile and malnourished, Santos the young explorer enters surreal worlds in Mexico built on danger and violence. Rail yards inhabited by soot-faced men crazed with drink and sex. Jungles dense with animals of all species, including predators armed with machetes and rope and the rejection of mercy that comes from having no witnesses. The child memorizes this perverse landscape while trying not to let it devour him. Sleep comes in alleys and under bridges. Adventure comes on the top of barreling boxcars. The child begs, borrows, and steals to stay alive. Santos comes of age alone, with increasingly vague notions of what home is and what it means to live.

At sixteen he is tied to a chair with filthy rope. A man in a ski mask methodically slices designs into Santos's forearms like some cruel and ancient rite of passage. "All you have to do is give us a phone number," the man whispers. "Who is going to save you, *loco*?" But there is no one for Santos to call. There is no money and no savior. There is only *la letra Z*, the last letter. The unnamable.

"God, please don't abandon your child," he begs.

Santos counts himself lucky as he limps bloody and beaten down a highway outside San Fernando, Tamaulipas, a town known for the mass murder of hundreds of migrants and locals over the years. The Zetas, one of Mexico's most brutal cartels, have had their way with him, and miraculously he is still breathing, with his genitals and fingers intact. He looks at the deep red parallel lines cut across both his forearms. It was like his torturers were keeping score. The police pick up Santos from the side of the road and bring him to the hospital. He's underage, so they feel sorry for him even though it might have been cops who did this to him. After two weeks of hospital recuperation, he is handed 4,000 pesos ($200) for a bus ticket back to Honduras.

Foot Soldiers | 101

But there's no going back. There is nothing in Honduras except poverty and the teenage gangsters who will kill him in broad daylight if he refuses to do their bidding. The future is forward, even if it means facing death again. If he moves forward, at least he faces death on his own terms. He takes the money they give him and buys food and water to get through the South Texas backwoods. He is carrying those supplies when Border Patrol catches him a few days later just outside San Antonio. He eats his leftover rations on the deportation flight back to Central America. A week after failing to enter the United States, he uses what is left of his hospital money to buy a bus ticket out of Honduras.

By the time Santos approaches the *mareros* in Pakal-Ná, asking for work, he is a hardened young soldier who knows how to follow orders and how to swallow pain. He has been on the train tracks for several years and understands what it's like to fail crossing into the United States. While he's had shit luck getting to America, he has become an expert at clandestine movement on the tracks. He has learned how to pass for Mexican. He has gotten good at being invisible. The *mareros* give him a cell phone, instructions, and a handful of migrants. "Get this group to Celaya," they tell him. "A man will be waiting for you in a truck." He thinks this will be easy money because Mexico has yet to start the intensified hunt for Central Americans that will begin under Programa Frontera Sur. This feels like a job he's been training for his whole life, which is partly true. He helps his clients onto a train leaving Pakal-Ná. Seven days later, his cargo is tired and hungry but safely in Celaya. They pile into a waiting vehicle. Someone hands Santos 8,000 pesos ($400).

He will subsequently make many drop-offs in Celaya in the years to come. He will get smarter about whom to trust and whom to avoid. He will follow simple orders and get the job done over and over again. The work will become steady enough for him to save a little cash before he decides he's had enough of the tracks and heads north toward Arizona. He will pay for his own clandestine passage by carrying a *mochila* full of marijuana across the desert.

Santos's brief experience as a drug mule forces him to question his own morals and the limits of what he is willing to do to survive. He successfully crosses the U.S.-Mexico border and takes solace in the fact that he didn't leave that kid from Honduras to die under the Sonoran sun. He also didn't leave any part of himself in the desert because of greed or selfishness. The trip was worth it because he soon finds that life in Phoenix brings a newfound sense of peace and tranquility. He rents a room with friends he has met on the street. He sleeps on a bed—his own bed. He finds pride in steady employment. Building houses in the suffocating Arizona heat is rough, but the $180 he sometimes earns in a day is more than he would make in a month cutting sugarcane back home. Life away from the train tracks is good even if the American dream is not perfect. He might live in constant fear of deportation, but that's better than the constant fear of being murdered. For months, he tries to live the quiet and under-the-radar life of the undocumented and go where the work takes him. He gets nervous one morning when his boss accepts a job in Tucson, where Border Patrol presence is an order of magnitude more intense than in Phoenix. "Don't worry, I go down there all the time," his employer reassures him. After their vehicle changes lanes without using a turn signal, Santos finds himself handcuffed and on an airplane soaring toward San Pedro Sula.

His *pueblo* is different after so many years away. Kids he grew up with now rule the neighborhood with impunity. MS-13 is the law. Santos is offered a job collecting extortion money from his friends, neighbors, and family. He refuses. The gang threatens him. He asks to speak directly with Spider, the clique leader he has known all his life. He pleads his case. Spider gives him an ultimatum: "Join us, leave, or we kill you. Those are the rules." Santos has spent his youth trying to avoid gang life, and after all he has seen

Foot Soldiers | 103

in Mexico and Arizona, he knows it is a road that dead-ends. He begs Spider to let him stay. Spider is not an unreasonable person. He gives Santos three weeks to get his affairs in order before he must vacate the premises.

ANA TIJOUX'S VOICE grumbles out from a cell phone speaker. *Crisis of men. Crisis of those who want to be happy. Crisis of people with scars.* Santos mixes a pool of black ink, cloudy with dirt and blood, while curious strangers hover over him in awe. A train screams in the distance as he wets the needle and continues the delicate surgery on his own flesh. "That's fucking badass, *perro*," Chino tells him. "You think you can tattoo me?"

And just like that, two desperate young men on the hunt for quick money and a better future randomly collide on the train tracks in Mexico. Chino and Santos bond over their mutual feeling of abandonment and a childhood partially spent on the migrant trail. They show each other their scars and talk about the difficult lives that have brought them to Chiapas. The two of them have grown up in an environment in Mexico where friendships are fleeting and betrayal is the norm. Trust is not something either is very familiar with, but something clicks between them. They find a fast kinship they hope will end differently than their many previous failed relationships. "A wise soldier doesn't die in war," Chino often says. A wise soldier has a sixth sense. A wise soldier finds a homie who has his back, which is exactly what he and Santos find in one another on that day in Pakal-Ná. Soon they are making plans to move clients who need help getting across Mexico.

Chino and Santos become thick as thieves as they laugh and talk shit and watch the Mexican countryside flash past them from the tops of freight trains. If you listen closely, you can hear the train schedule of the cursed being whispered into the wind: Chancalá to Pakal-Ná. Tenosique to Pakal-Ná. Corozal to Pakal-Ná. Benemérito to Pakal-Ná. Pakal-Ná to Salto de Agua. Pakal-Ná to Coatza. Pakal-Ná to Celaya. Days, weeks, and months go by as the two young men make trip after trip, escorting migrants through a maze of dangers. They are spiders clinging to train cars. Teenage pilgrims guiding the meek through a jungle Babylon. Brothers in a shared battle against poverty and the random violence that characterizes their occupation.

Some clients are arranged via anonymous phone calls and money wires. Others come to them on the tracks, hat in hand, with the phone number of a relative in Houston who can help cover the costs of the next leg of the journey. Either way, Santos and Chino never make more than a few hundred dollars per trip, but that's enough to buy food, weed, cell phone credit, and a few nights' rental of a dirty mattress in a cinder-block room on the tracks. The quick bursts of money are intoxicating, and they don't mind the low moments when they sleep on the street or have to pass themselves off as needy migrants so that they can get a free meal at a shelter. They inhabit a world of boom or bust, but it's not so much the money as the freedom and the adrenaline that keep them tethered to the tracks. For the two of them, their shared nomadic lifestyle is addictive, and so is the intense feeling of being alive and briefly in control of something.

SANTOS HAS BEEN MISSING for more than a week and no one in Pakal-Ná can give me a straight answer about his whereabouts. I stop asking Chino and others because every day I get a different answer. *He went north to start a job in the United States. He's in Guatemala bringing a group of migrants up. He is in Salto de Agua and will be back tomorrow.* People prefer to lie than admit they don't know something. Misinformation is a currency constantly traded on the tracks out of malice, ignorance, or the fear of coming across as naive. It's always better to give the impression that you know things, because uninformed people are targets. In the end, the answer I am looking for is simple and predictable.

"It Used to Not Be Like This"

The darkness pretends to bring calm to the jungle. Insects serenade each other and faraway stereos send lullabies into the late night. The quiet radio rhythms are seductive, hypnotic. They give a false sense of security. Work has been slow lately because Immigration has put up a security fence around Pakal-Ná: highway checkpoints, train raids, jungle hunts for people walking on the tracks. If you can't get out of Chiapas you can't make any money. *Where the hell is Chino?* Santos asks himself. *Probably off on one of his benders. That guy needs to slow down on the drinking. It's gonna kill him. Don't fall asleep. Don't fall asleep.* Santos knows better but can't help it. His eyelids are heavy. He just needs a couple of hours to recharge.

In the distance, gravel crunches underneath slow-moving tires. Streetlights bounce off the shiny paint of brand-new immigration vans creeping around street corners. Escape routes are blocked. A quarter of a mile north of where Santos is sleeping, the combat boots of federal agents begin their midnight march down the tracks. Whispers. Hand signals. The soft squelch of radios with their volume on low. Suddenly, yellow beams of light appear out of nowhere. Torches interrogate the jungle foliage. The scared eyes of men crouching in the dark reflect the light back. *¡No te muevas, culero!* If you run, we shoot!

The screams shake Santos awake. He instinctively sprints blindly into the darkness, making it only a few hundred feet before losing a shoe. As he turns to recover it, the weight of a man slams into his back. Muscular hands pin him to the ground. His own hands claw at the dirt as he tries to break free. The agent pushes on the side of his face, forcing him to look down the tracks. He can see flashlights dancing through the blackness as migrants flee into the jungle. Dogs bark in the night as if cheering for the home team. Santos closes his eyes and exhales.

HIS FINGERTIPS ARE ROLLED in black ink. He scratches a fake name onto a deportation form. Then it's three days in a filthy cell in Palenque, followed by three more days in an even filthier cell in Tapachula. He and his fellow travelers are handcuffed when they board the bus. Honduran men with demoralized faces watch the Mexican countryside roll by. The prisoners are given bread and water, like in the movies. Santos whispers to a young man across the aisle from him. They nod in agreement about their next steps. Soldiers greet the bus in Corinto, Honduras. His country is now a foreign land. A curse to escape from. "*Mamá*, I'm at the border," Santos says over a staticky phone line. "I wish I could see you, but I can't. Those guys are waiting for me there."

When the sun starts to show its face above the trees, Santos and the guy he met on the deportation bus are five kilometers into Guatemala. He gives half his money to police officers who stop them on the road. Later, he gives the other half to Guatemalan federal agents who board the bus he is riding. Thirty-six hours after leaving Honduras (again), Santos is being chased by Mexican immigration officials who come running out of the jungle near Chancalá. This time he doesn't lose a shoe. They scream at him, but he refuses to look back as he makes his way full speed toward Pakal-Ná.

"IT USED TO not be like this," Santos tells me fifteen days after being arrested and deported. His black hair is greasy and uncombed. His clothes are muddy and he looks ten pounds lighter. He has been deported from Mexico numerous times, but this recent trip seems to have taken a toll on his body and his psyche. He speaks to me with a newfound sense of weariness.

Foot Soldiers | 107

Santos: I'm scared now. Before when I would leave Honduras, it would take me six days to get from my house to Coatza [Coatzacoalcos, Veracruz]. Now, I've been in Pakal-Ná almost a month and I still haven't gotten to Coatza. Before, it was a lot easier because you could travel on *la bestia* and they didn't charge a *cuota*. There also weren't any immigration agents guarding the train. If you wanted to, you could also go by bus and there wasn't a lot of immigration there either. But now all this stuff has started. They say that the United States has an agreement with the Mexican government to detain Central Americans. So now they aren't letting anyone pass, especially those from Honduras. Our president says that in Honduras there is money and work, so we shouldn't be leaving. But that is only true for his people. His people have resources, but there is nothing for us. Our government doesn't support the poor.

Santos's recent arrest and deportation are the direct result of Programa Frontera Sur, an enforcement shift that has changed the entire migration landscape. It is now significantly harder to cross Mexico because of this initiative's heightened security measures and mass deportations, but people are still coming for the same reasons: poverty, violence, political instability, environmental catastrophes.

Programa Frontera Sur has increased reliance on guides to cross Mexico while creating new moneymaking opportunities for cartels and gangs, who for many years were already heavily invested in taxing, extorting, kidnapping, and generally brutalizing migrants. This program simply exacerbates a preexisting problem by encouraging cartels to become even more invested in controlling all aspects of smuggling between Central America and the

United States. To meet customer demand in the wake of Programa Frontera Sur and safely net a profit, smugglers have had to adjust to this changing milieu, which now includes raising their prices and sharing more of their income with criminal networks that monitor and tax their movements. For Santos and Chino, Pakal-Ná is a relatively safe space because of their connection to the local MS-13 clique. However, all bets are increasingly off when you enter foreign territory. For Santos, the new stress created by Programa Frontera Sur is overwhelming.

> **Santos:** Truthfully, [*he takes a drag from a cigarette*] it's not easy to be down with this lifestyle. There is always some *cabrón* who shows up and is like, "Who among you is the guide?" That's always the first question they ask. The next thing you know they have a gun to your head and are asking everyone to pay the *cuota*. If you don't have the *cuota*, well . . . it's hard and these guides gamble with their lives. Sometimes *guías* bring people who say they have money, but it turns out they don't and there is no one who can help them pay for the trip. Other times you connect with someone who says, "I'm going with you because I am afraid, but I can pull my own weight." But then they turn out to be useless on the trail and don't help out at all. Then you end up having problems with the people you are bringing. Believe me, working with migrants is not easy. Plus you have to deal with the *mafiosos*. You have to work with them, but you can't trust them. They have no problem killing you. If you don't pay the *cuota*, they kill you. If you pay the *cuota* but you don't get along with them, they may just take your money and kill you anyways. That's how they are . . . It's seriously a lot of work getting from Honduras to Chiapas. It's a hard job and you work daily

just to get something to eat. In the end, you never really accomplish anything with this job.

Jason: But there are people who enjoy the lifestyle, right?

Santos: I think a lot of them like it, but I can't handle it. I don't feel anything noble about getting money from being a guide. The job is hard, and you never know the truth about what is happening. You never feel safe. I don't think I was born for this type of work.

CHAPTER SIX

Papo and Alma

The motorbike skids to a halt. The engine idles and coughs exhaust while the dilated pupils of the rider peer out from behind the helmet's dark visor. The Honduran sun is high overhead as his scrawny arm takes aim with a small-caliber weapon that's larger than life in this moment. No words. No warning. A rapid cadence of clicks and pops creates a soundscape of aggression and everyday horror. The neighbors will ask *Why?* but they know the answer. Perhaps a young man looking for a place "to carry his anger." Perhaps no fathomable reason at all for this carnage. Papo's motorcycle disappears down the street, leaving behind a trail of dust and death smoke. This moment will derail his entire life.

Yo Vengo del Hoyo

The group watches the grass crystallize around them as if time itself is coming to a stop. Complicated geometric shapes of ice form on the plastic sheet they huddle under. *In the movies it's always hot in Texas*, Papo thinks to himself. *There's supposed to be vultures and cactuses and shit. No one said it would be this fucking cold.* It doesn't help that he is wearing a thin jacket and his lanky five-eight frame has zero body fat to help him stay warm. Every time they hear a car pass the group gets quiet. *Cállate, cabrón.* They listen to the darkness in hopes that it will reveal something to them. A huddled mass dreams and fantasizes. Heartbeats pulse in syncopated rhythms with moving shadows and distant echoes. It's come to this after so much time and money. A waiting game, a listening game.

A vehicle creeps. "I didn't hear the signal, did you?" someone asks. Heavy soles crunch gravel and ice. Cylinders of light break open the darkness. A peckerwood with a flattop yells in badly pronounced Spanish, "*¡No te muevas!*"

WHEN PAPO'S MOTHER handed him over to her little sister in Honduras, she didn't imagine that twelve years would pass before she would hug her son again. But that was how long it took her to save up enough money to pay a smuggler to get him to Texas. In the meantime, she couldn't have imagined the things he would experience coming of age in La Ceiba, Honduras. Or maybe she could and that's why she had to leave. She had to find a new world that she could pull her son into.

As a child in Honduras, Papo develops the understanding that horrible things can happen to anyone for no discernible rhyme or reason. Violence can come for you at any time, especially if you are a young man. As he grows, so does his fear of death, like some vicious and insatiable vine that follows him everywhere. It creeps under his bed and into his dreams. *Maras.* Bullets. *Machetes.* By the time he is a teenager, he has collected mental images of pooling blood on sidewalks and people walking through the bodies of bullet-ridden ghosts that seem to haunt every street corner in his neighborhood. His is an imagination forged by gunfire and panic. He watches as his generation goes on a quest for hope that is met with the metaphorical and literal dead ends offered up to young men like him.

Papo is rounded up on a freezing Texas night and thrown into the back of a Border Patrol vehicle. Not yet sixteen years old, he already knows what it's like to be a fugitive, a target, a wetback, an OTM,* a detainee, a prisoner, a survivor. He pleads his case to immigration agents and judges. He tells them about the bloodshed in Honduras. A lawyer scribbles his childhood sagas onto yellow notepads. Customs and Border Protection release him to a guardian mostly because of his age and not because they care or comprehend what he has been through. Everyone else in his group is sent back to Mexico or Honduras or Guatemala or India or Sierra Leone or some other place that has become increasingly unlivable. So many places where life is not sustainable for the unlucky. Those women and men will have to start their journeys all over and once again sit in a ditch on the side of the road, freezing to death, awaiting their ride to a better future. When Papo steps out of the migrant detention center in South Padre Island to greet his mother, she has to reach up to hug the man that her little boy has become in her absence.

A judge orders Papo to enroll in high school in Texas. That's where teenagers are supposed to be. Papo doesn't speak the language, so he ends up in remedial English classes. *Hi, my name is Papo. I am from Honduras.* Starting a new school is always hard. It's probably a lot harder when no one will take you seriously because you speak broken English and walk the halls with the other damaged children from Third World countries like foreign explorers awed by this *tierra lucida.* Most of his American classmates worry about whom to ask to prom or if they will pass their driving tests. It's a world away from what Papo left behind in Honduras.

---

* The Border Patrol refers to non-Mexican migrants as "OTMs," or "Other Than Mexicans."

Papo and Alma | 113

Papo: I've seen people assassinated on the streets. It's happened right in front of me. I was getting off the bus and saw people running and hiding. I watched it happen. People were falling to the ground. I watched and couldn't believe what bullets could do when they hit someone's face. I couldn't talk or breathe. All I could do was run.

His American classmates make post-graduation plans. Papo had plans once too. He imagined some good job prospects after completing a computer certification course in Honduras. He imagined going to college. Those days are gone. School is a fantasy he can no longer believe in. As soon as he turns eighteen, Papo runs away from high school and into the workforce. He breaks his back loading trucks inside a warehouse. He breaks his back learning construction. He does whatever comes his way so that he can start handing his mom some cash to help cover the $7,000 debt she incurred paying for his passage from Honduras. The jobs are menial, but at least he has a car and at least he is alive. "The majority of the kids I grew up with are dead," he tells me. "The only reason I'm not dead is because my mom got me out of the hole that I was falling into. My friends didn't have that opportunity, so they went down into that dark hole. A lot of them died in the worst fucking way." For a few years, he considers himself lucky not to be at the bottom of that hole.

The cop only finds a few grams of weed in the car, but it's enough for Papo to end up in handcuffs. This is Texas after all. It's a minor offense, so he easily makes bail. Aside from this arrest, his record has been clean for the three years he's lived in the United States. His shitty court-appointed lawyer thinks he will only have to pay a small fine and do some community service. Papo is optimistic when he arrives at the courthouse for his hearing. His optimism quickly turns to panic when he gets lost in the cavernous building.

He can't decipher the wall map mounted in the lobby. He can't find his lawyer. People try to be helpful by giving him confused directions in English and Spanglish. He walks in terrified circles before finally entering the correct courtroom. They have already called his case number and moved on. He begs and pleads and tries to explain his tardiness. The judge is unimpressed by this skinny young man with long hair and tattoos caught with marijuana in his car. A young man who can't even be relied on to show up on time for his court hearing. Being fifteen minutes late earns Papo a direct flight back to Honduras via Obama's deportation airlines.

For three years, Papo knew a life outside the black hole that threatened to destroy him. For three years he knew a life not plagued by the fear of some kid passing a bullet through his skull while waiting for the bus. For a brief moment he reveled in a life away from the gangs that give people few options and only one warning. All of that was erased in fifteen minutes. He is back in the hole he thought he had escaped from, and nothing has changed. Through a window in his aunt's living room in Honduras he can see out onto the street. He knows that the neighborhood monster with a thousand eyes still remembers him and that motorcycle. That day seems to follow him everywhere. Papo can feel all those eyes looking at him. He can hear whispers building into something dangerous that is coming for him. He grabs his backpack and begins the slow crawl out of that hole again.

Someday Never Comes

When she handed her four-month-old baby to her sister, Alma's mother told herself it wouldn't be long before she could save up enough to send for her daughter. *Everyone has a job in the United States. People earn good money there. They live good lives there. It will be easier to raise a family there.* Someday soon she will come back for the baby.

Days and months and years go by. The passage of cruel and numbing time blurs the ink on some imagined promissory note, making it almost illegible. Almost. Baby Alma becomes a little girl from some grim fairy tale who grows old waiting for a knock at the door, a surprise visit from the stranger who swore a blood oath to return. But no one sends for her. Someday never comes.

Alma finds happiness in her aunt, the kind woman who has cared for her since the day she was left behind. She is the only mother she's ever known. Another woman sometimes calls on her birthday, but that person is just a voice from a faraway place where promises go to be broken. Alma has never really met the person on the other end of the line, but when she thinks about her, she is reminded that the only thing in this world her mother ever gave her was a sense of abandonment.

THE OVERCROWDED ROOM is sour with sweat. There's a filthy toilet in the corner splattered with piss and excrement. Exhausted people lie down on any available floor space while fingers tap out messages into cheap cell phones. *I'm in a place called "Tapachula." I need $200 to try again. Ayudame.* Two women whisper to each other in K'iche'. A guard reeking of cheap aftershave asks a teenage girl if she is traveling with anyone. A baby wails and a mother coos. "Don't worry, Dulce," Alma reassures her daughter. "Everything is going to be okay." Alma thinks about her own mother and how nothing was ever okay. *"No pasa nada, mi amor,"* she tells her child. "This is a hotel, where we are going to stay for a little while. I promise we will leave here soon. Everything is going to be okay."

In Honduras, nothing is okay for Alma. For her, it's a land polluted by trauma and bad memories and more years of struggle than she cares to remember. When she tries to conjure up the good times, the thought of her murdered husband, who never did anything bad to anyone yet still ended up dead, comes back to haunt her. He didn't live long enough to see his daughter Gaby blow out the candle on her first birthday cake.

Alma thought falling in love again would change her luck, but it made things worse. She winces at the flashbacks of a drunken boyfriend's bony knuckles and the unrelenting beatings. It was as if he released a demon every time he cracked open a bottle. But demons don't live inside bottles; they live inside us. They are always there. The booze just unlocks their flimsy shackles. For Alma's entire life she's been a fighter, but her abuser turns her into a new person, someone who will now die in battle rather than sit back and passively accept her fate. A screwdriver, a pair of scissors, a stress-induced dissociation that allows her to defend herself. She will use whatever it takes to stop the blows. ("After so many years of beatings, I could pick up a knife and attack someone without even knowing it," she laments as her light brown eyes well with tears.) She won't take shit from him or anyone else, even if it means losing control of herself in the process. Thankfully, she hasn't seen her ex-boyfriend in years. He might be dead now. If so, it's a miracle he didn't take her with him to whatever hell he currently occupies. The only good thing that drunk ever did was help her make Dulce and then immediately run away. He didn't stick around long enough to sign the birth certificate.

Alma soon finds herself a thirty-year-old working single mother trying to feed to two small kids. She's a scrappy businesswoman who takes to selling clothes from a street-corner stall. It's not much, but it gives her a sense of control, which is hard to find in San Pedro Sula. On a good day she can bring in 600 lempiras ($25). But it's not long before the gangs take notice. They notice everything. An offer is made. *Pay us 200 lempiras a day to operate in this neighborhood. Pay us or die.* It's an impossible proposition that cannot be negotiated. Like so many before and after her, she closes her business and makes an escape plan. Whatever awaits her in Mexico has to be better than what she is running from.

"Gaby, you're a big girl," she says to her five-year-old, "but Dulce is too small to stay here. We will be back soon. Dulce and I will find us a new place to live in Mexico, and then I will come back for you. I promise I'll come back for you."

In that moment when Alma leaves her daughter with the aunt who raised her, she does not hear the voice of her own mother making that same vow three decades earlier. This is because she knows that no matter what happens, she will return. She is many good and bad things, but she is not her mother. Sitting in a polished-concrete holding cell in Chiapas surrounded by dozens of other migrants, she tells Dulce that everything is going to be okay.

Breakfast of Champions

"This place is fucked. My whole life is fucked."

"Shut up, Chino," Alma commands. "No one wants to hear your complaining."

"I'm serious. I'm gonna buy some bleach and drink it and get it over with."

"You're just drunk. Stop complaining."

It's early in the day, but Chino is somehow already fucked up. It's probably a carryover from last night's bender. Alma is having none of it. "You're not funny, Chino."

"I'm not trying to be funny," he says. "I'm serious."

"That's not what I'm talking about. *Oye*, Jason, this fucking guy thought it would be funny to come running down the street last night yelling, 'Immigration raid!' You should have seen everyone scatter. It was a mess."

Chino is a little embarrassed by this revelation, although it is clear he is trying to hold back his laughter. He can't help laughing at his own jokes. Alma cracks a grin and rolls her eyes. Even she can't stay mad at him for long. "Go get us something to sit on," she commands him. Chino leaves to scavenge the neighborhood for impromptu furniture. The Breadman tends to a small fire he has started in the dirt.

Alma: What the hell are you doing?

Breadman: What do you mean?

Alma: You're burning Dulce's cardboard. What is she supposed to sit on?

Breadman: I'm sorry, I didn't know.

Alma: How could you not know that it was hers? That's what she sits on!

Breadman: I'll get her some new cardboard after breakfast.

Alma looks at me and shakes her head. The Breadman silently pokes at the fire with a stick.

Usually when we sit in front of the migrant shelter, Alma pretends to be a weary mom traveling alone with her daughter. Other migrants tend to trust a woman with a kid. Locals and gringos feel sorry for a woman with a kid. *Please help me and my poor little girl. We have nothing.* People don't notice that Alma and her child are always wearing clean clothes, much cleaner than the poor bastards trudging toward the door of the shelter who have just crawled out of the jungle. No one asks why the shelter won't open its doors

Papo and Alma | 119

to this woman and her kid who sit outside on the dirt every single day. In the beginning, I too bought into Alma's story because she's so good at it. It's what helps pay the rent on the room that she and Papo live in down the street. This fictitious role allows her access to information and trust; the former can be sold and the latter can be abused for profit. Alma is a mole, a secret conduit for data about newly arrived migrants that helps the local chapter of MS-13 stay in business. She knows who comes and goes. She knows who needs to pay the *cuota*. She knows which migrants have family in New York who can be persuaded to send money if someone they love happens to end up bound and gagged in a room on the outskirts of Pakal-Ná. Alma is not unique, though. Many locals (and languishing migrants) in places like Pakal-Ná collect information and pass it along to criminals, both as a way to make a little extra cash and to guarantee that they and their families don't get fucked with.

Alma can be a good actor when it suits her, but she and I have come to an understanding. She no longer pretends to be a newly arrived migrant when it is just me and the Pleasure Palace crew.

The mood this morning is tense. A train has just arrived in Pakal-Ná. Dozens of people are milling around the tracks, waiting for the first signs of movement, like runners listening for the starter pistol to fire. Several fair-skinned Mexicans in tight jeans and polo shirts pull up in a shiny F-150 truck. They are here to assess the situation. These men with their masculine overconfidence and out-of-place wardrobe give off a scary vibe. They control this territory and have recently initiated a head tax. These men are the reason that migrants now coming up from Guatemala have to pay $100 per person to get through Pakal-Ná and begin the long journey across Mexico. Alma talks to these men in private for twenty minutes. After they drive away, she takes a walk with Dulce and Papo so that she can start collecting money from those planning to ride the train.

The Breadman finally has a good fire going. We start to prepare the breakfast I brought. Tortillas, refried beans, cheese, chiles, and instant coffee. Someone produces a plastic one-liter Coke bottle filled with water from a nearby spigot. The cap is loosened so that air can escape. The bottle is placed directly into the fire. Like some kind of migrant sorcery, the receptacle is engulfed in flames but refuses to melt. The water comes to a boil and soon we are all drinking plastic-flavored Nescafé out of styrofoam cups. Alma and Papo return with money collected from train hoppers just as food is starting to be handed out.

"This place is a mess. You need to clean up your room, Chino," Alma jokes. Chino starts picking up small pieces of trash and some of his scattered personal effects on the ground.

The Breadman taps Alma and points to a group of men nearby. "Those guys don't have a guide."

"I know," she says. "I already checked." Someone comes to talk to Papo. He hands off 50 pesos' worth of marijuana wrapped in newspaper. Santos grabs a tortilla and makes a taco. He mumbles under his breath that the Breadman literally sleeps in a bakery yet never puts anything in the collective pantry. The Breadman ignores this slight. He makes a taco and walks away.

Chino: Jason, can you loan me thirty pesos?

Jason: For what?

Chino: I want to put some credit on my cell phone.

Jason: Okay, but you better not use this money to buy bleach.

Chino: I was just joking. *En serio*, I need credit for my phone.

Jason: If you come back with bleach, it better be because you're gonna wash some fucking clothes.

I place a few coins in his palm and fake like I'm gonna punch him in the stomach. We slap hands and laugh. "That kid is crazy," Alma tells me as Chino runs to a nearby market. "He gets fucked up and starts acting wild."

"It's true," Papo says as he puffs on a joint and rocks to music playing from a cell phone. "He's a good kid, but he starts smoking weed and drinking that *guaro* and then gets out of control." Papo often gives off an aggressive vibe, but it's clear that he has a soft spot for hard-luck cases.

Jason: How did you meet Chino?

Papo: I met him on the tracks in Pakal-Ná. He told me he was a migrant and asked if I could give him some weed. I think he was afraid of me at the time, so he lied about who he was. We smoked some weed together and then he left on the train. I saw him a few days later back in Pakal-Ná, and I said, "Hey, I thought you were leaving." That's when he told me he was moving people, and then we started hanging out more.

Jason: He seems to be having a rough time right now.

Papo: Yeah, he gets like that sometimes. He comes through Pakal-Ná moving people and has a little money. He comes through and he is happy. Then a few days later he comes back with no money and is all fucked up. I think the people he works for often rip him off and don't pay him what they promised. That's when he starts begging me for money. That's when he's like, "Papo, give me five pesos, bro, so I can get a *botellita*." He drinks that *guaro* and gets all fucked up. It's sad, bro. I feel bad for him.

Reggaeton starts playing on someone's cell phone. "I love this *rollo*," Papo comments as he continues to puff on his joint. "Hey, Jason, is it true that in California you can just go to a store and buy marijuana?"

"Yeah, there are lots of places that sell it now. You can get all kinds of different types."

"That's crazy. I got deported because I had weed in my car. It's crazy you can now buy it in a store."

He smiles as he looks at the burning joint between his slender brown fingers. "Man, my dream is to be able to smoke weed anywhere and not get in trouble. If I come visit you, you have to take me to one of those stores."

"Sure, I'd be happy to," I say. I can see Papo on Venice Beach telling jokes and rolling blunts. Waves crashing. Reggae music playing. His wiry, tattooed arms have a golden-brown tan. His long, curly black hair shines in the California sun. He is a young man enjoying a few simple pleasures as he momentarily forgets about death threats and hunger and the specter of deportation. Papo also seems to be in this imaginary place as he closes his eyes and rocks his body to the music.

"Man, I love this song," he says again.

Alma turns to me with a serious look, as if to bring us all back to reality. "Jason, you see us here acting happy, but we don't want to be here. We are just trying to survive."

Soon we hear the whistle and grinding metal that signals the train is preparing to leave. Young men in ragged shoes and sweat-stained shirts sprint past the Pleasure Palace. The crowd cheers. *¡Con ganas!* As *la bestia* pulls away, people huddled on the metal grates between train cars flash by like frames from a silent movie. Hands reach down to help a few last-minute passengers grab hold. I count only eight cars on the train. Too few for a trip of any distance. "Those people are stupid," Chino tells me. "That train is gonna go five kilometers down the tracks and then it's gonna stop so that immigration agents can jump out and arrest everyone." Several men watch the clattering machine disappear around a curve and then start chasing after it on foot. They will hide in the jungle and watch the raid happen from a distance. Once the immigration vans leave with their prisoners, the men will continue walking on the tracks. Later, as we sit in the Pleasure Palace finishing breakfast, we hear the train returning to the Pakal-Ná depot. The eight cars arrive empty.

Visa

A camera-wielding Mexican social worker recently visited Papo and Alma's place to document the squalid conditions the family is living in. Alma is hopeful the photos they take will prove that they are needy and strengthen their petition for help from the government. Mexico recently provided some hard-luck Central Americans with temporary humanitarian visas that allow them to legally stay in the country for finite periods of time. The visas don't permit people to legally work, but they do enable them to travel freely and access some federal programs. Alma thinks that a visa will help facilitate her two daughters' entering public school. She and Papo have to submit to an interview at the Honduran embassy in Mexico City as part of the application process. Later I will learn that the best way to secure a visa is to give cash to one of the hustlers who hang out in front of the embassy, who will then put in a good word for you with those who conduct the interviews. For now, I'm hunched over filling out paperwork that is dense and exhausting. We spend hours trying to get Alma and Papo's story straight.

Jason: They are going to ask you where you two met.

Alma: What should we tell them?

Jason: I think you should tell them the truth. If you start lying to them it's going be hard to keep your story straight. I also don't think you need to lie.

Alma: Okay, we will tell them that we met in La Técnica, in Guatemala. I was traveling with Dulce when I met Papo. He helped me send for Gaby.

Papo paces the room, clutching a beer and nervously switching back and forth between cigarettes and a joint. Many people on the tracks are wary of Papo because of his connection to MS-13. He sells drugs for them and relays information, but his relationship with the gang seems to be one that was forced upon him and that he begrudgingly accepts because he has little choice. He does their bidding and in return is able to make a little cash. More important, his job guarantees some form of protection for Alma and the girls. Plus, he gets all his weed for free. As we prep, I worry that he is going to say something to accidentally sabotage the interview.

Jason: Papo, they will ask what you have been doing for work in Mexico.

Papo: Write down that I have been working construction and also selling tacos. Just don't write down that MS-13 made me sell weed for them. Don't put that on the form [*laughing*].

Jason: Should I put down "*marijuanero*" for your occupation?

Papo and Alma | 125

We laugh and take sips of our beers. I tell myself not to worry. Papo is going to do fine when he gets in front of an immigration officer. He is a smart guy with a disarming smile, and despite all he has been through, he tries to do right by people, even strangers. Still, he has that rough-around-the-edges look and vibe that comes from being raised on the street. Tattoos run across his ropy arms and up his neck. He has the lean physique of someone who appears simultaneously underfed and prone to throwing a quick punch. On his own, he doesn't make for a sympathetic migrant. I am hoping that Alma with her soft smile and kind eyes will do most of the talking.

Jason: Alma, the questionnaire asks why you came to Mexico.

Alma: For a better future. Write down "for a better future." Look, I'm just going to tell people tomorrow that we can't live in Honduras. It's too dangerous. Here my kids don't have a TV or go to school, but at least they are alive. I don't care if they don't want to give me a visa. I just want visas for the girls so that they can go to school. I feel bad because they keep asking when they are going to start school and learn how to read.

Jason: Papo, they will also want to know why you left Honduras. You will have to talk about that stuff.

Papo: What should I tell them?

Jason: You should tell them the truth.

Papo: I'm gonna tell them I came home one day and my aunt was crying because there was a note stuck to our door that said they were going to kill me and my whole family. She was yelling at me, asking what I had done. But I didn't do anything, bro. I was kind of laughing about it because I thought it was a joke. But I was on the street the next day, and someone came up to me and said I should leave the neighborhood because I had a *clavo* and they were going to kill me. I had loaned my motorcycle to a neighbor and he used it to go out and shoot someone. He was wearing my helmet, so everyone thought it was me. I tried to explain that I didn't do it, but they said it didn't matter. It was my bike and they were going to kill me. So I had to leave. Those bastards ruined my life. My life is shit.

After he says this last line, Papo starts crying. He tries to get more words out as he pauses to fight back tears. It's the first time in our relationship that I have seen him show any sign of vulnerability. He has just turned twenty-four years old, but he suddenly looks like a child to me, like a scared teenager running for his life.

Jason: They are going to ask why you want a visa.

Papo: I'm going to say I want a visa because I want to get a better job, a legal job. I'm tired of living a life where I am always afraid. I am tired of hiding. I've been afraid in Honduras, in the United States, and in Mexico. I don't want to be afraid anymore.

Part II

KINGS OF PAIN

CHAPTER SEVEN

Duke of Earl

The camera comes in for a close-up of the twitching severed head on top of the railroad tie. A pool of blood slowly expands underneath it. Crimson runs over the MADE IN THE USA stamped into the gray concrete. A desperate mouth gasps for jungle air, but there are no longer any lungs to fill. Death spasms work to reanimate dying muscles, but nothing can be done. It's too late. Flaco pokes at the bloody head with a knife and yells, "*¡Somos sicarios!*" (We are assassins!) He discharges a cloud of marijuana smoke into the open mouth of the dying face. An intimate exchange of final breath. "*Mira*, he still wants to smoke weed!" Flaco laughs at his own stupid joke and then kicks the iguana's head into the bushes like a miniature soccer ball.

"I'M SORRY, *HERMANO*. Nothing could be done," Flaco tells me. "Papo's dead. They killed him."

"Who killed him?" I ask.

Flaco shakes his head. He doesn't want to say. They might be listening.

"What happened?"

He grimaces and makes a cutting motion across his throat.

"They say he was a snitch, so they cut off his lips and his ears. Then they cut off his tongue. They say they did it while he was still alive, bro. Someone killed him for 500 pesos [$25]."

I look at him in disbelief. This is a bad joke. But he is not joking. A suffocating pressure builds in my chest. The sudden smell of stress-induced sweat. A search for words that comes out meaningless.

"Papo was a good guy. We were friends," I say with a breaking voice.

"I know, *viejo*. He was my homie. It's fucked up."

I look at Flaco and then close my eyes and turn my face toward the Chiapas sun. My body tenses. My breathing is labored. I want to run, but there is no outrunning this. This is why Papo stopped answering my texts. This is why his Facebook account became inactive. But where is Alma? Why hasn't she called me? Did something happen to her too? Where are the children? This whole thing is fucked. I want to scream. I want to crawl into a hole and disappear. I push a tear out of the corner of my eye with the palm of my hand and try to steel myself. Not here. Not now. There will be time later for me to curl up into a ball and weep.

Flaco looks at me. His eyes start to water, so he turns away. He cracks open a Modelo.

"This is for Papo and all the dead homies."

He draws a cross on the ground with beer.

I stare at the dark and holy stain in the dirt and then open a beer and make my own cross.

FLACO IS INTENSE. A man who sends me videos of himself harassing decapitated iguanas. A man who sends me videos telling me he loves me like

Duke of Earl | 133

a brother. Loud and disorderly. Charming and reprehensible. Overly confident in that annoying, hypermasculine way. They call him skinny, but he is not *flaco*. His thick frame competes with his outsized personality. A booming laugh, a tasteless sense of humor, an unbridled propensity for talking shit. He's a lot to handle, like a drunken and completely inappropriate relative whose comments you take with a grain of salt because they make you laugh (most of the time) and because there is nothing you can do to change their attitude or delivery. Flaco's obnoxious charisma creates a powerful orbit that is hard not to get sucked into.

The day we first meet on the tracks he tells me of Papo's death. Seeing how this news upsets me, he tries to share in my grief. We talk and drink and make liquid offerings to ghosts. We reminisce about Papo, the kid who couldn't outrun death no matter where he went. He wasn't supposed to die on the tracks. He was the one who was going to crawl out of that hole in Honduras that took so many of his friends. Instead, that demon on a motorcycle finally caught up to him. But how? What did the end look like? Where is he buried? Flaco responds to my many questions about the murder with vague answers, headshakes, and a quieting finger to the lips. *There are too many ears on the tracks, hermano. You never know who you can trust. It happened right here, so we shouldn't speak of it.*

I will later search in vain for published news of Papo's death. Was he carrying ID? Did they identify his body? Is he buried in Palenque's potter's field with the other nameless Central Americans? How many migrants die on the tracks in Mexico and go unnoticed? The thousands of missing persons reports filed in Mexico and along the southern U.S. border suggest that people disappear with a high frequency. As of July 2023, the Pima County Office of the Medical Examiner listed 1,517 unidentified migrant bodies in its database. This number represents only recovered individuals. It fails to account for the thousands more who vanish while crossing Mexico and those who die in remote areas of the border, where their remains are never found.

I think about something Papo once told me after I lost contact with Santos: "He is either dead or in jail." So where is Papo? Is he dead? Is he in jail? Flaco deflects my questions with his own. Am I a cop? Why am I here? Who do I know? He is intrigued that I am writing a book about smugglers, about his occupation. Flaco believes he is an important figure and that I should be writing about him. Before I know it, I am in the audience, along with a cadre of young men, as he holds court on the train tracks in his aggressive and charismatic and occasionally sensitive way.

Flaco: Hey, *caquero* [shit man], we're almost out of beer. You better go to the store soon.

[*Flaco's underling, Acid, shrugs because he has no money. I hand him a hundred-peso bill.*]

Jason: Flaco, why do you keep calling Acid *caquero?*

Flaco: Cuz that nigga crazy. He crazy. We were sleeping on the tracks last night and that foo found an outhouse and decided to sleep inside of it. He slept in a shitter, bro. When he came out this morning he was stretching and you could see that he had a bunch of shit-stained pieces of toilet paper stuck to his face [*laughing*]. He's the *caquero!*

Acid: [*Mocking a serious tone*] Don't laugh. It was a lot warmer in the shit house than sleeping outside. [*We all crack up.*]

Flaco: I told you that foo's crazy.

Duke of Earl | 135

Flaco turns to Jorge, one of the young Honduran men he is smuggling. "Hey, tell the gringo* about the *caquero*." Jorge musters a nervous laugh and shakes his head. He's an early twentysomething with a baby face and unassuming ways. He sits on the edge of the group, wanting little to do with this scatological conversation. A cloud of death chased him out of his home in Olancho, Honduras, a few weeks earlier. These men he is paying to escort him to the U.S.-Mexico border make him nervous. Their wildness reminds him of the *mareros* who recently murdered his father. Unfortunately, he has no choice but to put his faith in them. He must accept that theirs is a complicated relationship of (mis)trust that requires maintaining a healthy fear of both his surroundings and his traveling companions.

Pirate's delicate dark brown fingers put the finishing touches on an artisanal-looking joint.

A bone-white crucifix swings from his neck. The dangling Jesús competes with the hollow-eyed monsters and oversized weed leaves etched across his bare chest and arms. On his leg, someone has taken a needle and tapped out *Fuck da police* in dull blue ink. Pirate talks of his future.

> **Pirate:** This is it for me. I've been on the tracks for fifteen years. I'm done, *perro*. This is my *última misión*. Once we get these guys to the border, I'm gone.

> **Jason:** How many times have you crossed Mexico?

> **Pirate:** I don't know. I lost count. Maybe somewhere between fifty and a hundred times.

> **Jason:** So what's next for you?

---

* Although I am Latino, many migrants and smugglers often called me "gringo" (the American).

136 | SOLDIERS AND KINGS

> **Pirate:** Flaco is gonna get me across to California. I brought my wife and daughter up two months ago and they turned themselves in to Immigration. They are waiting for me.

I've heard plans like these before. Most of the time it's a pipe dream. I try to imagine him holding a straight job, flipping burgers with a name tag that says *Pirate*. He lights up and takes several quick puffs. He considers the smoke emanating from his handiwork as if he can divine something from it. He reaches over to Payaso, who stabs two large metal needles into a ball of yarn and accepts the joint.

"Why do they call you Payaso?" I inquire.

He turns to me, his dull black eyes lifeless in the afternoon sun.

"They call me Payaso because I used to be funny."

Prolonged silence. No reaction in his face. Then both of us start laughing. Even if it wasn't funny, I'd still laugh because he is scary as shit, the kind of scary you have to laugh at because you don't know what else to do. Flaco warns me not to ask about Papo's death around Payaso, so I don't. Behind Payaso's back they tell stories about watching him bring a machete down on people's heads and coolly cutting off testicles to make a point. They say if you dig around the train tracks in Pakal-Ná, you will find the remains of those who thought Payaso was joking when he said, "Pay the *cuota*, or else." The joint keeps moving. Payaso picks up the needles and returns to his knitting. When the police later arrest him for a series of murders, he will begin texting me photos from prison of his various knitting projects. This includes a SpongeBob SquarePants bag he made for me. In our many communications Payaso will mostly avoid talking about his crimes, except to update me when they add new victims to his growing body count. Given what I know about his occupation, it's hard not to wonder if it was his tattooed hands that were responsible for the removal of Papo's lips and ears. Was it his knife that ran a red line across my friend's Adam's apple? I have visions of Payaso's hands blackened and slick with mess. I hallucinate Papo's face, and it is no longer recognizable. What kind of stain does that much blood leave on the ground? I tell myself it's better not to think about it.

WE SKIN AND GUT the decapitated iguanas with a rusty knife and pitch their bodies into a boiling pot of vegetables and coconut milk. One of the lizards is pregnant, so Flaco cooks the eggs separately. When we bite down, the rubbery ova explode in our mouths, releasing a sour fish flavor.

> **Flaco:** Careful, bro, eating these eggs will make your dick hard for days. [*He makes a firm motion with a closed fist.*]

> **Jason:** Oh yeah? Then why you are trying to make me eat so many of them?

> **Flaco:** *Jajaja. Pinche* gringo. They're good, though, right?

> **Jason:** Not really.

> [*One of his phones buzzes.*]

> **Flaco:** *¿En serio? No mames.* What time? Shit.

> [*He hangs up.*]

> **Flaco:** The train won't be here until tonight.

> [*A few people grumble.*]

Jason: How do you know?

Flaco: Because that was the conductor that just called me.

Unlike foot soldiers, Flaco makes relatively big money doing this. He is someone who temporarily hires out street kids like Chino and Santos to do his bidding on the tracks. He pays them low wages for their help moving across different segments of the migrant trail and supplements their income with free food, alcohol, and drugs. In turn, he can make thousands of dollars per trip, taking people from Honduras all the way to the U.S.-Mexico border. While low-level guides stew in the jungles waiting for a train that might never come, Flaco lies shirtless on a couch in his nearby apartment, watching soccer on a flat screen and smoking weed with one of his *morras* who maintains the place. Multiple apartments across Mexico serve as his home base for different legs of the journey. He's a traveling salesman who peddles safety from the goblins looking to consume migrants. A salesman whose many phones incessantly vibrate and chirp, the sounds of thousands of potential dollars to be made if he can survive the gauntlet one more time.

All day long he brokers deals with clients. He chats with train conductors on the payroll who give real-time updates on arrivals and departures. He gets warnings from corrupt cops about pending immigration raids. He also deferentially takes phone instructions from high-ranking gang members who oversee movement on the tracks. These gangsters decide if and when he can cross through places like Pakal-Ná, Coatzacoalcos, or Lechería. Flaco is sometimes bitter that other people dictate his movement, especially since those he has to get permission from can turn on him in a heartbeat. Flaco will never graduate to the level of calling the shots remotely while his soldiers do the grunt work of moving people. He lacks the patience needed to oversee logistics. He is the traveling salesman who just can't seem to move up the promotional ranks, so to make ends meet he will forever be on the road.

Acid makes a ringing sound with his mouth and picks up a box of cigarettes. "Excuse me, it's a personal call." He turns away from us and starts talking into his pack of Marlboro Reds.

Flaco shakes his head. "I told you that nigga crazy. Hey, *caquero*! Get off the phone and go get us some beers!"

Acid apologizes to the person on the line and then hangs up.

> **Flaco:** *En serio*, that nigga crazy. You gotta watch out for the *caquero*. All this fool wants is dick. The last time I saw him in Coatza was in December when he was hanging out with these two fags. He had his arms around both of them. One was holding his beer and the other was giving him lines of coke. I'd never seen this foo so happy! But you better watch out, man. If he sees one of us in our boxers, he gets horny and starts rubbing his dick. The other day Jorge was wiping his ass in the woods and Acid saw him and was like, "*¡Que rico el culo!*"

I look over at Jorge, who is clearly blushing.

Sex is often a topic of conversation among smugglers. Heterosexual sex is something to boast about, and many proudly describe ongoing sexual relationships with women in different locations. This is especially true for people like Flaco who maintain multiple houses across Mexico and Honduras. On the other hand, homosexual sex is joked about among these men, as both an outward expression of homophobia and an indirect way to discuss potential taboo desires. Honduran smugglers will tout their heterosexual prowess and appetites while jokingly questioning the sexuality of others.[*] Relatedly, many of them openly seek female sex workers on the tracks,

---

[*] The humor is similar to the hypermasculine teasing associated with the working-class Mexican humor called *chingaderas*.

especially at the end of a run when the men's pockets are full of cash. Paying women for sex is often seen as part of the smuggler lifestyle. For this reason, Flaco and Pirate always have condoms in their backpacks. Conversely, few are willing to discuss male sex workers on the tracks, other than to condemn the behavior with homophobic slurs. However, a few people (e.g., Acid) openly flaunt both their bisexuality and their willingness to trade sex with men for drugs and alcohol. Chino also hints to me during various conversations that men sometimes pay him for sex on the tracks and that many straight-passing men he knows are also engaged in that behavior.

While migration to the United States can be seen as a path to freedom for those trying to escape homophobia in Latin America, the hypermasculine conditions of smuggling often make open discussions of homosexuality a forbidden subject and a source of ridicule. In Flaco's crew, it is fine for Acid to have sex with men, as long as others are able to crack jokes in order to express their personal discomfort, biases, and perhaps secret wishes. Because he is considered a good soldier, Acid's sexual behavior is tolerated by his crew and simply described as him just being "crazy."

"Watch out for Acid," Flaco jokingly warns. "I'm serious, man. This *vato* gets horny when he sees someone cleaning their *culo*. You gotta be careful. He'll put a machete in your back and try to fuck you."

Everyone laughs and Acid wags his tongue and starts chasing us around as if to grab our asses. Flaco lovingly puts his arm around him. "It's cool if you're gay, though. You're my friend, foo, and I can't change you. But *hijo de puta*, this guy is nuts."

"Hey, Acid, I think your phone is ringing," someone says. He again picks up the pack of Marlboros and begins a conversation with a phantom on the other end of the line.

Flaco points at Acid and says, "That foo's crazy, but you gotta have *hermanos* like that on the tracks. If you get on the train and some *loco* starts firing off a gun, you gotta have your people with you. It's always better to have some crazy motherfuckers with you. But I don't get messed with. My people never get robbed, because I'm crazy and I'm connected."

Foos Gone Wild

The tinted-out Civic crawls over the blacktop, seemingly immune to minimum speed limits. The driver's seat is fully reclined. All you can see through the open window is a single brown hand gripping the steering wheel. Art Laboe's soundtrack for cholo hopes and dreams fills the Southern California air with harmonies from an era of pony boys and switchblades and golden sunsets. *As I walk through this world nothing can stop the Duke of Earl.* Flaco is looking for ladies who want to party. Cholas with big hair and thick eyeliner. Thick gringas that like to drink and smoke weed and fuck brown dudes. He's not looking for trouble. But there it is. There he is. He sees him and thinks to himself, *Fuck that nigga. Fucking puto.*

Well, I'm an alley cat, some say a dirty rat . . .

Flaco reaches for the *cuete* under his seat and calmly steps out of the car. The *vato* doesn't see it at first because he's holding it low when he enters the front yard.

"What the fuck are you doing?"

"I need my money, foo."

"I don't have your fucking money. Get the fuck outta my house!"

"What, bitch? What the fuck you say?"

The butt of the 9mm makes a dull sound against the side of the dude's skull. Flaco is quickly on top of him with an unbridled rage, a rage that makes him laugh out loud. A *vecina* screams for help as the men tumble off the porch and square up in the yard. Flaco rips a gold chain off his opponent's neck. By the time *la jura* rolls up, both men are bleeding and dirty. An unregistered gun lies in the grass.

Flaco doesn't have much of a case to plead to the judge. *Your Honor, I advanced the victim a sizable quantity of methamphetamines and he failed to pay me for it. When I saw him entering a house, I thought it an opportune time to inquire if he had my money. I was merely seeking monetary compensation or the return of my property.* Rightfully, the judge has no sympathy. All he sees is a twenty-five-year-old Honduran immigrant accused of invading someone's home, pistol-whipping them, and then demanding money. Breaking and entering. Assault with a deadly weapon. Armed robbery. The person standing before the judge is a suspected gang member and drug dealer who has already served time in California for previous crimes. It doesn't look good. The court-appointed attorney visits him in jail and brings bad news. The prosecutor is pushing for twenty-five to life. Flaco breaks down in tears when he hears the projected sentence.

THE BLOATED EXCESS of the Rose Parade plays on a tiny TV. A family huddles around the screen, captivated by the surreal scene. Marching armies in white uniforms blow silver trumpets and whack snare drums. Oversized lions, elephants, and jesters glide across the screen. Oversized Americans cheer from lawn chairs. A giant Esnoopy made of flowers and metal wire dances to music. The price to build one of these floats could feed his entire community for years. It's January 1, 1996. Twelve-year-old Flaco points at the television. *"Mira, Mami,* I'm going to be there. I'm going to California someday."

She hugs the boy and laughs. *"Mijo, estás loco."*

There is little keeping young Flaco tethered to Honduras. It's a simple plot. No money. No school. No father. No future that doesn't involve

Duke of Earl | 143

cutting sugarcane. He lives in his *abuela*'s house with his mother and his siblings. *Abuela* is not kind. *Abuela* hates his guts, treats him like a dog. He has to find a way out. He calls an aunt in Los Angeles, "*Tía*, I need your help. I'm heading north."

"*No, pendejo*," she responds. "Keep your ass at home! You're too young to leave!"

He ignores her warning. His mother hugs him and cries the day he says goodbye. "Please don't go, *mijo*," she implores.

"I have to," he responds in a child's voice. The boy is thirteen when it all starts. *Un Huckleberry Finn*. Except there is no river to navigate. It's *puro tren*, pure train.

Flaco falls in love with *la bestia*. It's a love that will stay with him forever. How can he not love the machine that opens up worlds of adventure to a child searching for meaning and a way to feel alive? His skinny frame balances atop the metal monster as he screams, "I love the beast!"

A thousand awe-inspiring landscapes pass by. The sticky coastal heat of Coatzacoalcos. The urban grime of Mexico City. The vast deserts of Hermosillo. Flaco learns train routes and shortcuts. He parties along the way. His name and face become known to the suspicious characters lurking on the tracks. *That kid is fucking crazy. That kid is down for his shit. That kid has a mean right hook.* He grows into a tall frame and his infectious laugh develops a bass quality. You can hear him a mile away howling his ass off at the absurdity of life on the tracks. It's an absurdity that will come to define him. The United States was the dream, but it soon becomes the long-gone fantasy of a thirteen-year-old with no money and no family willing to support a border crossing. The streets of Mexico become his playground, his home, his future.

And then, in 1998, the deadliest hurricane in Central American history destroys Honduras. Like some demonic Poseidon bringing terror from the deep, Hurricane Mitch unleashes nature's fury across the country. Unrelenting rain. Biblical floods. Catastrophic landslides. A few weeks before Mitch makes landfall, Flaco decides to return home to see his family after a prolonged stay in Mexico. This poorly timed visit means that he soon finds himself standing on high ground and watching the roofs of houses and the bloated bodies of livestock and neighbors float by. The streets are filled with the stench of the dead. Over a million people displaced. Billions of dollars in damage. No one is spared. For a brief moment, the United States recognizes that Central America is unlivable for many and invites close to sixty thousand Honduran nationals to enter the country under Congress's Temporary Protected Status. Flaco heads north and crosses illegally through Tijuana. He begins walking to Los Angeles and gets picked up by a gringo in San Bernardino who speaks no Spanish. Through hand signals and broken English, Flaco explains where he is going. The gringo buys him a hamburger and drops him off at his *tía*'s house. The same *tía* who told him to keep his ass at home two years earlier. A few weeks later he presents himself to Immigration and asks for help. At fifteen years old, he is given refuge. His California dream is realized.

The trajectory from homeless street kid in Mexico to LA gangbanger does not require much imagination. Like the many child refugees from a previous generation who fled civil wars in Guatemala, El Salvador, and Nicaragua in the 1980s, Flaco finds shelter among the thriving gangs in Southern California. MS-13 was started in Los Angeles by displaced and disenfranchised kids from Central America. It naturally provides a new home for a displaced Honduran kid who came of age on the train tracks in Mexico.

Temporary Protected Status offers a safety net for many Hondurans, a way to stay and legally work in the United States. But there is little focused or nuanced outreach to help newly arrived undereducated kids who grew up poor and fostered by street violence. Many of these refugee children have little education to begin with, so the idea of putting them into a normal school system and expecting them to thrive is ludicrous. Flaco is already wild when he lands in California. LA gang life simply provides a new (but familiar) setting where he can mature into an adult criminal.

Duke of Earl | 145

In "Califas," Honduran slang mingles with the homies' Spanglish. *Perro.* Dawg. Doggie. *Vato. Vos.* My nigga. Califas brings new beginnings. New soundtracks. New stage dressings. New vices. Hip-hop and low-rider old-ies. Forties of Olde E. *The Chronic.* Coco Puffs. Dickies with knife-edge creases. Blinding-white T-shirts. Socks that rise above your knees. *Vatos* who can get you a *cuete.* Lil homies that need to get jumped in. Newly dead homies to pour out beer for. *Cristal.** Cocaine. A gun in your face. A gun in some other dude's face. Fast cars. Faster cars. Armed robberies. Drug deal-ing. Drug robberies. *Pura droga, hermano. Pura droga.*

Flaco puts in work for almost a decade. A self-described *delincuente* who becomes an O.G. A *veterano.* He lives a life of clichéd crime, a caricature of *Blood In Blood Out* and *The Godfather: Part II.* Nothing can stop the Duke of Earl. And then everything comes to a screeching halt when he stands in front of a judge who starts talking about twenty-five to life.

THE CARDBOARD has been measured and cut so that it will fit around his growing stomach. They still call him *flaco* even though he's gained al-most a hundred pounds since arriving in prison. His cellmate watches as he takes pieces of trimmed plastic and slides them between the cardboard and his gut. Duct tape cinches everything tightly together. He then pulls three thermal shirts over his homemade armor. By the time Flaco enters the prison yard, sweat is starting to form on his forehead and upper lip. Convicts mill about, segregated by phenotype and linguistics. Concealed hands fidget with abraded metal and flame-hardened plastic, tools of the dark trade. A silent countdown fills the air with uneasy energy. Finally, someone yells, "*¡Dale gas!*" and all hell breaks loose.

His court-appointed attorney was ready to accept a twenty-five-to-life

---

* Crystal meth.

sentence, but Flaco manages to cobble together some cash to get a second opinion. Thirty-five thousand dollars later, a private lawyer tells him his sentence has been reduced to seven to fifteen years. It's a long time, but at least it's not forever. He does his bid like most imprisoned gang members. He hangs with the homies and tries to kill time with various activities: contraband smuggling, beatdowns, prison riots, vacations in the hole, improvised culinary classes, wine-making workshops. He learns new skills and expands his gang connections. He tries to stay alive and keep his sanity. Sixty months into his sentence, the United States government makes him a deal.

> **Flaco:** It was in *dos mil hoyo*,* bro. I mean 2008. My lawyer said that if I wanted to go back to Honduras I could, but they would take my papers away. I was like, "I don't give a fuck. *A la verga*." They threw my *residencia* in the trash. I was like, "Fuck that shit, nigga. Let's go." They deported me back to Honduras. I went straight to my grandmother's house and after three days she kicked me out. I'm the one that sent her the money from the United States to build that house [*laughing*]. I built her house and she kicked me out of it after three days [*laughing*].

At thirty years old, Flaco finds himself once again leaving Honduras and headed for the Mexican train tracks.

---

* People affiliated with MS-13 tend to avoid using the word "*ocho*" (eight) because of its linguistic connection to the 18th Street gang. So instead of saying "*dos mil ocho*" (2008), they might say "*dos mil hoyo*," whereby a similar-sounding word (in this case "*hoyo*," or hole) replaces the number.

Duke of Earl | 147

La Cementera

The white line burns red hot. It rattles his head. His tongue pops out of his mouth, his fingers and limbs freeze in gnarled and palsied poses. A twitch followed by the release of a cocaine-induced guttural sound of pleasure. *Aahhhhhhh!* Flaco grabs my voice recorder and screams, "A big salute to my comrade Jason! White Power! To the almighty gringo! We are here on the train tracks eating iguana with all the migrants who are trying to get to *la USA*," he says, laughing, "but *la migra* won't let us in!"

Jason: Seriously, would you ever want to go back to the United States?

Flaco: Go back? Me? I can get across in ten minutes if I want to. It's nothing. It's easy. But what would I go back for? I make more money now than I ever did there. I can make $8,000, $10,000, $12,000 here in fifteen days. I got three women now and three houses. You think I want to be back in *la USA*? Fuck no! I used to make a lot of money there, but I had to do it with a gun. Thank God I don't do that stuff any-more. But listen, you got family in Honduras? Tell them to call me and send me some money. I'll get them to the U.S. In December, I made $4,000* at the border. I spent it all on bitches, coke, beer, weed—everything, homie. I spent it in two days. Four thousand dollars. I don't give a fuck! Shit! [*He sniffs coke off his hand.*] If I had that money right now, I'd be getting crazy all day. Drinking. Fucking. Partying. I'd

---

* This is after all fees and expenses have been paid.

spend it all on my friends. I don't give a fuck. If your money runs out and you come up to me and say, "Hey, nigga, loan me a hundred bucks. I need it," I'd give it to you because we're friends. I mean if I tell you to fuck off, what do I gain? Nothing. No, man, if you don't have friends, you have nothing. So I would rather have a shit ton of friends than a shit ton of money.

Despite the fact that they've just spent two days walking through the jungle to avoid an immigration raid on the outskirts of Pakal-Ná, everyone in Flaco's groups has their spirits up. They now wait for the train in La Cementera, a sleepy village named after a nearby cement factory. There is currently enough weed, beer, and cocaine available to keep everyone temporarily entertained. Flaco is clearly blowing through the cash that Jorge and the other three migrants in his care have advanced him for the first part of the trip. He is spending all his cash so that he can have a good time with his friends. By the time he leaves La Cementera a day later, he will have spent over $600 on partying. It's one of the things he likes most about this job. It allows him to wildly consume drugs and alcohol, the stereotypical behavior expected of *coyotes*. But his exuberant spending isn't just about self-indulgence. Maintaining the party atmosphere helps keep his drug-addicted foot soldiers, young kids like Acid and Chino, loyal. It also keeps one's mind numb to the many risks on the tracks. The Border Patrol often describes smugglers as dangerous because they are "always high on drugs." Few consider the fact that the dangers of the job encourage (if not necessitate) drug and alcohol consumption to deal with the constant fear that things can turn very bad at any moment.

Pirate reaches into a burlap sack and produces an iguana. Its little feet are bound with twine like a prisoner in a child's game. The animal is motionless, seemingly resigned to what is about to happen. Jorge fetches some

Duke of Earl | 149

wood and ignites a small fire. Acid pulls a machete from his backpack. Ranchera music plays while Flaco brokers a deal. *"Cuatro varones,"* he says into his phone. "Don't worry, they're skinny. They can fit in a car or a truck. Maybe even the trunk. I'll send the pictures right now."

He hangs up and calls Jorge over. Flaco snaps a headshot of him with his cell phone. He then lines the other three migrants up and they each smile for the camera. The photos should prevent any misunderstandings with the Zetas in Coatzacoalcos. The photos are receipts for the $200 *cuota* Flaco has just paid for each of his clients. A romantic Mexican ballad starts playing.

> **Flaco:** Acid, what the fuck is this music? What are you listening to, *puto*? Are you gonna start crying on me? You want to slow dance? Change this shit! [*He resumes a story he was telling before the phone rang.*] As I was saying, Jason, this fucking *culero* kept calling to say he was going to kill me. I told that foo that he couldn't fucking touch me in Mexico. But I can't go to Honduras. That's where they'll catch me . . .

Fifty feet away, a hunchbacked old woman in a checkered dress and apron waddles out of the jungle. She carries a plastic bucket sloshing with cold *horchata*. Upon her approach, Flaco's demeanor and language change. "Hello, *madre*," he says. "How are you? It's very hot today. What are you selling?" She offers us libations. Flaco buys a round of drinks. "This is delicious, *madre*. You don't by chance have any cold beers at the bottom of that bucket, do you?" She giggles and pats Flaco's tattooed arm and then disappears down the tracks.

> **Flaco:** So, look, like I said, I told that nigga to come find me, but he won't come here. He called me up and said, "Where you at?" I said, "I'm in Palenque, *güey*. Come get me, *puto*!"

Fuck that piece of shit. Fuck those *putos*. I just have to make a phone call and that foo is fucking dead.

Jason: Do you like doing this work even though people want to kill you sometimes?

Flaco: Hell yeah! Cuz every day it's weed, coke, and beer for me, foo. I fucking love coke! I mean I like this job, but it is dangerous. You just gotta have faith in God to protect you.

Jason: How much longer do you have on this trip?

Flaco: We should be in Mexico City in six or seven days. After that, another week to get to the border. Come see me in Mexico City or Mexicali, foo. When we get paid, I'm going to buy a bunch of coke and we are going to party.

CHAPTER EIGHT

Kingston

Our faces are dripping with sweat, our breath sour with the aftertaste of a long night of irresponsibility. The humidity of coastal Veracruz chokes and infuriates. We fantasize about a breeze to cool us off, calm us down. Something to make us better men. Instead, we are aggravated. We pace and posture and collectively exhale tension into the air. These moments are always reckless and juvenile. Dangerous games that foolish and prideful men play to feel powerful, to feel alive, to wind up dead. I know better but still somehow manage to find myself caught up in this catastrophe. An eternal search for a momentary high, a story later poorly justified as the cost of doing this type of ethnographic fieldwork. An excuse perhaps to temporarily be something from my past that I can never truly run away from.

I have to look up at the Russian because he's a full head taller than me. Bloodshot eyes. Dirty stubble. Hair so blond it's almost white. Of course, rough words are exchanged in Spanish. That's how it always starts. They are exactly the type of words you might expect strangers to trade at two a.m. in front of a run-down club that caters to local and international degenerates. Nothing good ever comes from these exhibitions of testosterone and aggression, except maybe a lesson in humility or remorse. I raise my hands in surrender. I try to step away and avoid escalating the situation. The Russian lunges and pushes me backward. Before I can decide whether to walk away or moronically charge him, a black fist rattles his jaw, sending him crashing to the filthy pavement. Kingston moves fast. He is on top of him, his fists beating a staccato rhythm into the man's face. The bouncer who'd been trying to get the Russian to pay his bar tab halfheartedly grabs Kingston's arm. He immediately gives up when he sees how committed the assailant is to giving this beatdown. The bouncer steps back to let the lesson continue. We scream for Kingston to stop, but he is deaf to our cries. The sounds of flesh on flesh and a cranium bouncing against the sidewalk blend with our voices.

I've witnessed many bar fights, but nothing close to this. This feels personal and cathartic. Rage unbottled and completely unrestrained. The summation of an entire life lived in the shadow of cruelty and hyperviolence now manifests itself on the sidewalk. It's obvious the Russian has had enough before it even begins. "You're not talking shit now, are you?" a voice screams. He tries to roll away, but Kingston has not yet had enough. He picks up this giant man and tosses his huge frame through the entrance of the club. The doorman steps back and calls for help. Bottle-blond Central American waitresses in neon miniskirts and bulging tops scream as they seek shelter behind the bar. A bouncer foolishly grabs Kingston and is quickly thrown into a nearby table. This moment feels unstoppable. Once again, Kingston is straddling the Russian, landing blow after blow. In a state of desperation and confusion, the man tries to squirm away, but there is nothing to take hold of. His writhing body slides across the checkered ceramic floor tiles that are glossy with industrial cleaner. The Russian reaches for a table leg, but Kingston pulls him back. The man's exhausted forearms try to block blows that are unrelenting. I wonder if I am witnessing someone getting beaten to death.

Kingston | 153

I grab one of Kingston's sinewy arms. Snoop grabs the other. We try to pull him away, but it's hopeless. He is still punching, even with us clinging to him. A new bouncer steps forward to intervene. That's when I see Chuy jumping on his one leg and swinging his crutch like a sword to keep people back. "Let's go!" Snoop yells. Suddenly, Kingston's arms go slack in our grip like a switch has been turned off. He pushes off the Russian and screams, "You don't put your fucking hands on nobody when I'm around!" I yank on Kingston's shirt, pulling him down the street toward the car. We pick up speed as panic sets in. Looking back, I see Chuy with an arm around Snoop's neck as he hops after us. In the distance, the Russian is bloody and drunkenly crawling out of the club on his hands and knees. The bouncers make no attempt to help him. *You should have paid your bill, culero.* Chuy starts up the car and slams the gas pedal with his crutch. We burn around a corner in a screech of tires. "Did you see how my negro threw that *vato* through the door?!" Snoop screams. Chuy reaches under his seat and produces a rag damp with paint thinner. He places it over his mouth and nose and breathes in all that goodness.

In the front seat Kingston cradles a hand with bloody and swelling knuckles.* He turns back to look at me. "I'm sorry, Jason. I didn't mean to do that crazy shit. I just don't want nobody putting their hands on you." From the back seat I stare at my weary reflection in the rearview mirror. Who do I think I am? What is it that I think I am doing here? When will I know that I have gone too far?

At this point I am already more than three years into this project, and a lot has changed for me. I've learned more than I ever imagined about the inner workings of human smuggling. I've developed intense and productive friendships with people whose lives revolve around making money moving

---

* Three days after the fight, Kingston runs into the same Russian at a medical clinic: "That nigga looked at me with two black eyes, but he didn't say shit."

migrants while simultaneously trying to evade their own early and unnatural deaths. But this enlightenment and these relationships come at a cost. I keep telling myself that I can handle things even as they keep getting more violent and out of control. I hope that my newfound sense of paranoia and hypervigilance will eventually dissipate. I try to ignore the troubling flashbacks that come to me when I am eating dinner with my family or walking my dog. I foolishly tell myself that all of this awfulness is simply part of the job I committed myself to doing a long time ago. I just need to accept these things and everything will be okay. But on the nights when a dark figure glistening with blood chases me down the train tracks and jams a blade into me, I wake up in a cold sweat and remember that things are not okay. I am in over my head.

As we escape into the blackness of night, Arcángel's rasp comes out of the car's speakers: *I've been a son of a bitch since I was born . . . You don't live like this.*

Garifuna

The dark room is dingy and overcrowded. Stained bedrolls, cracked plastic chairs, improvised furniture. A thick blanket covers a tiny barred window. It muffles the cacophony of Mexico City outside and keeps out the prying eyes of immigration officials and thieves. The only light in the room emanates from an opaque bare bulb in the ceiling that gives the impression that it is eleven p.m., not eleven a.m. Snoop sits at a small wooden table working through a hangover and fiddling with the makings of a joint. Ramos, who looks fifteen but is pushing twenty-two, lies on a yellowed mattress, playing DJ on his phone, which is connected to a nearby portable stereo. The deafening volume from the speakers has been shaking the walls since early this morning. Biggie. T.I. Wiz Khalifa. Kevin Gates. Young Thug.

In this tiny room, phones are always ringing, accompanied by a relentless thumping bass, a television on full blast, and a lot of screaming, dancing, and singing. It's the soundtrack to young men killing time while living on the edge of something dangerous. The twenty-four-hour party vibe makes this place feel like a fraternity, not a migrant safe house. There are some nights I worry that the floor is literally going to cave in from all of us jumping up and down while singing along to 2Pac. There are other nights I'm genuinely concerned someone is going to take a knife to the chest because they didn't speak to a stranger properly or they looked at someone sideways. The working-class Mexican neighbors never complain about the noise made at all hours by the black Honduran smugglers who occupy several rooms in this apartment complex. This is because the entire building (and *colonia*) is controlled by MS-13, who make good money collecting rent and a head tax from the many smugglers and migrants who come and go. This isn't a place where you call the police. This is a place where you mind your own business.

Andy stirs a crackling pan of plantains and shakes his ass to the music. At thirty-one, he is den mother to the many young soldiers temporarily staying here. He cooks. He cleans. He keeps the peace, which isn't always easy when you are surrounded by a rotating cast of rowdies fueled by beer, weed, cocaine, crack, and testosterone. Andy is far from intimidating in his neon board shorts, rubber sandals, and tank top that clings tightly to his beer gut. He is pudgy and jovial, but people respect him. He is the voice of reason, the purveyor of a gentle smile that exudes kindness in this often chaotic space. He's been smuggling people off and on for a decade but lately prefers to hold down the fort here in Lechería, a gritty neighborhood on the northern outskirts of Mexico City. This is partly because he is one of the few in this crew

156 | SOLDIERS AND KINGS

who currently doesn't have a visa. The best smugglers have gamed the system and persuaded the Mexican government to grant them temporary permission to stay in the country for humanitarian reasons, which isn't that difficult given that they usually have the same hard-luck stories as their clients. *They killed my brother. They killed my mom. They're gonna kill me.* Andy's application for a visa was recently denied after it was discovered that he had filed a complaint against an immigration official who pistol-whipped him in detention on a previous arrest for suspicion of smuggling. The problem with humanitarian visas, though, is that while they offer a reprieve from deportation, they don't allow a holder to legally work in the country. People with these visas often end up laboring undocumented in Mexico for subpar wages. On the bright side, smugglers can use their visas to move freely across the country with their clients, making it easier to deal with police, Immigration, hotel owners, and taxi drivers.

Instead of transporting people, Andy currently makes ends meet by asking motorists for change at stoplights (what people refer to as *charol*). This is an often-lucrative activity that almost all the black male smugglers I know practice periodically. Snoop and others say that they can sometimes make $25 a day, which is significantly more than they would earn working under the table for a Mexican employer. I asked Papo about it once and he tried to explain it in racial terms: "That's what the *morenos* [dark-skinned people] do. They make a lot of money doing it. They make more than the *güeros* [fair-skinned people]. Other Hondurans don't really do the *charol*. It's mostly the *morenos*. I think Mexicans feel bad for the *morenos* because of slavery and shit." One thing that Papo's explanation fails to account for is the fact that because of skin color, it is difficult for black people to blend into the Mexican workforce. Employers don't want to hire illegal workers who are easily identified as foreigners, which subsequently forces people to beg on the streets. However, competition with other migrants can sometimes be intense at traffic lights, reducing everyone's overall earnings. Lately, competition coupled with the fact that Mexican immigration agents have increasingly cracked down on the practice of *charol* has made it an unstable source of income. When Andy is not on a street corner, he is at home making sure that there is food in the pantry and a place to sleep for arriving smugglers and their clients whom he charges for room and board. In general, managing a safe house can be lucrative because people on the migrant trail always need cheap accommodations. Low-level smugglers like Chino and Santos are usually willing to shell out a few pesos for the opportunity to sleep indoors on a piece of cardboard, as long as there is protection from the elements and the authorities.

Kafu Banton's Panamanian reggae hit "Discriminación" begins to play on the stereo. Andy turns away from the frying pan and starts singing loudly into a wooden spoon turned microphone. "Listen to these words, Jason," he tells me while tapping his ear. Snoop and Ramos soon join in for the chorus: *I don't like how the government abuses us . . . It's only because of our color.*

For many years, the stereotypical American image of an undocumented migrant was a young Mexican male scrambling over a barbed wire fence or trudging through the desert. Since 2014, that popular image has morphed into a collage of children wrapped in silver Mylar blankets on the floor of migrant detention centers and mothers with toddlers clinging to rafts in the middle of the Rio Grande. In all of these scenarios, the people have brown, not black, skin.*

When I began this project in 2015 in Pakal-Ná, I was surprised by the

---

* One of the rare popular media moments that exposed the racial complexity of migration was the circulation of a photograph of Border Patrol agents on horseback chasing down Haitian migrants in South Texas in 2021. See Joel Rose, "The Inquiry into Border Agents on Horseback Continues: Critics See a 'Broken' System," *All Things Considered*, NPR, November 6, 2021, https://www.npr.org/2021/11/06/1052786254/border-patrol-agents-horseback-investigation-haitian-immigrants.

number of black migrants showing up at the shelter and on the train tracks. The majority of them are Garifuna* (plural Garinagu), an Afro-Indigenous group from Central America† descended from enslaved people shipwrecked off the island of St. Vincent at the end of the seventeenth century. These Africans settled on the island and intermarried with Indigenous Kalinago (also known as Caribs). In 1797, after years of fighting European colonization in the region, over five thousand Garinagu ("Black Caribs") were loaded onto boats by the British and abandoned on the Honduran island of Roatán. These displaced people eventually migrated to the mainland of Honduras and can now also be found in small communities in Guatemala, Nicaragua, and Belize. The largest concentrations of Garinagu in Latin America (approximately 200,000) are on the Bay Islands and Caribbean coastal cities of Honduras. A similar number of people are estimated to be living in the United States, with major enclaves in New York City, Houston, New Orleans, and Miami.

My introduction to Garifuna smugglers happened when I first met Snoop on the tracks in Pakal-Ná while hanging out with Chino and the Pleasure Palace crew. He was headed north with a small group of fellow Garinagu who were hiding on the edge of town. Snoop was around only long enough to buy some groceries, get some weed from Papo, and smoke a few joints on the tracks with locals he knew. But after chatting with him for an hour, a few things became clear. First, because of the intense discrimination that black migrants face on the trail, Garinagu move across Mexico in ways that are socially and spatially distinct from other Central Americans. Unlike fair-skinned Hondurans, who can sometimes pass for Mexican, Garinagu are

---

* "Garifuna" typically refers to language, culture, and people, with "Garinagu" the plural form of "Garifuna." However, the people I worked with tended to use "Garifuna" as a catchall phrase.

† There are also black migrants from other parts of Central America (e.g., Panama) and an increasing number of Haitian and African migrants who fly to Latin America and then make the trek north to the United States.

easily identified as foreigners. As Andy would later tell me in Lechería, "People try to mess with us because of our race. People think we are exploitable, especially the police." Because of this, you are not likely to run into Garinagu spending extended periods of time in places like Pakal-Ná, where they are easy targets for the police, immigration officials, and gangs. They tend to move quickly through towns and seek refuge in the jungle, in less-populated villages, or in safe houses away from the train tracks.

Second, to combat racialized abuse, Garinagu primarily rely on smugglers from their own communities and tend to travel only with other migrants who are known to them (i.e., relatives or close neighbors). As Snoop noted in our first conversation, "I only move people I know, people from my *pueblo*"—the implication being that people he moves are black just like him. Snoop would eventually introduce me to Andy in Mexico City, who would more directly address the issue of race and smuggling:

> White guides don't want to help you if you are black. If you are white and want to travel from Honduras they might charge you $6,000 for a good trip. But if you are black and you get a white guide, they'll say, "I'm going to charge you $9,000 or $10,000 because your color causes a lot of problems." They know that our color is problematic for them, so it's better to get a Garifuna guide.

He's right. Black smugglers have a more nuanced understanding of how skin color can cause issues with law enforcement and locals. They also know what to expect *en el camino* and have strategies (such as hiding in the woods or in Garifuna safe houses) to deal with harassment. The different needs of black and brown migrants are also visible among the criminal organizations that smuggle people across Mexico. Garinagu tend to use members of black transnational gangs such as the Bloods for guide services, while mestizo Hondurans (i.e., people of mixed Spanish-Indigenous heritage) often rely on MS-13. This racialized smuggling industry also has a geographic component. Black Hondurans usually want to head to New York, Houston, or New Orleans, so their guides bring them up through South Texas. Mestizo Hondurans are often headed to the West Coast of the United States, so their smugglers utilize routes through the Sonoran Desert of Arizona.

The tendency of Garinagu to exclusively travel with members of their own ethnic group has several benefits. It helps guarantee that people will work together en route. It also makes it unlikely someone will be abandoned or betrayed by a fellow migrant or by their smuggler, who is usually a known member of their community. Moreover, large groups of Garinagu tend to stir up fear among Mexicans, who often find them completely foreign and may buy into various stereotypes about black people. As Andy explains:

> People know that the Garifuna are united. We know our history and the racism that our ancestors experienced. That's why we don't take no shit. Mexicans know this. They see a big group of *morenos* and get scared. But also, the guys who collect the *cuotas* on the trains sometimes don't even want to look us in the face because they think we will use *brujería* on them [*laughs*]. Sometimes the people who are robbing migrants on the train see all these *morenos* standing up together and they don't say anything. They just keep on going.

Trust

When I see Kingston walk through the apartment door for the first time, everyone straightens up as if a commanding officer has just appeared. I half expect the music to stop to add more drama to his entrance. There is no doubt that he is in charge. All of the young soldiers in the room greet him with deference. There are complicated handshakes and masculine hugs. Someone hands him a burning joint. I reach out and offer a beer. He looks at me with curious eyes and says in English, "A'ight. Thank you." Like Flaco, Kingston is more than a decade older than almost everyone else in his crew. He's an O.G. A veteran. Someone who understands things because he has worked his way up the ranks from a lowly foot soldier to the leader of a gang of young men. He began moving people informally just like Chino and Santos. Through hard work and luck, he managed to stay alive while gaining a reputation. Over the years as he has watched smuggling evolve, he has been able to carve out a leadership role for himself through his connections to high-ranking gang leaders in the United States and via his ability to command the respect of his underlings.

Kingston is tall, lean, and muscular, a physique shaped by years of incarceration and the homemade workout regimen one develops to keep from going insane while locked in a cage. This included hundreds of sit-ups and push-ups every day to maintain his muscle tone and his speed. It's a workout he is still dedicated to each morning. "You've gotta have discipline," he will later constantly tell me. "Discipline is the key." American prison tattoos run across his arms and chest: the names of sired children and dead homies; skulls, numbers, and dripping letters that attest to his longtime membership in the Bloods, a black American gang that has many chapters among the Garifuna in Central America. Increased migration in recent decades between the Bronx and the Caribbean coast of Honduras has expanded the influence of the Bloods abroad and allowed the gang to corner the market on the smuggling of black migrants through Mexico.

As a leader, Kingston exudes a potent mix of charisma, fearlessness, and the street smarts that are needed in this business if you want to see your late twenties. His intimidating physical presence is balanced by his handsome face and childlike grin, and the silver caps on his teeth that shine when he playfully talks shit in a mix of Spanish and Bronx-inflected English. For the record, he talks a lot of shit. Every other phrase out of his mouth is either "Get the fuck outta here!" or "What the fuck?" Sometimes these phrases are uttered with a laugh and a smile. Other times with a growl. No one can escape his catchphrases: taxi drivers, store clerks, elderly waiters, bartenders, little kids. They all seem to laugh him off, either because they think he is ridiculous or because they are slightly afraid. There is something about Kingston that lets him get away with being irreverent at all times. It's hard not to be charmed by him. A young Garifuna woman staying in the apartment next door walks into the room and immediately approaches him. "What's your name?" she coyly asks. He smiles and says, "My name is Satan." She blushes and makes eyes at him. Somehow this line works. I watch this interaction and find myself captivated by a man who seems to fill up the entire room with his persona. Over the years, I will see him work his charm effectively on practically everyone he meets, including a whole bunch of scary motherfuckers.

We sit for an hour drinking beers and eating the lunch that Andy has prepared. Kingston and I make small talk in Spanglish about Mexico City and some of his experiences in the United States. He looks at the camera around my neck and says, "You wanna take a picture of me?" I nod and gesture to the door. We leave the cinder-block room and enter the apartment building's small courtyard. He stands in the afternoon sun as it warms his dark brown skin. He looks away from the lens, showing me his profile and firm jawline. I snap photos. He then turns and looks directly into the camera. His expression is cold. I crack a joke to lighten the mood. He tries to fight back a smile but ends up grinning. I finish a roll of film and put the camera down. Kingston's tone then gets serious.

Kingston: I got a question for you.

Jason: Okay.

Kingston | 163

Kingston: You not police, right?

Jason: Me? Police? Fuck no, man. Never. Have your soldiers told you about me and what I'm doing here?

Kingston: Yeah, they told me about you.

Jason: I'm an anthropologist. I want to write about what it's like being a black smuggler in Mexico. That's why I gave you my business card. I'm hoping you will call me because I want to hang out and learn about your job. I want to hang out so that we can chat and you can learn to trust me.

Kingston: A'ight, I got you. I got it. I believe you, man.

Jason: Look, if you call me up, I'm going to say, "Hey, can I come hang out with you? Can I ask you some questions?" But if there is ever a point where you say, "I don't trust you," I promise I will throw this camera and voice recorder away.

Kingston: Look, I don't care what you do with the pictures. That's your business. I just need to know if you police.

Jason: I'm not police. If you don't think you can trust me, this won't really work and I won't bother you.

Kingston: Okay. Okay. *No hay problema. Todo bien.* I'm just asking, man. I just want to know what's going on because we just came from the fucking jungle and you know what that's like. That's why I am asking. You keep it official with me and I'll keep it official with you.

Jason: I want to write a book about guides. I've been in this safe house for over a month and I'm hoping that you guys are starting to trust me because I really want to be here and understand your lives.

Kingston: I appreciate that because not everybody would be doing the shit you've been doing. Not everybody would want to be here with us. Believe me. Look, come to my house in Veracruz. We can chill out. Go to the beach. Play soccer. Chill with some Mexicans. I got people there.

Jason: Thank you. I hope that you know that I'm here to try and tell a story. I'm not here to get anyone in trouble. I've been talking to your soldiers, but I am not sure if they really understand what I'm trying to do.

Kingston: Look, I made those guys. I brought them into this group, but they're young and don't know shit. I'll tell you what you want to know.

Meeting Kingston, a veteran gangster turned guide, would open up new worlds for me into the relationship between smuggling, gangs, and violence. It would also bring me closer to understanding death and those who traffic in it. At the time, though, I couldn't foresee how my soon-to-be complicated and emotionally draining relationship with him would eventually make me question just how close to the sun I was willing to fly.

Escuela

From the apartment courtyard, we can hear the slamming of dominoes onto a plywood table and the requisite cackling and shit-talking that accompanies such moves. While antsy young men gamble and smoke weed inside, Kingston and I sit in the shade with a styrofoam cooler of beer between us. The Mexico City sun is a flaming yellow orb fighting to break through the smog overhead. Stereos from surrounding apartments compete with each other. Vicente Fernández tries to outsing Bad Bunny and Bob Marley. After just a few weeks, Kingston has fully embraced his role as my teacher and begins to explain his perspective on the smuggling game.

> **Kingston:** *Mira, mi rey* [Look, my king]. I'm going to tell you something very important. They say that people getting ripped off at the *frontera* is the fault of guides, but I don't think that's the reason. Well, in some cases, yes. There are some guides who are fucking worthless. There are some guides who agree to move people and then they leave them at the northern border or never get them to their final destination. Those guides are just thieves who are doing their job poorly. That's bad for business because the people you are in charge of often know you because you've been recommended by someone. This job is all about recommendations. It's like if you have someone paint your house and I walk by and say, "Hey, who did that?" If I like the job, I want to work with that *vato*. If the house is painted poorly, I'm like, "Who did that shit?" Recommendations are very important.

> **Jason:** How does somebody get started in all this?

Kingston: In my case, I already knew Mexico. I probably knew like 90 percent of the country. I knew it because I was going all over the place. I was going everywhere. I was doing the *charol* because it used to be good. You could make good *lana* doing it, but now it's worth dick. There's a lot of immigration raids that make it hard to be on the streets, so you end up going back to Honduras where you meet people who want to go to *el norte*. I knew Mexico, so I started talking to *polleros* in Honduras who wanted my help. I asked them, "If I bring people with me, will you pay me?" They said they would, so I was like, "*Firme*. Let's go!" I knew the routes and told people, "I'll get you there. You just gotta pay me." A few agreed and I brought them on that first trip. I got them there safely. Then people started recommending me . . . The next thing I know I had two or three years doing this shit.

Social scientists studying clandestine migration have long confirmed Kingston's point. If you have the money to contract a smuggler, your preference is to find someone who is connected to your home community. That way if a person disappears *en el camino*, families have some ability to track down the guide or the guide's family and hold them accountable. This doesn't mean that something bad can't or won't happen en route, such as kidnapping by the cartels or arrest by immigration officials. However, it does provide some assurance that any calamity that occurs won't be due to the bad intentions of your *guía*. Unfortunately, the rising costs of smuggling often lead people to migrate alone or contract unknown guides they meet at different legs of the journey when they periodically have money. This is often how people like Chino and Santos pick up work. As Kingston notes, the staged nature of migration means that people pass through many hands, which is where problems can arise.

Kingston: People love me because I treat them right. For example, if someone seeks me out and pays me, I'll get them to their destination. It's only if something bad happens in the *camino* that's outside my control that I won't be able to get them there. But it's also not always a question of whether the guide is good. It's also a question of the *polleros*, the people who are receiving migrants at the border.

Jason: How so?

Kingston: If you are a *pollero* and you live at the U.S.-Mexico border, you control that area. You have me bringing people up from Honduras or someplace else. I charge $7,000 to bring my people. [*He takes a sniff of coke off the back of his hand.*] In Honduras, I ask for $1,000 up front. When we get into southern Mexico, I ask you for another $500. When we get to Mexico City, I ask for another $500. That's $2,000. With that $2,000 I'll get you to Mexico City. You still owe $5,000, and so far I have only made maybe $300 or $400 per person. In Mexico City, I'll ask for half of the $5,000. With that money I'll get you to the northern border. What happens next? People get to the border and their family sends the rest of the $5,000 to the *caminador* [walker], the person who will get you across the river or the desert.

At this point, it is important to note that the *caminador* is not Garifuna or Honduran. He is usually Mexican and has been subcontracted by someone like Kingston (a guide) or most likely the *pollero* back in Honduras who initially brokered the entire deal. The *pollero* in Honduras has to make contact with a *pollero* at the U.S.-Mexico border who will then arrange the contract with a *caminador*. These subcontracted individuals are usually controlled by Mexican cartels. As Kingston notes, these third-party smugglers are often wild cards in terms of how they will treat a client.

> **Kingston:** There are people who are sick in the head. People who will rob you *en el camino* or ask for another $1,000 at the northern border and then run off with your $3,500. Or they just kidnap you and ask for more money. You have to pay them because they don't play around. Business is business. But in the beginning, you think you are gonna pay $7,000 and you end up paying more than $9,000 because you got ripped off and had to pay someone else to get you across. This is the fault of those at the northern border, the Mexican *polleros* and *caminadores* and even the *levantadores*, the gringos and Chicanos who will drive you to a safe house. Too many people aren't trustworthy. They will ask for more money and try to rip people off. There are also some guides who charge $9,000 or $10,000, and you end up riding on the fucking train! Not even in a car! *Chinga la madre*. You pay all that money to eat well and sleep in hotels but end up on the train tracks and in the jungles eating tortillas and sardines and iguanas . . . Some of these guides get a lot of money and they get crazy and do whatever the hell they want. They end up leaving people stranded. Then those people have to go back with no money and start over.

In many ways, Kingston is describing the typical approach to smuggling: ask for as much money as possible at every stage of the trip and when the time is right, find a way to rip off the clients that you have little loyalty toward. As ugly as this process sounds, this is standard practice. At the end of the day, Kingston is correct when he asserts, "Too many people aren't trustworthy." This issue of trust has been exacerbated by both the increase in security measures by the Mexican government and the rise in overall violence on the migrant trail. Initiatives like Programa Frontera Sur have made the already dangerous process of migration more hazardous and expensive. People now have to deal with many more actors seeking to deter, arrest, and make money off of them. For Kingston, the best smugglers to navigate this increasingly complicated process are those willing to get their hands dirty.

> **Kingston:** Guides now have to do business with people who you don't ever want to fucking run into. This is what people don't understand. Some people who think they are guides will say, "I'm headed north and I'll take you." They think it's easy. They think they know what is going on, but they don't. Those aren't real guides. Real guides need to be motherfuckers because shit is coming. Real guides know it's coming. People will kick down your door and say, "*¿Quién es el bueno?* Who brought you?" You gotta man up and say, "It's me, *carnal*. What's up?" Then they put a gun to your fucking head and say, "All right let's do business." I want people to understand that being a guide is not easy. All kinds of fucked-up shit happens *en el camino*. It's a process where you are always waiting for someone to show up or for money to arrive. When you're bringing people it's always a motherfucker. But that's how life is. It's a tough story and you have to be from the streets and be down for anything to do this work. That's how it is now.

Several factors have led to the violence Kingston speaks of. First, Mexican drug cartels (e.g., the Zetas) and local gangs have increasingly become involved in extorting and abusing migrants as they pass through different areas. People thus seek out smugglers who can negotiate safe passage. This has led to the increased involvement of groups like MS-13, or in the case of Garinagu, Bloods. They possess the necessary skill sets to broker deals with cartels while also fending off rival gangs looking to kidnap or rob migrants. However, a gangbanger-turned-smuggler's history in a region may sometimes cause problems and require that they take circuitous routes through some territories to avoid certain people or neighborhoods. This is often where recruiting young soldiers becomes important, especially if they are familiar with certain stretches of the migrant trail—like Chino, who moves primarily between the Guatemala border and Pakal-Ná. To complicate matters, robberies and assaults at the hands of locals (who are often very young) have gotten more severe and out of control over the last decade.

Kingston: Man, shit is crazy now. Now the ones who are fucking your shit up are little kids who are killing people on the tracks. They'll take your money and your life. That's why you need to respect the young kids, because you never know what they are capable of.

Jason: Let's say that I want to be a soldier right now, what do I have to learn?

Kingston: You have to learn discipline and how to be down with crazies. Guides need to know how to talk to people. For example, I'm *loco* and I can get crazy if I need to. I can enter a territory with *puro locos* and know how to fit in. There are some guides who show up to a new place and mouth off. They will say to strangers, "I don't give a fuck!" I say to them, "Really [*laughing*]? You think you don't give a fuck?

There are real *locos* here. How you gonna act crazy with these real motherfuckers who will kill you?" In those cases, you gotta watch how you talk. You have to study everyone and pay attention. You have to be looking out all the time. If I'm in a place and some *loco* starts bossing me around, like sending me on a shopping trip to get food or beer, I go so that I can learn what's really going on. They send me on errands and I learn. But to learn like I'm telling you, you have to listen and pay attention. Sometimes you meet people on the tracks and all they do is talk and talk. Blah blah blah. [*He makes mouth gesture with his hand.*] People talk too much trying to convince you they know shit. It's better to listen and be aware, because there are some places where they won't accept you. They'll just throw you off the train. You have to know how to listen so that you can learn and know where not to go.

Jason: I would imagine that as a soldier on the tracks you learn this stuff pretty quickly.

Kingston: Well, you start out just fucking around. You start out thinking you are playing. But you soon realize that you can't change the train tracks, but they can really change you. The tracks are like a dog you keep fucking with. You keep fucking with it again and again until eventually it bites you and then it's over.

Jason: How have you managed to survive this long?

Kingston: My story is not an easy one, *hermano*. My whole life has been a clusterfuck.

CHAPTER NINE

Genesis

The child's bony body swings in the wind, a tiny man condemned to the gallows. From his upside-down position, all Kingston can see are his mother's legs and sandals. This view is so familiar, though, that he can read the movement of her feet. He knows when she is preparing to strike. *You worthless piece of shit. Why don't you ever listen?* An electrical cord whips across his bare back. He screams as his eight-year-old frame absorbs the blow. The cord hurts a hell of a lot more than the flat side of a machete. He wishes she would go back to using the machete. His mother winds up to deliver another lash. He squirms and desperately tries to untie his feet from the pole. It is futile. This is unstoppable. This is forever. The whip cracks against his skin again and again, creating a soundtrack to his upside-down world.

Twenty-five years later, summer raindrops thick as quarters pound out machine-gun fire on a zinc roof. Tired women stand in doorways, tightly gripping shopping bags and holding newspapers over their heads for protection. A momma dog with teats dragging on the ground scrambles under a car in search of shelter. Kingston packs a crack rock into the end of a cigarette and puts flame to it. The humidity makes his thick exhalations linger in the

Genesis | 173

air. The room fills with smoke as we talk of life and death, our conversation shrouded in a growing caustic fog. He speaks of choices that defy notions of right and wrong. He sketches origin stories into the air that he hopes will explain and justify bad deeds. He paints the worlds that have made him.

THE BEATINGS BECOME too frequent, too intense. Even at eight years old, Kingston recognizes that this is no way to live. He has to get out because no one will save him from his mother's wrath. His father has been dead a year, but it doesn't matter. He was just a stranger from a faraway place, a man he met only once, when he knocked on the door and tried to take his son away to America. His mother refused to give Kingston up. If she couldn't escape poverty, then neither would her child. They would suffer together. But Kingston knows that life is not sustainable at home. No one should live like this. He has had enough of these whippings taken while hanging by his feet.

> **Kingston:** Me and my mom didn't get along, so I started leaving the house when I was eight years old. I had to become independent. I left home and started coming and going. I was running around on the streets doing my thing. I used to sing for money with a friend of mine. We would sing at night in front of people's houses. They would pay us to go away or they would throw water or piss on us to make us leave [*laughing*]. Somebody later killed that friend.

He starts looking for work so that he can feed himself.

> **Kingston:** The first real job I had was at the bus depot washing buses. Later, there were even moments when they would

let me drive. I was driving the bus as a little kid [*laughing*]. I was going everywhere at that time. That's also when I started to be around drugs.

Kingston finds himself a child on the streets looking for a new family, a story that parallels the early experiences of Flaco, Chino, and Santos. He is eager to fit in and be accepted. Older gang members in his neighborhood see potential in such a precocious young man. They begin to indoctrinate him and seemingly help predetermine what his adulthood will look like.

Kingston: The first time I shot a gun I was nine or ten. The gang in my neighborhood tried to get me to kill someone. They wanted me to shoot somebody on the street. It wasn't a job. It was just me trying to feel important. I picked up a gun and someone grabbed my hand and aimed, and I started pulling the trigger. I started shooting everywhere but didn't hit anyone. We were just playing around then.

For a few years Kingston plays around on the streets and gets into minor scrapes with the law. Perhaps under normal circumstances, this would have just been a phase. Something to grow out of. Unfortunately, nothing about Kingston's young life would ever prove normal.

Kingston: I lost my dad when I was eight, but I didn't care. I didn't really know him. My mom died of cancer when I was twelve. When she died, I said to myself, "Now I don't have anyone left. I'm alone." The rest of my family didn't give a fuck about me. They'd see me on the street and just walk by. From then on [*he lets out a big exhale of smoke*], I told myself that it was gonna be okay. That's just how it's gonna be. I

Genesis | 175

started to get serious with robbing. I started stealing milk and bread in the *barrio*. People would see me enter the neighborhood and they would get scared because they knew if they were going to get past me, they would leave empty-handed. I'd be running off with their milk and bananas and shit [*laughing*]. People started talking about me, saying, "That nigga terrible. That nigga trouble."

Completely alone in the world, Kingston gets bolder with his street hustling. He also starts making brief forays into Mexico, El Salvador, and Guatemala in search of thrills. Like many smugglers I come to know, he wanders aimlessly across international boundaries, both coming of age and accruing a deep knowledge of Latin American geography that will later become a crucial resource. It is at this juncture that I sometimes imagine an alternate reality for him. Maybe he ends up in Mexico and falls in love with someone who helps turn his life around. He leaves the game before things get too out of control. His story gets written with a happy ending. But that, of course, does not happen. Instead, a high-ranking member of the Bloods comes to his neighborhood and starts recruiting young people. This phenomenon is similar to what happened when members of MS-13 began getting deported from Los Angeles to El Salvador in the late 1980s, bringing American gang culture with them. What had previously been a loose collection of hoodlums in coastal Honduras turned into a formalized organization with international connections to Belize, New York, and beyond. "Once we started that gang shit, it got really crazy," he tells me. "We were running around with guns, robbing people in the *barrio*. We were really bad. That's why the military came and rounded us up and took us to a base. I was twelve or thirteen when I joined the army."

In the 1980s, American fears regarding the spread of communism from Nicaragua's newly installed Sandinista government were being felt across

176 | SOLDIERS AND KINGS

Central America. Because of its long history of subservience to the United States, Honduras was viewed as a perfect partner in the region to help Ronald Reagan fight his growing Cold War. For Honduras, this meant an influx of large amounts of foreign money to help expand its military presence throughout the country. As tensions rose between the United States and Nicaragua, Honduras began to feel pressure from Washington to increase the size of its military. Although the 1982 Honduran constitution confirmed that military service was obligatory for unmarried males between the ages of eighteen and thirty, the low wages and poor living conditions offered to soldiers discouraged many from enlisting. To make up for this deficit in recruits, the army periodically carried out "manhunts" (often outside high schools and soccer matches in poor neighborhoods) where they rounded up youth and forcibly conscripted them for service. These young recruits were subject to "two years of often brutal training at almost no pay." Kingston was underage when he was grabbed by the military in the early 1990s,* but it didn't seem to matter. He was an orphan who looked much older than his years and had no parents searching for him. There was no one to mount a rescue party. Besides, many members of his gang, including Andy and several cousins, were captured at the same time. Kingston figured he was better off staying with them. The military would feed and house him and provide new skills. The military would also turn him into a different person.

> **Kingston:** They came to the *barrios* and started rounding up kids. I remember someone grabbing me and being like, "I ain't playing with you. Let's go." So many kids got kidnapped. People's mothers were crying when they took us away. Later we were all crying for our mothers when they cut our hair off. There were a lot of Garifuna there. I never

---

* This practice was suspended in 1993.

Genesis | 177

saw so many *morenos* in one place. There were also a lot of young kids in the army, like ten years old. *Chinga su madre.* That shit was fucked up. I was a little kid doing crazy shit in the army. They knew I would do whatever they wanted, so they put me in a special unit with other crazy motherfuckers. They treated me bad. They tortured me mentally and physically. They fucked me up. You have to understand that in Honduras the military is a lot different than in the United States.

Kingston was the perfect candidate for a child soldier: young, poor, impressionable, an orphan. As Schauer and Elbert note in their analysis of the psychological damage inflicted on youth in the military:

Becoming a fighter may seem an attractive possibility for children and adolescents who are facing poverty, starvation, unemployment, and ethnic or political persecution . . . Former child soldiers and commanders alike reported that children are more malleable and adaptable. Thus, they are easier to indoctrinate, as their moral development is not yet completed and they tend to listen to authorities without questioning them.

At age twelve, Kingston had already been on the streets for almost four years and was no stranger to brutality. However, his time in the military formalized and rewarded his ability to be violent, while also creating devastating long-term effects for his adulthood.*

---

* "Child soldiers are raised in an environment of severe violence . . . and subsequently often commit cruelties and atrocities of the worst kind. This repeated exposure to chronic and traumatic stress during development leaves children with mental and related physical ill-health, notably PTSD and severe personality changes. Such exposure also deprives the child from a normal

Kingston leaves the military at age fourteen and returns to the streets a changed person with new skills. He now can fieldstrip a weapon in just a few minutes and has a working knowledge of explosives. No longer does someone have to hold his hand while he fires a gun. He has become a professional marksman who can hit a moving target while on a dead run. His brain is also now wired to mentally plan ambushes for maximum potency. His world has become one of concealment, subterfuge, and hypervigilance. For the rest of his life, he will sit with his back against a wall, both literally and figuratively. Trust no one. Trust can get you killed. Kingston reenters civilian society a damaged child with a commitment to discipline and a refined sense of how to effectively be violent.

THE YOUNG MAN walks up and aims as if it is the most natural movement in the world. A metallic click. An explosion of flame and smoke. There is no time to react. He turns and points the gun at a teenage Kingston: "You see what I just did?" Kingston nods his head in shock. Brain matter and blood are everywhere. His ears ring, but he hears the next question clear as day. "What are you gonna do about it?" This is a defining moment in Kingston's young life, which has already been characterized by gunshots, beatings, and a thousand other unspeakable lessons. This question is both real and philosophical, paralyzing and energizing. This is the moment that breaks his young world open, forging a dark chasm that he will try to fill for the rest of his life with blood, hatred, drugs, and self-loathing.

---

and healthy development and impairs their integration into society as a fully functioning member." Elisabeth Schauer and Thomas Elbert, "The Psychological Impact of Child Soldiering," in *Trauma Rehabilitation after War and Conflict*, ed. Erin Martz (New York: Springer, 2010), 311.

Genesis | 179

Kingston: Someone came and killed my best friend right in front of my face, and I couldn't do anything about it. After that, I was like, "Fuck this shit." I just went crazy. I started hurting people too. It seemed like the whole world was going crazy at that time. Because of my friend getting killed, I started to do really terrible things. Things you don't want to hear about.

The trauma of watching the murder of a friend or family member is enough to send anyone over the edge. Coupled with a lack of psychological care or familial support, it is easy to imagine the dark places one can travel to in response. I often think about the fact that everyone I spoke to for this book knows someone who has been murdered, and practically all of them (Flaco, Papo, Chino, Alma, Jesmyn) have witnessed someone being killed. Given Kingston's early adolescent experiences and military training, his reaction of hyperviolent behavior should come as no surprise.*

After the death of his friend, Kingston goes on a rampage. His fury becomes reckless and unstoppable. He cares little for life and death, his own or that of others. All he knows is that he will never be helpless again. Now when a gun is pointed at his face and someone asks, "What are you gonna do about it?" he has an aggressive response. But his violent tendencies build a notorious reputation, one that starts to catch up with him. At fourteen he becomes a wanted man. "I had to leave home because the police were looking for me," he says. When he flees Honduras, there is no one to say goodbye to.

---

* "Research shows that former child soldiers have difficulties in controlling aggressive impulses and have little skills for handling life without violence. These children show on-going aggressiveness within their families and communities, even after relocation to their home villages." Schauer and Elbert, "The Psychological Impact of Child Soldiering," 335.

THE GUATEMALAN POLICE OFFICER dumps the contents of Kingston's backpack on the ground and begins to rifle through his clothes and toiletries. There is no money to pilfer. "Go home, kid," the officer tells him. "You'll never make it." The young man imagines what is waiting for him in Honduras. Hunger. Despair. A bullet.

"I got nothing to go back to," he responds.

Kingston mumbles obscenities under his breath as he watches the cop speed away with his backpack and all his clothes. He is kicking gravel on the side of the road and watching heat lines rise up in the distance when an old man in a rusted-out truck pulls over. The old man takes pity on the lanky black teenager who seems to be running away from so many things. He drives the kid all the way to Guatemala City, where he buys him some clothes and hands him enough quetzales to get to the Mexican border. A few days later Kingston is in Tapachula, Chiapas, pulling himself up onto a speeding freight train headed north. He is now a migrant on the trail. He sleeps on the streets in Ixtepec and does odd jobs for a few pesos and a hot meal in Orizaba and Tierra Blanca. He steals food off restaurant plates in Apizaco and Lechería. These are locations he will later come to know intimately as a smuggler. For now, the world is new and full of hope for a kid trying to leave so many nightmares behind.

In Monterrey, Mexico, Kingston spends several days on a farm caring for livestock. It is there that he meets up with others just like him. Children headed to Texas to connect with relatives who made the journey before them. This is the early 1990s, before border enforcement reaches the hyper-militarized levels that begin in the wake of 9/11. He and his friends easily cross into the United States through Laredo. Four days later, Kingston is sleeping on someone's couch in Houston, but he knows he can't stay. His father had family in New York who can maybe help him. He borrows money

Genesis | 181

for a bus ticket. Seventy-two hours later he is walking around the Bronx looking for Garinagu who might know his people.

The Wonder Years

New York is everything he had imagined, a fast-paced drama full of excitement and possibility. He finds support through a long-lost half brother who helps him secure his Green Card. The legal process is aided by the fact that Kingston is an underage hard-case orphan with an American-born father. He enters the workforce and starts making good money painting cars. But going straight doesn't last long. His half brother is a Blood who connects him with a crew in the Bronx. Kingston's exploits in Honduras are well known to New York gang members, and they welcome him with open arms. He begins spending his evenings and days off selling weed, coke, and crack. His military training serves him well as he takes command of dozens of young gang members, kids who rob, sell drugs, and do his dirty work. He is the same age as or younger than most of his crew, but everyone recognizes that the world of hurt he has already waded through at such a young age puts him in a weight class all his own. He is also now over six feet tall and full of muscle. People listen when he talks. No one questions his leadership or whether he is down for his shit. Business is good. He moves up the ranks. His numbers begin to increase. Within a matter of months, he has dozens of soldiers working under him. But despite all his abilities, Kingston lacks restraint. There are some things he just can't let go.

The blade runs quick and hot across the kid's face. Metal pares off flesh. Muscle and tissue and bone looking so foreign without the protection of skin. The kid screams as if he's dying. Maybe he is. His hands try to cover the gaping wound as blood pours out through his fingers. Kingston looks at his friend writhing on the ground and then to the person holding a bloody knife. "What's up now, motherfucker?" the knife-wielding stranger asks. Déjà vu.

"THAT REALLY BOTHERED ME, man, because we was just drinking and this dude came and cut my friend's face and nobody did shit," he tells me late one night in Veracruz. "He cut it down to the bone. That shit was fucked up, so I pulled out my .22 and I clocked that nigga."

BY THE TIME Kingston is done retaliating, the gun is a bloody mess and the person's face is hard to recognize as human. It's a miracle he didn't kill someone that day. This isn't Kingston's first run-in with American law enforcement, but even if it were, it's too serious a crime to excuse, even for a sixteen-year-old. On the day of sentencing, Kingston tries to look hard in front of the judge, but he isn't fooling anyone. He knows things are bad. When the words ring out in the courthouse, "Attempted first-degree murder; twenty-five to life," he can't hold back the tears.

> Kingston: Man, my life was over. I had no family to help me and I was serving twenty-five to life. They took everything away. No more pussy. No more nothing. I was in Rikers and then they shipped me to a medium-security facility until I turned eighteen. Then they sent me all over the state: Buffalo, Sing Sing, Attica.

Although he has no family to visit him on Sundays or fill his commissary, there are plenty of Bloods from his crew already locked up who welcome him into the fold. Gang life gives him structure and purpose in prison. He

Genesis | 183

finds himself a student in a new laboratory for violence. Kingston starts doing things that are familiar: assault, drug smuggling, extortion. Income is generated by manufacturing shanks and taxing the drugs smuggled in through various orifices. He reads books and gets tattooed. He does hundreds of thousands of sit-ups and push-ups. He builds a routine and seeks peace through discipline and his own form of transcendental meditation.

> **Kingston:** You can survive anywhere, and that includes prison. You just have to control yourself. You have to control how you act. Prison torments everyone. No one wants to be in there, but if you know how to live and do your time, then everything is fine. Your body is in prison, but your mind is free.

One of the things that gives him hope early on is a chance encounter with an inmate.

> **Kingston:** I was in my cell one day and I started smelling *mota*. There was an old guy in the cell next to mine who was always smoking weed. I heard he had killed a bunch of people and was serving a life sentence. He started talking to me like, "Hey, you wanna smoke some weed?" I didn't want to accept no favors from him because that's how you end up giving up the *culo*. But we kept talking and he started asking me about my case. We eventually started smoking together [*laughing*]. We became friends. He was like a lawyer because he helped me write letters to the governor about my case. He started writing all these letters to Albany to have my case reconsidered. This went on for a couple of years until I was transferred.

184 | SOLDIERS AND KINGS

Kingston tries to stay positive, but after almost a decade of the same day on repeat, the weight of his sentence begins to take a toll. His meditation starts to fail him. He begins to lose his precious discipline. During his eighth year of incarceration, he finds himself at the lowest point in his life and unaware that things are about change.

> **Kingston:** I started to give up hope in prison. I started going crazy. I cut someone and they added time to my sentence. I started fighting with the guards. They kept throwing me in the hole, into isolation. For several years, it was just a bed and a toilet. No window. No sunlight. That's when I really started to give up. Then I was in my cell one day and a letter arrived. It was marked *Legal*. I threw it on my bed and just looked at it. I didn't give a fuck about no legal mail. I wanted to hear from my family. So that letter just sat there for days, unopened. I remember I was sitting in my cell reading a book when a guard came by and said, "You need to get your shit together because you are leaving on Monday." That's when I finally opened the letter and realized that they were going to release me. I had forgotten about the things we wrote to Albany. I guess it worked. This happened on a Friday and I couldn't sleep that whole weekend. The guards brought me out on Monday morning. It was like nine a.m. and two guards had me by the arms when they opened those doors. I saw the sun for first time after so long and I just fell to the ground. They had to pick me up and carry me.

Within a matter of days Kingston goes from a state prison cell to a federal immigration detention center. Two months later he is on a plane flying to Honduras. He doesn't care that he loses his U.S. residency. He doesn't care that he has to return to a place that might still remember his violent exploits from a previous life. None of it matters, because he is free.

The return to Honduras is better than he ever fantasized. His appetite is insatiable. Alcohol. Drugs. Sex. All consumed with the unbridled enthusiasm one stores up after almost a decade of isolation. The celebration of life goes on for weeks in the coastal city of La Ceiba. When the money finally runs dry, Kingston returns to his home village. It's been ten years since he ran away. He walks the streets and tries to reconnect with friends. A few weeks after his homecoming, someone breaks into the house where he is sleeping. The pressure of a .22 caliber pistol against his forehead startles him awake. He flinches just as the gun fires. The bullet burns across the side of his head, goes through his shoulder, and rips into the mattress. His ears ring as the gunman escapes through an open window. Is this retribution for something he did as a kid? Is this payback for a dirty deed carried out in New York? Maybe it's just a case of mistaken identity. Regardless of the reason, Honduras is not safe. He goes to the hospital to get treated for a bullet wound and then plans his escape. In no time at all he is standing on the tracks in Pakal-Ná, pushing a client onto a Mexican freight train headed north toward the border.

CHAPTER TEN

Apocalipsis

Chino and Jesmyn are looking rough. She's been wearing the same clothes for several days and the dark circles under her eyes signal restless nights of sleeping on a concrete patio just a few feet from the train tracks. Chino is pale and abnormally sweaty, even for the tropics. His skin is on fire and every bone in his body aches. "We were riding the train and I lost Santos near Salto de Agua [eighty kilometers west of Pakal-Ná]," he tells me as we congregate under a scrawny tree in search of relief from the sun. "I was trying to cut the train's brake line to slow it down so that I could jump off to look for him. The train slammed to a stop and threw me off. That's how I got this." He lifts his shirt to reveal a dark purple bruise the size and shape of a small mango. There is a deep rectangular puncture wound in the middle of the bruise that makes it look like he's been stabbed. The wound has started oozing pus and Chino's fever is likely the result of a growing infection. Santos looks at his friend and shakes his head. "I was kind of fucked up when it happened," Chino says, laughing.

"I know," Santos replies. "That's how you almost got yourself killed."

Despite his injury, Chino is surprisingly cheerful as the four of us sit by the tracks and enjoy a slight breeze. A melody of chirping birds fills the

Apocalipsis | 187

jungle air. Pakal-Ná is weirdly peaceful at the moment, except when the nearby train thunderously clanks as it adds new boxcars in preparation for departure. At this point, I have known Jesmyn only a few days. She is still quiet around me and mostly just listens to our conversation as she decides whether I can be trusted. Chino, though, is both talkative and more relaxed than normal. He's not nervously pacing or taking enthusiastic slugs from a plastic jug of *caña*. Even the fingers on his machete-ravaged arm aren't twitching like they usually do. At first I think maybe the fever has slowed him down, that he's too exhausted and sick to be his boisterous and chaotic self. But it soon becomes clear that Chino is changing. He is starting to contemplate a different kind of life in Mexico, one that now seems to include Jesmyn. "I might stay in Pakal-Ná," he tells me. "We're thinking about renting a room and looking for work. Either that or maybe we will head to Guatemala. Jesmyn's mom does some business there and might be able to help me find a job."

This statement catches me off guard. Just a few weeks earlier he was running around the tracks shit-faced, talking about drinking bleach as a way to escape his troubled life. Now he seems clearheaded and optimistic about the future. I listen in slight disbelief as he speaks seriously about finding normal employment. He puts his arm around Jesmyn, who blushes and tries to cover up her smile with her hand. She and Chino are clearly smitten with each other, love at first sight on the migrant trail. As we sit and listen to the birds and the clanging of train cars, I wonder if this is how he gets out of this life. After so many years of hard luck and bad decisions, someone crosses Chino's path and offers a new direction. But can it be this simple? Can he and Jesmyn rent a room in Pakal-Ná and both get a fresh start? Can they make a life for themselves that doesn't involve sleeping on the ground or running scared from machete attacks? Together maybe they will no longer feel restless or abandoned. The birds continue to chirp all around us, and for a moment the train tracks feel like a place of optimism.

A few hours later, Chino and I stand in front of a nearby pharmacy while I play doctor.

> **Jason:** *Oye, mano*, you need to take these pills. And don't go off and give them to your friends. You can't get fucked up on these things. This is Advil. It's medicine. It will help with the pain and lower your fever.

> **Chino:** Okay, okay. I promise I'll take them and won't give them away.

> **Jason:** I also need you to drink water. A lot of water. All day long. The word of the day is "water." [*I hand him a bottle.*] Look, just pretend this is *caña*.

> **Chino:** [*laughing*] Okay, *en serio*. I promise I'll drink water.

I hand him a bottle of Electrolit, a pharmaceutical-grade hydration liquid. Millions of people crossing the Sonoran Desert of Arizona have used it to try to stave off dehydration and death during their treacherous journeys across the U.S.-Mexico border. Prior to my work with smugglers, I spent six years in the desert researching the experiences of migrants. During that time, I encountered thousands of empty containers of Electrolit, including one that I found next to the body of Carmita Maricela Zhagüi Pulla, a thirty-one-year-old mother of three from Ecuador who died from dehydration just a few days before. Maricela had managed to cross the length of Central America and Mexico only to meet her demise in southern Arizona when she became sick and was abandoned by her smuggler. It's hard not to think of that encounter with death every time I see a bottle of Electrolit. As

I pass it to Chino, I wonder if he too will eventually try his luck that far north.

> **Jason:** Drink this. It will help, and if you don't feel better soon, I'll take you to the doctor.

> **Chino:** Okay, thank you. I'll see you tomorrow, right?

> **Jason:** Yes, I'll be back in the morning. Are you leaving soon?

> **Chino:** No. I'm really thinking about staying here with Jesmyn. *En serio.* I want to rent a room for us. It costs like 200 or 300 pesos [$12 to $19]. Do you think you can help me with that?

> **Jason:** Of course. But you have to promise me you will drink water and take the medicine. And don't smoke any cigarettes right now. That shit doesn't help.

> **Chino:** Okay, no cigarettes for now, I promise. I'll just smoke weed [*laughing*].

SANTOS'S TATTOO GUN has been rattling all afternoon. He is busy cutting into the arms and legs of members of the Pleasure Palace crew and anyone else who wants to sit still for thirty minutes: a Batman logo; a fat joint; the names and initials of longed-for children, wives, and parents. Santos etches these things into brown flesh as reggaeton plays, marijuana smoke fills the air, and young smugglers wait for phone calls from bosses or the next freight train carrying migrants to arrive. I watch for hours as different people go under his needle, which is a guitar string that never gets changed and is only occasionally dipped in rubbing alcohol to sanitize it. My lone contribution to the afternoon festivities is to act as an English spell-checker and prevent someone from getting the word "weet" tattooed underneath a drawing of a weed leaf.

When Santos finally runs out of customers, we break for a lunch of re-fried bean tacos and start up a game of cards. Around the time that our third hand is being dealt, his phone starts buzzing. "I got to go," he tells me as he starts loading clothes, his tattoo gun, and some food into a backpack. These goodbyes always seem so goddamn dramatic, especially since they can happen at the drop of a hat. Guides like Santos who specialize in particular segments of the journey (in this case the 1,200-kilometer route from Tenosique to Celaya) are often on call for higher-level smugglers who use him as a subcontractor. To stay in business and in good standing, Santos has to be ready to move at a moment's notice. In this case, he has been summoned by Sombra, the guide that he, Chino, and Jesmyn traveled with from Guatemala several weeks ago.

After Santos is packed, he makes one last taco and pulls out a pocket Bible. "I always read this before I set off on a trip," he tells me as we squat in the dirt. "My favorite is the Book of Revelation." The passage that he points to is a bit grim for someone about to walk into the unknown:

> When he opened the Abyss, smoke rose from it like the smoke from a gigantic furnace. The sun and sky were darkened by the smoke from the Abyss. And out of the smoke locusts came down on the earth and were given power like that of scorpions of the earth. They were told not to harm the grass of the earth or any plant or tree, but only those people who did not have the seal of God on their foreheads . . . During those days people

will seek death but will not find it; they will long to die, but death will elude them.

Santos is a believer, and he prays that his faith will protect him on the journey. Still, he is suspicious of the world of smuggling and is vying for a way out.

> **Santos:** You can meet people here on the tracks and never fully understand what their motives are and why they want to be your friend. I could be asleep and someone could rob me. They could drop a rock on my head and take everything. People can kill you for the smallest things. That's why I prefer to spend my nights alone. At least alone I know who I am and where I'm going. I know that I am not going to hurt anyone.

> **Jason:** What is it that you are looking for?

> **Santos:** I just want to get to the other side [of the border] and live a normal life. I want to get away from all this stuff. I want to sleep whenever I want. I don't want to be lying on the ground afraid to close my eyes. The truth is that I just want to work. I'll do whatever it takes to follow my own destiny. I have battled a lot in this life and I just want to keep moving forward.

In many ways, Chino and Santos have led parallel lives: Both came of age on the train tracks. Both found themselves alone and somehow tangled up in the world of smuggling. They found kinship in one another because of their shared sense of abandonment and an existence that has always been about surviving in hopes that there is something better on the horizon. They are young soldiers at their individual crossroads. Do they take the path that leads toward the lives of Flaco and Kingston, or do they try to walk away? Twenty-year-old Chino sees a future in Pakal-Ná with Jesmyn. Twenty-year-old Santos sees a future that he still has to chase down. Chino stays behind. Santos heads north and doesn't look back.

CHAPTER ELEVEN

Dinero, Dinero

Flaco waves his hand in the air with disgust. "Lalo, take that fucking cigarette outside. There's a baby in here. Secondhand smoke is bad for the baby, foo." Lalo sheepishly walks to the front door of the tiny apartment and exhales into the courtyard. He obeys the order despite the fact that we are in Lalo's house and it's Lalo's baby. "I don't let anyone smoke in my place in Honduras," Flaco proudly tells me. "I even make my father-in-law smoke outside. No cigarettes in my house, only weed. Weed is good for you, foo. Hahaha."

In the corner of Lalo's living room, a toddler stacks empty beer cans into a pyramid that keeps collapsing. A three-month-old baby naps on a nearby couch. I think of my own children, who are the same ages and who at this moment are comfortably playing in an upper-middle-class neighborhood an hour south of this Mexico City safe house. When I get home I will have to explain to an inquisitive three-year-old what Dad has been doing all day and whom I have been talking to.

A skeleton in dirty clothes appears in the doorway. He hands Lalo some crumpled bills and then skitters away with a tiny handful of product. This drab gray concrete-block building reminds me of the apartment complex from the movie *New Jack City*. This place is run by Goodwin, a high-ranking member of MS-13 who taxes all business transactions and has a propensity for collecting assault rifles. The bottom-floor apartments are rented out by Mexican families, many of whom have side hustles catering to the needs of transient Central Americans who occupy the upstairs rooms. This involves selling meals and other things out of their domiciles. *Baleadas* for the *catrachos*. *Pupusas* for the *guanacos*. Televisions can be rented by the hour so that you can catch the soccer match before leaving on the next train. Weed, cocaine, speed, and crack are available for all interested parties.

Flaco has arrived in Lechería with severely blistered feet, the result of several days of walking through the jungle with damp socks. His crew and clients are upstairs partying with other smugglers and some visiting gang-bangers. This gives us a few quiet moments to converse. His physical condition and Lalo's kids playing in the room seem to inspire him to contemplate his own family and express concerns for the future.

> **Flaco**: Children are a blessing from God. I love my kids, bro. Whenever I'm at home with my son, I like to give him money to buy stuff because when I was small I didn't have anything. I didn't have a dad. I didn't have nothing. No clothes. Nothing, foo. I had one notebook for the entire school year. I would go to school and all my stuff was broken. My ass would be hanging out of my ripped pants.

> **Jason**: How many kids do you have?

> **Flaco**: I have six children in the States and one in Honduras. We call the one in Honduras Flaquito. He is my *perrito*, bro. I love him so much. That's why I do this job. It's all business.

It's all about the money. If there is no job, there is no money. If there is no work, how is my kid going to eat? We are poor, so I have to work for my son, but it's getting dangerous.

Flaco is affiliated with MS-13 but not a full-fledged member. This means that he still has to compensate them for protection at various points in the journey and hire soldiers like Lalo to act as assistants in Lechería and elsewhere. The gangs control the train tracks, so Flaco pays Goodwin a head tax in Mexico City for the migrants he is smuggling. This will provide safe passage to his next destination, which is usually Guadalajara, where he keeps an apartment. But these gang affiliations don't guarantee one's safety when dealing with Mexican drug cartels like the Zetas who control the route through Veracruz.

Flaco: The Zetas almost killed me in Coatza, so now I'm starting to think that maybe I'm done with all this. I had to pay them 15,000 pesos [$750] to get through because they were going to kill me. They beat the shit out of me. That was money I needed to feed my wife and my kids. *Puta madre*, I think I'm done. Three or four more trips and I'll have enough to build a house in Honduras. All I have in this world is my kid, so I have to get out for him.

Jason: Is it easy to get out?

Flaco: Sure. That's what Pirate is going to do. He's getting out. He moved people for five years but never made it to the U.S. He got caught trying to cross the border seven times before. But he knows I'm crazy and I can get him through.

Lalo's three-year-old child walks over to us and says, "Can I have some beer?"

Flaco shakes his head and yells, "Hey, Lalo, your kid's over here asking us for *cerveza*. Come grab this kid, foo." Lalo stands in the doorway laughing as he hands off a small plastic baggie to a newly arrived customer. Flaco points to the child and says:

> You have to set a good example for your kids or they end up all crazy. I knew this *vato* in LA that had a four-year-old who used to get all fucked up. We would be partying and that kid would be yelling shit like "*¡Puta madre, papi!* Let me hit that forty!" That kid would be walking around yelling, "I'm drunk, motherfuckers!" I'm telling you, foos is crazy.

Given what I know about Flaco's childhood and that of others (e.g., Chino and Kingston), it's hard not to imagine the worst for the young kids growing up in safe houses and on the train tracks. Flaco is acutely aware of what the future could hold for his own young son back in Honduras. Although smuggling is illegal, he views it as a noble profession because it involves physical labor and puts food on the table. It is not necessarily easy money, so he sees it as an occupation that can potentially set a good example for his children.

> Flaco: I want my kid to see me working. I don't care if I have to walk five or six days through the jungle moving people. I don't care if my feet get all fucked up. At least my kid will see that I am working. I'm not out robbing people. I'm not doing bad things to be able to feed him. My kid has never seen me do anything bad. I know that I have to set a good example. I want my kids to see me working and helping people

get across. If you are on the tracks and are robbing people and doing bad things, those are the things that you will end up teaching your kid. But if you teach him to study hard and work hard and earn everything he gets, then that is what he will learn from you. If you are out robbing all day long and your kid turns out to be a thief, that's your fault. But it's hard because a lot of times if you were raised a delinquent your kid is also going to turn out to be a delinquent.

Flaco seems to gloss over the fact that a major component of smuggling is extracting as much as possible from clients and their families. He doesn't want to admit that fleecing people for money could be considered stealing by many.

Jason: But sometimes on the train tracks it seems like you have to rob some people to survive.

Flaco: Me? No. Here on the tracks? No. Thank God, I don't do that. Because if you steal, you end up eventually having to pay for the bad things you do. If I pray and say, "God, please help me move these people," and then I start stealing from them, God is going to say to me, "How can you be robbing people but you want me to protect you?" In the Bible it says you shouldn't steal. It says you shouldn't do bad things. So if you are asking for help and also doing bad things, it doesn't work. I was a *delincuente* when I was in *la USA*. I was stealing cars and stuff. But not anymore. I have my kid and I don't want him to see me doing horrible stuff. I don't want him to think bad things about me.

BY THE TIME Flaco and I head outside, the mood has changed from somber and introspective to drunken and boisterous. It's a Friday afternoon and everyone is feeling the effects of several hours of drinking and smoking. From the top floor of the apartment building we bask under the hazy Mexico City sky. For a brief moment we are graced with a soft breeze that counteracts the heat coming off the smoking blacktop and the suffocating feeling created by the drab concrete buildings enveloping us. Flaco pulls me aside and whispers, "Don't mess around with those guys on the stairs," as he makes a slight nod toward three skinny young men in soccer jerseys sharing a joint. "Those guys are heavyweights. I vouched for you and explained why you are carrying a camera. Just don't ask any questions about gangs or *sicarios*. Those guys just got here from El Salvador to do some jobs and they are scary, bro."

"Thanks for the heads-up," I tell him. "You know I don't ask about that shit. I'm not that stupid." He laughs and gives me a big hug.

This is the first time I have seen Flaco genuinely afraid for me. After months of meeting in sketchy locations, it's a little unnerving. I've grown accustomed to the simple fact that one cannot be in a migrant safe house in Mexico without having interactions with some of the more intense *mareros*. But I have never had problems before. For some reason, though, Flaco is nervous for me. I consider leaving but recognize that my sudden departure could make me more suspicious and potentially complicate any return visits. So I do what I always do when I run into these types of difficult situations. I introduce myself and start making small talk. Twenty minutes later I'm sitting between the three young men as we share pictures of our kids stored on our cell phones. An hour later, I am snapping portraits of everyone.

The sun begins to disappear behind a Mexico City horizon of dilapidated and half-constructed buildings. Shadows move across dozens of unfinished top floors of houses, the half-realized dreams of migrants living in the United States who send money home to build their retirement nests. Many will remain unfinished. Many will never be occupied by their builders, who work themselves to death in pursuit of the American fantasy. The exposed rebar of these buildings reaches to the sky like fields of metallic cornstalks, metal hands grasping at dreams. Flaco's two phones buzz and chirp. Goodwin calls and says it's going be $500 for a car to get Flaco and his crew to Guadalajara, where they can catch another train. A wire transfer for half the money is arranged. As night begins to fall, Flaco gets animated, the cocktail of cocaine and beer working its magic. He begins telling stories of his wild childhood and adventures on the tracks. In the middle of a tall tale about a time he was kidnapped by the Zetas, an enormous rat runs across his bare foot and then sails onto the apartment rooftop next door. Flaco leaps into the air and shrieks like a child. I spit out my beer. Someone falls off the steps, laughing. "You see that shit?" Flaco asks us. "Nigga, that shit was the size of a rabbit."

After several more hours of revelry, I start to say my goodbyes. "Flaco, I gotta go soon," I tell him.

"Okay. Hold on a minute," he responds. He walks over to use the rooftop bathroom, which is a five-gallon water jug. Despite the fact that the jug is already overflowing, people continue to try to urinate in it, sending waves of fluid splashing onto the ground.

"Flaco," I say, laughing, "you might as well just piss on the floor at this point."

He turns his head to look at me midstream. "You better come see me at the border, foo. When I get paid, we're going to party."

One of the *sicarios* looks at me and shakes his head. He points at Flaco spraying urine all over the place and laughingly says, "Does your family know about the kind of people you hang out with?"

Flaco walks me to the door as my ride is pulling up. We hug several times. I think about the last time I said goodbye to Papo and it hits me like a ton of bricks. I think that there is a real possibility I will never see Flaco again.

"When this is all over," he says, "I want you to come to my house in Honduras. When my kid turns two I'm going to butcher a cow for the party and I want you to be there. God willing, everything is going to be okay. I believe in God and I believe that He will help me."

Flaco starts to cry.

"I love you, *hermano*," he says.

"I love you too," I tell him as my own tears start to fall.

"I'll see you at the border as long as I don't get deported," he says.

"If you get deported," I respond, "I'll only charge you $5,000 to get you back to Lechería. That's my friends and family discount."

Controlando la Bestia

For the next several weeks, my phone fills up with videos of Flaco's exploits. Grainy footage of bucolic country that he films while sitting atop and between speeding boxcars.

Village after village blows by.

Armed guards with masked faces patrol the tops of trains.

The ever-present sound of grinding metal.

Flaco stands on the tracks as a locomotive passes him at sixty miles an hour. He's close enough to kiss it. His other phone buzzes in the background. *¡Mira, Yason! ¡La maldita bestia!*

Acid lies on a cardboard mat, puffing on a blunt and waving at the camera.

Brown-skinned men with backpacks chase the train. Fingers grab hold

Dinero, Dinero | 201

of metal handles greasy with thousands of fingerprints. *¡Mira, Yason, es la banda luchando con la bestia!*

A chubby brown baby in a Minions T-shirt takes nervous barefoot steps. The hands of an anonymous woman follow behind, ready to catch him. *This is my kid in Honduras, bro. I love my kid. God bless you, hermano.*

A video from Guadalajara shows Flaco shirtless and dancing for the camera. He waves buds of marijuana twice the length of his hands. Children in the background stare in wonderment at this bare-chested ogre wiggling for the camera. *We are making some salad for lunch! Check out the size of this lettuce!* Three days later he sends a video pleading for help. *I'm hungry, foo. I got no money. Send me some money for food, hermano.* Somewhere near Tepic, Nayarit, the crew parties in a train's caboose. Flaco narrates a video tour of their steel abode. *Check out our casa, bro. It's got two levels and even has Wi-Fi!* The camera pans over a toilet, several chairs, and a plate of fried chicken. *Hey, Pirate, say high to the gringo!* Pirate looks up from his phone, a joint dangling from his mouth. Acid shows the camera an enormous pile of broken-up marijuana on a paper plate. Jorge, the shy kid from Olancho, pops his head up from one of the beds and gives a thumbs-up. There are several new people in the group that I don't recognize. They smile and wave.

In a video from northern Mexico, Acid, Flaco, and Jorge surf on top of a speeding train. They hold on to their hats to keep them from flying off. Flaco and Acid scream at the camera to be heard over the wind. *¡Estamos controlando la bestia! God bless you, bro! God willing, we will see you in Mexicali!* Jorge smiles in the background and gives another thumbs-up. His other hand nervously grips the speeding train. It appears he has lost a lot of weight since I last saw him at La Cementera. He looks weary.

In the final video, the Sonoran Desert passes outside the train car's window. Flaco stands in the middle of the frame, smiling and eating a cookie.

Of God and Man

The Mexicali safe house is right across the street from a migrant shelter. A perfect place to drop off clients and pick up new ones. Fidel Rueda's voice comes out of a cell phone speaker. *With effort and work I achieved my status . . . I am no longer the errand boy.*

"You should have been here last night, bro," Flaco tells me. "It was fucking crazy." Bare-chested and hungover, he starts doing some calculations. "We spent $200 on booze. I think I drank thirty beers. There were four prostitutes, *cristal*, coke, and lots of weed."

Everyone looks like reheated shit. Pirate is shirtless and droopy-eyed as he meticulously rolls an afternoon joint. Acid is on fire, his pupils black like chips of obsidian. His mouth running a mile a minute. He picks up a home-made barbell from the corner and starts doing reps. Flaco points at him. "You should have seen this nigga last night, foo. He was crazy. He was in the bathroom forever with the oldest prostitute you've ever seen. She had cataracts and kept crashing into stuff cuz she couldn't see."

Acid puts down the weights and produces a glass pipe. His eyes bulge as he sucks in the acrid smoke from burning methamphetamines. Flaco shakes his head. "You're wasting all your money on that shit. You should be buying coke instead."

The television plays at a deafening volume, competing with the music. A Mexican reporter stands in front of a camera and gives updates on what is happening nearby:

> More than two hundred people from African countries have arrived at the port of entry in Tijuana, asking the United States for politi-cal asylum. They join Haitians, Central Americans, and Mexicans who are all coming from underdeveloped regions looking for better

alternatives for themselves and their families. There are more than one hundred migrants in line, including entire families with under-aged children sleeping on the floor in front of the port of entry to the United States. Authorities have had to temporarily suspend the acceptance of asylum claims.

I ask a stupid question: "What is the most important thing to understand about this life?"

Flaco rubs his fingers together. "Money, money, money. You know what I mean? Like Daddy Yankee says, *Dinero, dinero. Es lo que todo el mundo quiere*. It's always about money, foo. Yesterday I made $7,500."

"How much money was wired to you during this trip?" I ask.

Flaco smiles and says, "At one point, I had $21,000 in a bank account. I made almost $2,000 per person on this trip."

He produces Western Union receipts from his wallet and lays them out like tarot cards predicting some brighter future. He points to the receipts and says, "I sent $1,900 to my wife and kid in Honduras. I sent my other two women $1,500. I even sent some money to my sister, who is getting treatment for cancer."

Pirate chimes in. "People are always criminalizing what we do, but we are just working for our families."

Our conversation begins to delve into economics. Through a fog of weed and cigarette smoke, a hungover Flaco begins to outline some of the basics. People pay him between $2,500 and $3,500 per person to go from Honduras to the U.S.-Mexico border. The size and makeup of the group determines the per-person cost as well as the overall profit he can make. In general, it's worth his time only if there are several people traveling, although larger groups require the hiring of additional soldiers. Those soldiers (like Acid) can make between $500 and $1,000 per trip, depending on how savvy they are at negotiating. However, there is no guarantee that a group will stay

204 | SOLDIERS AND KINGS

together. Soldiers may disappear or get arrested before reaching a final destination. In those instances, Flaco can pocket the money he promised to pay them.

Minimally, a client has to deposit $1,000 into one of Flaco's bank accounts before the trip starts. The first cash payment covers initial expenses, including the various *cuotas* that have to be paid on the way up to Central Mexico.* Fifteen hundred dollars can get you to Mexico City from Honduras, but the rest of the money has to be paid before continuing. This is why people get stuck places. They can't come up with the second payment. It doesn't matter to Flaco. He will leave you in Mexico City and either keep going with other (or new) clients or return to Honduras and start the process over again. Migrants who break their contract with a smuggler mid-trip because of lack of funds might look to someone like Chino or Santos; they are significantly cheaper because they charge for shorter segments of a trip that can be paid piecemeal. If someone makes it all the way to the U.S.-Mexico border and wants to cross into the United States, it costs another $2,500 to $5,000, depending on where they want to go and how much walking through the desert they are willing to do. Flaco won't physically get someone across the border, but he will broker the deal with a Mexican *coyote* and charge a service fee. He offers a luxury package going from Honduras to Phoenix for around $8,000.

After his brief economics lesson, Flaco pauses to catch his breath and then says, "It's through God's grace that you can make money doing this job. I always liked being down with bad people, but I'm not a bad person. I always try to be nice. I try to be a giving person. I make *billete* doing this job, but there are times where I don't make any money. There are times that I have taken people and I've paid for their travel and food and they ended up not paying me

---

* There generally are no *cuotas* after Mexico City, although the cartels in the north charge between $100 and $200 per person for the privilege of entering the desert in an attempt to cross the border.

anything. If you don't pay me, all I can say is 'God bless you.' God knows what is in your heart . . . So if you act bad, bad things will happen to you."

As the afternoon drags on, everyone begins to shake off the side effects of the previous evening. The room heats up with smoke and music. Someone fetches ice and beer. Acid keeps hitting the glass pipe. Flaco cuts lines of coke with a phone card. Pirate says he is ready to walk away from all of this. He speaks excitedly about the deal he has worked out. "I've known about Flaco for a long time, so I know I can trust him to get me across. A van is going to pick me up on the U.S. side and drive me to California."

Jorge, the baby-faced migrant, is conspicuously absent from the safe house, and no one has mentioned him since I arrived. I turn to Flaco. "Is that what happened to Jorge? Did a van pick him up?"

"Yeah, bro," he says. "He's in *la USA* now. I talked to him. He already has a job." Flaco lights a cigarette and points at Pirate. "That's my homie, but I keep telling him to not put his faith in me to get him across. He needs to put his faith in God. I am only a man."

THREE DAYS AFTER I leave Mexicali, I get a call from an unknown number. The connection is bad. Jorge's tortured words are metallic and distorted. His voice breaks as he fights to speak through his tears.

> **Jorge:** Flaco told us it was $2,500 per person to get across, so my family sent him $5,000 for me and my friend. He went to pick up the money and never came back. Now he's not answering his phone. I can't be here in Mexicali. I have to get across. My wife and little girl are already [in the United States] waiting for me. It's been two months since I left home. I've been sleeping on the streets of Mexicali for ten days. I can't do this anymore. I have to get across.

CHAPTER TWELVE

Robin Hood

"What's wrong with my pants?" Kingston asks me.

"Nothing. I think your pants are fine."

"Why you smiling?"

"I'm not smiling."

"Why you laughing?"

"I'm not laughing."

Kingston adjusts the fedora on his head. He has traded his baseball cap, baggy pants, shirt, and high-tops (all red, of course) for a mesh tank top, leather sandals, and skintight shorts. He looks like he should be on a beach vacation in Cuba. I try to imagine him shopping for his fedora. *How much is this hat? Five hundred pesos? Get the fuck outta here!* I clench my lips to keep from laughing. Kingston glares at me. "I knew it. When I put these pants on this morning, I said to myself, 'Jason is gonna talk shit.' I knew it, mother-fucker."

"I'm not talking shit."

I turn and look out the window at the verdant Chiapas countryside rolling by. Staring at that sea of deep green helps keep me from laughing.

"I knew you'd be talking shit about my pants."

Robin Hood | 207

My longtime collaborator Mike Wells is in the back seat. In the rearview mirror I see him trying to contain his own laughter.

"Your pants are fine. It's just that, uh, they're a little tight and, uh, kind of short. I just don't picture you in shorts that small."

Kingston looks down at his legs and then looks at me. "You know my soldiers be saying the same shit to me. They be talking shit about my pants, saying they too tight. My shorty be saying the same shit too." He mimics a high-pitched female voice: "'Your pants are too tight.'"

At this point, I can't contain my laughter. In the back seat, Mike is cracking up too.

Kingston looks at me hard.

"Fuck you, motherfucker! That shit ain't funny."

Now all three of us are laughing our asses off.

"Fuck you motherfuckers! I like my pants." Kingston smiles and looks out the window and then suddenly yells, "Oh shit! Stop the car!"

I pull over to the side of the road. The sun is at midday and unforgiving. A handful of exhausted migrants huddle in the shade of a tree. Kingston jumps out of the car and approaches.

"*Muchachos*, how we doing?" he asks.

"You know how it is out here," someone grumbles.

"*Mira*, I'm here to help. Who here smokes marijuana?"

Every hand in the group goes up. They start to grin. Like a magician, Kingston pulls a joint from his pocket and lights it in one smooth motion. He takes a couple quick puffs and hands the joint off to a shirtless young man who proceeds to do a little dance while taking hits. Kingston then passes out cigarettes to the group while dispensing advice. "*Hermanos*, you gotta be careful around here. There's a checkpoint coming up that you need to go around. A *combi* [microbus] could get you to Pakal-Ná quicker, but it's probably going to cost you around 500 pesos [$25] per person. Do you have money to catch a *combi*?"

"No," someone replies.

It's clear these men don't have 500 pesos between the six of them. If they had money, they wouldn't be walking on the side of the road in broad daylight without a guide or any water.

They still have another fifty or sixty kilometers to go and a checkpoint to get through before landing in Pakal-Ná. They're fucked. The burning joint makes its way back to Kingston. He takes a final hit and recirculates it. "All right, *hermanos*, make sure you smoke all that shit so that you can walk fast like Speedy Gonzales!"

Everyone laughs and waves as we make our way back to the car. I start the engine and we begin to slowly roll past them.

"Oh wait, let's give them some water," Kingston declares.

"We're out of water," I tell him. "The only thing left is beer."

He reaches into the styrofoam cooler in the back seat and pulls out a dripping can of Tecate. "Hey, brother, come here. I got a cold one to help you with this heat."

Through the car window he hands the beer to a wide-eyed young man. As we drive away, I look in the rearview mirror just in time to see the young man kiss the beer and point to the sky in gratitude. As we pick up speed, Kingston pontificates, "Maybe I can start a shelter for migrants. That way I could really help people. They could come and rest and chill out. There'd be no problems. People could even party as long as they kept things under control. I would even give out cigarettes, weed, and *cerveza*."

I turn to him and ask, "Would you still be wearing those shorts?"

BY THE TIME I'm driving through Chiapas with Kingston playing migrant Robin Hood, he already has a decade of experience moving people through Mexico. Like many other smugglers I know, he has a temporary Mexican visa that allows him to freely travel across the country. He received the visa after participating in a riot in a detention center and then filing a complaint against a Mexican immigration agent who roughed him up during the melee. Our drive across Chiapas feels like a trip down memory lane as he reflects on a job he both likes and despises—a job he wants to get away from but seemingly can't.

Jason: Do you think it's hard to leave this life?

Kingston: Well, there have been a lot of times when I've said I'm not going to do this anymore. But then you find yourself in Honduras and you have no money and some dude wants to head north. People start asking for help. I know the *camino* and it would be easy. So it's like, "You know what? Let's go." It's hard to say no. You can say that you are retired, that you're out. But then you find yourself in a crisis and you know two or three people that are interested in going. You might as well take them, because if not, someone else will. That feeling is always there. It's a never-ending business.

Jason: Is it fun? Are there things you like?

Kingston: There are moments when the trip feels special. There are moments of joy but also moments of sadness. There are times when you get pissed off at the people you are moving or those on the other side waiting for you. Or you get mad at the people financing the *viaje*. Maybe they don't send the cash needed to pay for the next part of the trip, so you end up waiting and waiting and losing money. People are inconsiderate. They don't think about what your situation is like in Mexico when you got no money and have to wait another day. I think the best parts of the job are at night, though. From morning to the afternoon, forget it. You're busy. You're annoyed. There is a lot of pressure and panic. But at night, it's more relaxed. Things settle down. Maybe you got your money and you aren't moving for the moment. You feel safe. You can go buy some food and not worry. Your people also feel free for a little bit. They're not moving. They can chill out. And when it's all guys, there's lots of partying. You know how it is. You have your beer, your weed, your coke. It's a *desmadre*. You can party but you have to have some balance, some control. But when you're making money, everything feels right. You feel good. Like, motherfucker, I'm making it! $1,500, $5,000, $10,000. Goddamn!

Jason: How much money do you usually carry?

Kingston: Well, the road to Pakal-Ná is expensive, so you have to carry a lot of cash. If I have five people, I usually need 2,000 or 3,000 pesos [$100 or $150] per person to get from Corozal to Pakal-Ná. This means around 15,000 pesos [$750]. You use that to pay for bribes and rides. You can pay someone to give you a ride in their truck or maybe you grab a *combi*. Those *combi* drivers might ask for 500 to 1,000 pesos [$25 to $50] to get to Pakal-Ná [about 170 kilometers from Corozal]. Those bitch-ass niggas always ask for at least 1,000 pesos if you are traveling with a kid. So you pay them, but maybe they end up driving only like twenty minutes because they lie and say that there is a checkpoint coming up and they make you get off. Then you lose money because now you have to pay another driver. This is why you have to ask for a minimum of $1,000 to start a trip. Some people say they will take you for $500, but that is not enough because you always get robbed in Guatemala. They fuck you over there. They stop you so many times that it's easy to lose $300 even before leaving Guatemala. It's easy to be robbed of $500 before you even get out of southern Mexico. So if you ask for $1,500 to get to Mexico City, the guide might make $500 if they are lucky. The other $1,000 goes to expenses. In the end, it all depends on how fast you walk or whether you can contract a cheap ride. Shit is not easy.

Kingston's status as a high-ranking gang member turned smuggler puts him in the unique position of being both a protector from and a purveyor of violence.

El Show

Shadows scramble through the jungle foliage. Flashes in one's peripheral vision. The phantoms hold their breath and relay messages with hand signals and nods. Sunlight momentarily catches on the barrel of a gun. They listen for voices through the dense vegetation. They hear the laughter of men and boys with third-rate firearms and kitchen knives. They hear the clanging of unbuckling belts and the panting of ghouls with wild eyes and violent erections. The silhouettes of vengeful men circle and stalk these jungle marauders with military precision. Bravado and anger quietly build as the memories of previous abuses at the hands of these Mexican bandits are recalled. These smugglers turned avengers remember the screams of the vulnerable and the violated. Men, women, and children. So many black voices pleading for help. Their own people screaming for help that didn't come in time or come at all. The men emerge from the dark to collect unpaid debts.

The small, windowless room is throbbing with bass. The voices of singing men fills the room. *Roll one, smoke one.* A fat joint makes the rounds while beers are hoisted into the air like victory torches. Andy takes selfies and Snoop bangs dominoes onto a ragged wooden table while someone livestreams everything on Facebook. The room is filled with mostly young black men who, like Kingston, were robbed of happy childhoods. Young men who as teenagers found themselves living in alleys and on the train tracks, trying to make ends meet. They take joy where they can get it because tomorrow may not come. They celebrate tonight because tonight they are alive.

I take photos of these standard Tuesday night activities. I focus my camera on Priest, who glares and opens his mouth. A fog of ominous smoke billows out. Every time I take someone's picture, the go-to pose is either a scowl or an exhalation of marijuana smoke. This is an environment where looking hard is mandatory. Priest stares at me. Over the years, I have learned to be slightly afraid of those who don't talk and just stare. "Can we get just one where you're smiling?" I jokingly ask. Priest laughs at me and shakes his head no.

"Don't worry about that nigga," Kingston assures me. "He don't say much, but he a good soldier. I've known that dude for a long time. He is from one of the most dangerous neighborhoods in Honduras. He's fucking crazy." By "good soldier," Kingston means he can ask Priest to do his bidding with no questions asked. By "fucking crazy," he means that Priest is someone who can be relied upon to do the most serious jobs required by the gang. Jobs that often require blades or bullets.

Smuggling these days is not just about avoiding Immigration. It's increasingly about literal survival, especially in Mexico, where women, men,

Robin Hood | 213

and children run a gauntlet of assault, rape, kidnapping, and murder. As violence against migrants has ramped up, so has the need for a new breed of smuggler. These days you need at least one Priest in every crew, although it is probably more accurate to say that on the train tracks everyone has to have a little bit of Priest inside them.

> **Jason:** A lot of guides are in gangs, right?

> **Kingston:** *Muchos*, the majority of them. I would say 90 percent. *Maras* control certain parts of the train tracks, so it's hard to be a guide if you are not a *marero* because you need those connections. You need people backing you up. If you are not connected to a gang, it's easy to get robbed. Garifunas are usually Bloods, Crips, or Lion Kings. A few of them are even MS-13, but that's rare.

In an increasingly dangerous world of smuggling, the most successful guides seem to be those not afraid of death. This is why Kingston, the child soldier and ex-con with a history of violent behavior, excelled at this business upon his release from prison.

> **Kingston:** The *mareros* in Mexico started attacking migrants around 2007. They especially started attacking Garifuna, which made smuggling hard. So I declared war on the *maras* that were on the train tracks robbing people. That's when I had to become a different person to start doing some bad shit. We started traveling with machetes and guns, and I started bringing a lot of soldiers with me. I know it makes some people uncomfortable to travel with me because I carry a gun, but that's just how it is. People would come after us, so

we had to have a big Garifuna presence. They'd come after me on the train and I'd chase them away with a machete and say, "Don't try to play with me. Get the fuck outta here!" When they see a bunch of crazy niggas on the tracks, they know not to mess with us. *Mareros* talk a lot of shit, but I'm the one that will do something when necessary. I had a crew and I started to get down with them doing jobs. Because of all that crazy shit there are places in Mexico and Honduras that I just can't go through anymore.

During these conversations with Kingston about career trajectories, the line between smuggler and gangster becomes blurred. It also becomes clear that the train tracks are just as violent as the streets of Honduras and are now breeding grounds for murder, both random and contracted forms.

Kingston: There is no money in Honduras. With the crisis that is happening there, forget about it. There is no work. There is no life. Somebody comes by and says, "Listen, man, I got 500 or 1,000 pesos* [$25 or $50]. Go kill this mother-fucker." People are broke, so they go and do it.

Jason: But life on the tracks in Mexico isn't easy either, right?

Kingston: Here? People don't give a fuck. You can make money on the tracks, but you gotta do a lot of crazy shit. Everybody be killing people around here. Come on, man, you know this. You know how *el show* is here.

---

* Here he is referring to Mexican pesos but is talking about Honduras.

Jason: How much does it cost to kill somebody here in Mexico?

Kingston: It depends. On the tracks for $500 you can get someone killed like a motherfucker. That's a price that comes with a guarantee. But people will do it for a lot less. Seriously, it's easy to have somebody killed around here.

Part III

EXODUS

CHAPTER THIRTEEN

Resurrection

The dirty windows are covered up by thick drapes and pieces of duct-taped cardboard. Overgrown weeds sprout up from cracks in the driveway and the front porch. On the outside, this safe house in Celaya, Mexico, looks abandoned. This is by design so that neighbors and immigration enforcement don't suspect that Central Americans are hiding inside, sprawled out on stained bedrolls and rusty mattresses. The interior of the house is cool and dark like a catacomb, which is telling because I'm sitting across the table from a dead man, recounting to him the story of his demise.

> **Jason:** I started calling people to share the news. It was fucking terrible. Flaco and I were in Pakal-Ná, crying and pouring out beers on the train tracks. I was calling people who knew you to say, "Papo is dead. We don't know what happened. It might have been a case of mistaken identity."

> [*Papo, very much alive, shakes his head in disbelief as I continue.*]

Jason: Man, we were crying so hard. It was awful. We spent the whole *pinche* afternoon crying.

Papo: [*Laughing*] Thank God it wasn't me! I'm alive, bro! Papo is alive! But you know how things are in Pakal-Ná. They probably did kill somebody but got their name wrong and thought it was me. Or maybe they killed some other person named Papo. Those stories get confused all the time.

He is correct. The rumor mill is notorious. Lies and exaggerations are currency freely exchanged between friends, acquaintances, and strangers. *Didn't you hear? They killed so-and-so. It was the Zetas. They shot him in the face and left him by the tracks. No, bro. It was the maras. They threw him off the train and he got run over.* Stories of death injected with varying levels of truth float out into the air only to be revised and recirculated like a game of migrant telephone. It doesn't help that on the tracks, people come and go with little to no notice. Some disappear without a trace. Maybe they're dead or in jail. Maybe they've been kidnapped and are working on a ranch somewhere. Maybe they vanished for the simple fact that they needed to escape. My belief that Papo was dead is not an anomaly. He is one of many over the years whom I suspected of having met an untimely ending. It's easy to think this because a lot of people die on the migrant trail and no one ever knows what happened to them. Death and murder occur with such frequency that places like Palenque have dedicated part of their municipal cemetery to interring the unidentified bodies of border crossers.

In Papo and Alma's case, they both lost their phones, which contained my number and their only way to contact me. Soon after losing touch with them, I met Flaco in Pakal-Ná and heard the story of Papo's death. I spent more than a year mourning him and growing increasingly frustrated by a lack of information on the internet about what had happened. Online searches of news reports about migrant fatalities in Mexico resulted in an overwhelming number of cases where the dead were carrying no identification and the authorities were still looking for next of kin. If Papo was dead and unidentified, he was unfortunately just one of thousands of corpses in the same state of limbo. When news reports proved to be a dead end, I started doing some deep Facebook sleuthing to see if I could find one of Papo's relatives or a smuggler I knew who had been friends with him. It was during this search that I came across an old Facebook account of Alma's that appeared to be inactive. I sent her a friend request and numerous messages but heard nothing back for months. Then, out of the blue, she wrote a quick message to say that she had lost my number after leaving Pakal-Ná. She was now living in Celaya with Papo and the kids and I should come visit them.

> **Jason:** I was so relieved when I heard you were okay, but I was pissed at Flaco for convincing me you were dead. I'm telling you, man, we were all crying. It was fucked up.

> **Papo:** Flaco is a good dude. He's one of those *catrachos* that is always straight with you. He tells you what is really happening, so if he said I was dead, he must have believed it.

> **Jason:** I know. The way he was crying I could tell he was serious. But I was still pissed at him for believing so much in a rumor. We shed a lot of tears. I think we poured out a case of beer in your memory [*laughing*].

Alma lets out a cackle at this last line as she hunches over the kitchen table, separating the seeds and stems from a bud of marijuana. She has let her bleached-blond hair grow out to reveal her dark roots. She smiles easily and her face seems less weary than the last time I saw her. From inside this dark cave, we can hear the faint whistle of passing trains a quarter mile away.

The house is sparsely furnished and gloomy because of the blacked-out windows, but Alma happily reports that it is larger and has significantly fewer cockroaches than their previous Pakal-Ná apartment. There is also enough space to make a little money by providing temporary shelter for migrants and smugglers passing through. One unexpected irony of this safe house is that we are less than an hour south of San Miguel de Allende, a town where thousands of Americans have migrated and are living and working illegally in plain sight of Mexican immigration authorities.

Although they are all still undocumented after failing to secure humanitarian visas, Alma seems happier than the last time I saw her in Chiapas. The family is healthy and has been making ends meet through various legal and illegal odd jobs. Papo has even had some minor success finding semiconsistent work in construction. Each month is a struggle, but they have somehow managed to regularly cobble together enough cash to pay the rent and keep the lights on. However, Dulce and Gaby are still not in school. For now, the girls pass most of the day playing with a couple of busted dolls and an old three-wheeler in their barren front yard. Times are tough, but this move to central Mexico seems like an upgrade from the jungle.

Papo and I make a run to the store to buy treats for the kids. He uses the opportunity to give me a tour of the neighborhood. They live close enough to the tracks to make their home a convenient safe house for people hopping off trains, but they are far enough away not to be bombarded with the sounds of grinding metal and screeching brakes twenty-four hours a day. "When we got here to Celaya, the first thing we thought was just how different it was," Papo tells me. "It's more peaceful than Pakal-Ná, where we were living right next to the tracks. Here it almost feels like we are living out in the country."

As we walk, we see a few small groups of exhausted-looking migrants hiding in the bushes. Vagabonds with red-rimmed eyes and dirty clothes waiting for the next northbound train. In Pakal-Ná, migrants are often highly visible, and many are still fresh-faced and enthusiastic after only a few days into the trip. In the southern jungle you can stare down the tracks and see people huddled around small fires, warming cans of refried beans and passing joints. Music might fill the air, competing with roosters and insects. The vibe in Papo's neighborhood is different. It's quiet, somber. By the time people reach Celaya, they have spent weeks or months traveling more than 1,000 kilometers. They have arrived by some combination of foot, train, and vehicle and have likely experienced a range of traumas and humiliations. Most have lost the enthusiasm they began the journey with. Having made it this far is no easy task, and people will now work to be as incognito as possible. No one wants to attract the attention of immigration agents and end up back in Honduras at square one.

Papo and his family were able to avoid the dangerous train ride from Pakal-Ná to Celaya. But in some ways they might have preferred that mode of transportation to the one they ended up taking.

> **Papo:** We rode a bus from Chiapas all the way to Celaya, but we had to spend eighteen hours hiding in a small compartment underneath the luggage. It was so cramped and we had very little space down there. It was horrible. They never stopped the bus to give us food or water. We were in there so long that we had to pee in plastic bags. It was terrible because we couldn't really breathe. The driver knew we were there, but he wouldn't open the door to give us any air. At one point I thought Dulce was going to die. She was so pale when we finally got out of there. I thought I was going to die under there too. We paid 5,000 pesos [$240] each for the trip. It was one of the worst experiences of my life.

226 | SOLDIERS AND KINGS

Despite the harrowing journey, Alma and Papo both seem relieved to be out of Chiapas.

Jason: How long were you in Pakal-Ná?

Alma: Four or five months. I had a sister here in Celaya who invited us to stay with her. All we knew was that we had to get out of Pakal-Ná. It was starting to get really ugly there. The *mareros* were killing a lot of people. Pakal-Ná was starting to feel like my neighborhood back in San Pedro Sula. It now has all the same dangers we are running from in Honduras.

Papo: Pakal-Ná is a fucking hellhole, bro. The *maras* are now everywhere.

Jason: But most of them aren't tattooed anymore, right? It seems like it's harder to tell who is a *marero* now.

Papo: [*Nodding in agreement*] The *maras* are no longer all tattooed up. They are now in disguise. They are dressed normal. Some of the *maras* are the assholes walking around the train tracks preaching with Bibles in their hands, who then later attack migrants around the corner where you can't see what is happening. Jason, sometimes I would see you on the tracks talking to people who were *mareros* and it wasn't clear if you knew that.

He is right. Danger often hides in plain sight, and early on I was quite naive about whom to trust. Pato the friendly grocery store owner who offered me a room in his house, turned out to be the local head of MS-13. Some of the Mexican immigration officials in Palenque who showed an interest in my research ended up being implicated in migrant kidnappings and assault. After all the time I have spent on the tracks, it is still difficult to know whom to trust out there. People present many faces, some of them at different times, and others simultaneously: downtrodden migrant, benevolent smuggler, innocent bystander. There are the *mareros* who claim they are just as screwed as migrants and are only trying to make it north. There are the gangsters turned smugglers who say they want to do God's work by helping people and leaving all the violence behind. I've worked hard over the years to comprehend the complexity and fluidity of these overlapping and often contradictory categories. I have tried to limit my judgment and not fall prey to the simplistic narrative that wants to collapse these different categories into notions of good and bad. Still, there are some who rubbed me the wrong way from the start. People who exuded deception and treachery far beyond the normal levels you'd expect in a context where suspicion reigns. There are some I never liked from the beginning, and only later would I realize why. When Papo brings up *mareros* hiding in plain sight, I think about Bin Laden and the Breadman. I remember how they made everyone feel jumpy. I think about them and wonder if they have any remorse for what they have done.

CHAPTER FOURTEEN

Escape

Would you be an outlaw for my love?

—BIG STAR

The shot is framed tight around Chino's head and shoulders. His dark hair is newly trimmed, exposing his protruding ears and baby face. He looks fifteen. Behind him, a rusted train car's segmented body snakes deep into the Pakal-Ná jungle, a metal monster that goes on forever but seemingly goes nowhere. The director is asking serious questions about life on the tracks as part of a documentary film we are making. But Chino is stoned and finds being in front of a camera amusing. His terse responses are mostly punctuated with giggles, as if this is all a joke.

"What are your plans for the future?" the director asks.

"To try and conquer the world," Chino says, laughing.

"And what will you do after you conquer the world?"

He smiles and chuckles. "After that, I'll settle down."

But then Chino stops laughing and suddenly gets sober. "It's difficult when you are in a new place," he says, "because you never really know what's going to happen. You just know that it will be God's will. Whatever God says, that's what will happen."

After he says this last line, he quietly stares into the camera as if afraid of his own words.

I HAVE ONLY a few days left in Pakal-Ná before returning home to teach classes for the fall semester. Moving between the train tracks and the ivory tower of academia is an intellectual and emotional migration between disparate worlds that I find frustrating, disorienting, and often depressing. It's a movement that makes my own privilege hypervisible. Don't get me wrong, I love ethnography. I'm addicted to it. I love the closeness that it creates between me and the people I want to write about. I also like to imagine that my presence does something positive for those I interact with: it provides them with a sympathetic ear; a friend who might be able to help them navigate the complicated bureaucracy of migration; a lifeline they can use when things get really bad. But ethnography comes with a price. It comes with a hangover that lasts forever. This is because the people I work with are perpetually desperate. They have known struggle their entire lives and will continue to know it long after I am gone. I am just a tourist in that nightmarish world. I might leave with PTSD that my family and I will have to deal with, but I can abandon the train tracks whenever I want. But no matter how far away I go, I know that life on the migrant trail keeps going. Chino and others are potentially stuck there forever.

The Pleasure Palace crew and I decide to throw a party to celebrate the end of my summer fieldwork. It makes for a good excuse to buy cases of beer and a cake. We congregate on the tracks and use the shade of palm trees to escape from the sun. Los Tigres del Norte croon from a cell phone speaker. *Soy el mojado acaudalado pero en mi tierra quiero morir.* The Breadman dances and poses for pictures with Dulce. It's a potluck, so Papo provides attendees with free weed. Joints start making the rounds. Someone makes a gravity bong out of debris they scavenged on the tracks, a testament to migrant ingenuity. Alma takes a bong rip of such magnitude that she topples over from her seated position on a railroad tie. We die laughing.

When Jesmyn and Chino come walking toward us from down the tracks, the party is in full swing. The two of them are giddy and hold hands as new lovers do. They take a seat and eye each other as if they know a secret hidden from the rest of the world. Jesmyn clings to Chino's arm and traces the white scab that is now his *catracho* tattoo. He fills her cup with beer and makes sure the joints go to her before him. He tells bad jokes that she laughs at. Chino is beaming and Jesmyn is relaxed, seemingly less on guard. Life feels good for a moment. We dance and talk shit until our sides hurt from laughing.

A couple of hours into the party, Chino pulls me aside. Something has happened and he now has a problem with Sombra, the MS-13 smuggler he traveled up from the south with a few weeks earlier. Chino and Santos once took me to meet Sombra on the tracks, several kilometers north of Pakal-Ná. I immediately felt uncomfortable around him. He gave off a shifty and evasive vibe. Unlike many guides in their thirties, he seemed out of his element and devoid of the kind of charisma needed to command respect from his soldiers. It was clear that he didn't know the tracks very well, which was why he needed Chino's and Santos's help. He spoke aggressively to everyone. No one seemed to even remotely like or trust him.

Sombra was traveling with three women, including a fifteen-year-old and someone six months pregnant. He introduced the pregnant woman to me as his wife. He's a bad liar. It was obvious she was a client, and he showed little concern for her discomfort in having to waddle around on the train tracks with swollen feet. In general, he doesn't even pretend to care about the people under his watch. He ignores them except when he is barking

Escape | 231

orders. After half an hour of small talk with me, he disappeared into the jungle with his clients. Perhaps the biggest red flag I would learn about later was the fact that Sombra insisted the women stay with him on the tracks instead of entering the nearby shelter where they could get beds, hot showers, and free meals. He wanted to control all of their movements and interactions. He didn't want anyone questioning who it was they were traveling with.

Chino and Santos were guiding Sombra's group up from Tenosique when they met Jesmyn and invited her to tag along. The idea was that she would join their group and eventually travel farther north with them. Chino and Jesmyn falling in love in Pakal-Ná has complicated matters.

Chino: Sombra and Santos started getting everyone's luggage ready to go yesterday. They were asking for Jesmyn and saying it was time to leave. Sombra had her bags in his hands and was trying to force her to go. He knew that I liked her, so he asked me if I was going to pay her *cuota*. I told him that she and I were staying and he got pissed. He said he would kill me if I didn't do as he says. But I didn't want to go. I just didn't want to do it.

Jason: What did Santos have to say?

Chino: He told me I should go with them because it's not smart to disobey orders. When I told him I wasn't going, he said I needed to get out of Pakal-Ná now. He's my friend. He knows it's no longer going to be safe for me here.

Jason: If you had left with Sombra, what would have happened?

Chino: He's two-faced. You gotta understand that, Jason. Those girls he is traveling with are worth a lot of money . . . He says he is going to get them across the border for free, but he is tricking them. They don't understand what is really happening. He says he is going to help them, but he is actually bringing them to a brothel so that he can sell them. One of the girls is even underage. It's shameful. He says he's helping those women for free, but he is planning to give them to people up north who are dangerous, the kind of people who will cut off your fingers and do other bad stuff. Sombra got mad because I knew what he was up to. He was pissed at me because I asked him why he was doing that stuff. I said, "How can you do this to your own people?" I couldn't go along with him.

Jason: But it's dangerous to disobey an order, right?

Chino: Yeah, because now they will come after me. That's why I have to go. Gang law says that since I disobeyed orders, I can't be here. So now I'm worried they are going to start looking for me. A lot of people around here work for Sombra. [*He nudges his head toward a young man a few hundred feet down the tracks.*] That guy down there wants to fight me, so I have to watch myself. If I go to the police for help, they will deport me. They will put me in one of those giant detention centers where the gangs have people inside who know me. I have tattoos that mark me as a *marero* and they will start asking me who I'm with. Sombra's people can find me inside and kill me. Maybe if I head south they won't get me because he is headed north. But even if I go south they might sneak up on me later. You just never know. It's a bad situation.

Escape | 233

Jason: What about going home?

Chino: I spoke to my family and they said I should return to Honduras, but there the problems are the same. It's like a tree. Honduras is where the roots of all these problems are, and Pakal-Ná is just one of the branches. In Honduras, I worked for the gangs, but I tried to get away from that stuff. I want to retire now. I want to stay here and get my life together. But here it's just like in Honduras. If I don't go with them and do what they want and they see me on the tracks, they will kill me. Jesmyn thinks that maybe we should go to Belize or Guatemala. We can look for work there. The problem, though, is getting out of Pakal-Ná. I'm safe right now, but if they see me again, it's going to be bad. They are going to kill me. I want to leave, but I don't know how. I just want to live my life, a normal life like the people you see going to work and coming home to their houses and relaxing without any worries. I don't want to be in the streets anymore. There is a point where you reach a limit and that's where I'm at. I keep thinking that God is testing me.

Jason: What does your family say?

Chino: They know that I just want to be with them, that I want to do something else with my life. My sister Marina calls me every day and says to come home. I want to leave, but I don't know where to go. I just want to rent a room someplace where no one knows me. Maybe I can look for work and little by little get ahead. I told Jesmyn, "You are my girl and I want out of this life because they are going to kill me. I am still young and want to get my life together. Let's get out of here and fight for a better future." I told Jesmyn I don't care where we go. It doesn't matter. I'll go anywhere, even if I'm only earning 100 pesos [$5] a day. But in order to leave this life, I have to leave the tracks. I can't be on the tracks because that's where they're going to be. I don't know if something bad is going to happen down the road, but I do know that I don't want to be involved in this anymore. But like they say, once you get mixed up in this stuff you can't get out.

Despite the fact that Chino has been drinking and smoking weed, he comes across sober and serious in this conversation. He is not the same kid I watched drunkenly run across the tops of moving train cars. He is not running full speed toward self-annihilation. His eyes are now open to an escape into a world of new possibilities. He thinks that his moral compass can guide him down a better path.

Jason: So, what are you going to do?

Chino: I have to leave Pakal-Ná because they are waiting for me to put my guard down. When night falls they will try something. But maybe I'll go after them first. Maybe I'll start killing the people who are coming after me. I'll show them who the bigger man is. [*He shakes his head.*] But the truth is, I can't do that. I don't have it in me to do those things. Right now, it feels like God is testing me to see if I have a good heart. It's like he's saying to me that if I save Jesmyn, then my own sins will be washed away. That's the test he is giving me because, thinking about it, what does it

Escape | 235

cost me to keep going with Sombra? Nothing. I can just keep being crazy and go with him. Going with him is easy. But to not go with Sombra, that's the difficult thing. That's the test.

After this conversation, the going away party takes a dark turn. It's hard to celebrate knowing what is at stake for Chino and Jesmyn. I look around at this group of smugglers laughing and drinking, and I think about the potential for violence that is always bubbling under the surface of this social landscape ready to explode. Chino leans in to me and whispers, "There's a church in Palenque where I might be able to find help."

THE WINDOWS ARE ROLLED DOWN to let the hot jungle air pass through the car. The sun is beginning to disappear to the west as Jason Isbell plays on the car stereo. In the side mirror I see Jesmyn's head leaning out the car window, her dark, curly hair floating in the wind as she takes in the sights between Pakal-Ná and Palenque: Signs advertising discount rates for hotels that have swimming pools and Wi-Fi. Hand-painted billboards with offers for private tours of the nearby archaeological site. We pass an immigration van with the weary faces of migrants staring back at us through the vehicle's barred glass. I wonder if it is safer in there or out on the streets. I contemplate my options for helping Chino. Bring him to my house? Drive him to some other town and rent him a room? But where? How far is far enough to be safe from Sombra and his people? Do I just shove money at him and hope he can figure it out?

We drive endlessly through the narrow cobblestone streets of Palenque looking for a place that will take in migrants. Chino is indecisive and doesn't want to get out of the car. We find a church that has a few homeless people lingering outside. They tell us the priest is not in right now but to come back later and maybe he will let them stay. We pass Palenque's central plaza.

Couples the same age as Jesmyn and Chino embrace under brilliant white gazebos. Children devour melting ice cream and chase pigeons across the square. An out-of-tune brass band stumbles through a song from a distant decade. Chino nudges Jesmyn and points as we drive past. "I told you Palenque was beautiful," he says.

Defeated, we start driving back to Pakal-Ná. Back to the train tracks and the fate that is waiting for these star-crossed lovers. For the rest of my life, I'll wish that I'd gone in the opposite direction and never taken my foot off the gas.

CHAPTER FIFTEEN

Things Fall Apart

Dirty pants are down around his knees. His shirt is pushed up toward his chest, exposing a lean brown stomach. Light blue boxers cover his groin. Someone likely fixed his underwear before they took the photo. Even this kind of death deserves some dignity. He looks so young and frail but also hardened. A lithe body chiseled in cold stone; youthfulness permanently rendered immobile. The fragments of two people are visible on the edges of the image: a black leather shoe crushes the grass near his head; a latex-covered hand hovers over his legs, mid–forensic examination. They have rolled him over onto his back, exposing a bloody divot in the grass where his head initially rested. The bullet entered through the back of the skull. A protrusion just above his left eye signals perhaps where the projectile tried to escape. Blood has run down the side of his face and dried in a series of maroon rivulets. The blood is so shiny that I think you can see the Coahuila sun reflecting off it. If you listen closely to the image, you can hear things: feet marching over dry brush, an eleventh-hour cry for mercy, a meek popping sound that belies its ability to shatter so many worlds. I can hear 140 pounds of flesh falling and falling and falling to the earth. I can hear flies buzzing all around him. Dust and grass stick to his young face. I want to reach into the picture to clean him off. I want to shake him awake and back into this world. His dark eyes are open and staring at something just out of the frame. *What do you see, little brother?*

On the phone, Kingston is distraught and inconsolable. "He's fucking dead, bro!" he screams. "He's fucking dead! They killed him! Those motherfuckers killed him! Look how they did my nephew, *hermano*. Look what they did to him! Oh, dear God! Look what they did to him!"

I am afraid for Kingston and of what his sorrow might inspire. I am afraid of what he might do next. It's another moment when he is being tested. That voice from the past has returned to ask, *What are you going to do about it?* I listen while he rages over the phone. I listen while he plots. I try to offer alternatives to the bad ideas he puts forth. I try to calm him down by asking about the details of what happened. A teenage nephew was caught up in some bad shit in northern Mexico. It's the same bad shit that he and everyone else seems to be caught up in these days. The difference is that things went too far. The kid's luck ran out and now he is in the morgue. We discuss a plan to retrieve the body and return it to Honduras. He tells me that bringing the body home is his answer to the question *What are you going to do about it?* I look at the photo he sent me of his nephew lying dead in the grass under a Mexican sun and I can't but help notice the striking family resemblance. Twenty years ago, this could have been him. I wonder how many lives Kingston has.

LIKE MOST SMUGGLERS of his age and status, Kingston is heavily invested in portraying an aura of confidence, power, and longevity. Men like Kingston and Flaco have made it this far because they have the game figured out. They survive because they are always in control. They call the shots. But the truth is, life is precarious for them, perhaps even more so than for low-level smugglers like Chino and Santos. The young guys still have a

Things Fall Apart | 239

chance to walk away. Aspiring soldiers still possess the humility to admit that adventures on the train tracks aren't what they imagined. There could be something better on the horizon, even if it pays a lot less money and comes with serious responsibilities. But Kingston is in too deep. His years of heavy investment in this life, coupled with the pride that comes from being in control, make it difficult (if not impossible) to realistically imagine a future that doesn't involve the migrant trail and the wildness that many find addicting. This doesn't mean that he can't envision safer paths. The death of his nephew is the first in a series of devastating and cascading events that increasingly place him in a position to reconsider his options. He starts to look for a way out before it's him lying in an open field forever staring off into the beyond.

Bitch, Don't Kill My Vibe

A dying electric fan pushes a mix of hot air and crack smoke around the tiny room. Kingston exhales and passes the pipe to Snoop. "Go smoke that shit in the bathroom," he says. "It's getting hard to breathe in here." Chuy squirts a rag with gasoline and places it over his nose and mouth. He takes two deep breaths and then tries to pass the rag to me. I politely decline.

"No, thanks. I had a big lunch."

He cackles and points at Snoop walking away with the crack pipe. "The shit they smoke will kill you." We both laugh at the absurdity of his observation. In the background Kendrick Lamar's voice tells us, *Bitch, don't kill my vibe*.

Things have gotten more dangerous on the streets of Veracruz, so we have locked ourselves in Snoop's apartment to avoid the chaos outside. A new cartel has entered the city and is leaving a trail of blood as they battle it out with locals for control of certain neighborhoods and drug corners.

There is talk about gunmen sweeping through town, taking out low-level hustlers so that they can install their own people. Kingston is worried they are after him. He may have to leave town soon. It's unclear if this is just the generalized paranoia that accompanies smuggling and prolific crack consumption or if he is actually in danger. Regardless, he has recently grown more insistent that he needs to escape.

Jason: Is it too late for you to get out?

Kington: I don't think so, but then at the same time I think that maybe it is too late. I did some bad things in the past, and like they say, "You live by the sword, you die by the sword." I mean, I've been shot in my head, my foot, my neck. I've been attacked with machetes. But everything is okay, man. Life is life. I always say that there has to be good *and* bad things happening to you. If you don't have both, that shit is not real life.

Jason: But what's it like to think that every day there might be someone that wants to kill you?

Kingston: I worry about it a lot because I got my babies and my family.*

Jason: But you seem lucky. You made it into your thirties.

---

* Despite the depths of our many conversations, Kingston rarely talks about the multiple children he has with different women. This is largely a defense mechanism to keep their identities and locations hidden from people looking to take revenge against him.

Things Fall Apart | 241

Kingston: I'm older than Jesus now! [*We both laugh.*] I'm glad for that. I always thank God in the morning.

Jason: Do you think that means that you'll be okay?

Kingston: You never know. We could be drinking right now and I go outside and somebody comes up to me and "boom." [*He mimics shooting a handgun.*] You'd be like, "Oh shit, that motherfucker was just here drinking with us!" Life is like that. But I'm *tranquilo* now. I'm just biding my time. But it's not easy though, to be thinking that one day you could be dead. I'm just trying to be okay because sometimes I can't sleep, and I ask myself, "What the fuck is wrong?" Sometimes I only sleep every two or three days. I don't eat. I'm just thinking and thinking about the bad shit I've done. There are days where I be eating and I see things or remember things and that shit kills my appetite. But *así es la vida*.

Jason: What's next for you?

Kingston: Right now, I just want to kick back and maybe start a little business. I want to try and live a calm life, a good life. I'm just trying to live through all this shit. I'm not saying that I'm going to be a Christian or a pastor or none of that. [*Both of us laugh.*] But maybe God can find something else for me to do with my life.

Jason: But it's hard to find good work here in Mexico.

Kingston: You know how much they pay here daily? Like 90 or 100 pesos [$4.50 or $5.00] a day, and you got to be working under the fucking sun, carrying sacks of cement and doing that kind of bullshit.

Jason: What if you can't get your business going?

Kingston: If that doesn't work, I'll head back to the United States and get away from all this stuff here. I'll never come back to Mexico.

Kingston clearly wants out of smuggling and gang life, but his options are limited. He can't go back to Honduras because people want to kill him there. If he is caught crossing into the United States, he will face serious prison time because of his previous record. He doesn't have a Mexican work visa, so the only employment available to him is as a low-wage undocumented worker. While he has dreams of starting his own business, he lacks both the start-up capital and the social skills needed to run a legitimate enterprise. Kingston is not the kind of person who is going to apply for permits or pay taxes. He also does not have the patience to deal with the many setbacks he is likely to face while trying to get his business affairs in order. Like the highly motivated crack dealers described by anthropologist Philippe Bourgois or the business-savvy stickup kids sociologist Randol Contreras writes about, Kingston is smart, charismatic, and driven but has grown up in a world where these skills have been utilized largely in illicit economies. In an alternate universe, Kingston could be a successful and respected businessman. Unfortunately, it is unlikely that his aspirations for a straight job will ever be realized. His employment problems are further compounded by the fact that his daily existence is perilous and characterized by various calamities, both external and self-inflicted.

Things Fall Apart | 243

As night falls outside, we get antsy from being locked in the house all afternoon.

"You want to go to the club?" Kingston asks.

"That sounds like a really bad idea," I say, laughing. "Sure, let's do it. What could possibly go wrong this time?"

"Cool, I just have to stop by my house to feed my dog."

I'M STARING UP at the night sky as I relieve myself on a tree in the front yard. The whining horn of a nearby passing train cuts through the jungle air, reminding one that an escape is never far away. Kingston jiggles the key in the lock and pushes the metal door open. A few seconds later, I hear yelling and cabinets and doors slamming. He comes barreling out of the house screaming, "They took everything!"

Jason: What are you talking about?

Kingston: They stole everything. They came in and stole everything. I don't have nothing.

Jason: What the fuck are you talking about? Where's the dog?

Kingston: They stole my shit. They stole my dog, my fucking refrigerator, everything. They took everything!

I poke my head into the house and stare at emptiness. The place has been picked clean.

Kingston aggressively paces around the room. His aggravated voice echoes off the bare linoleum floor and concrete walls.

"They took everything!" he screams. "They even took my gun!"

244 | SOLDIERS AND KINGS

The place suddenly feels unsafe. We wonder who would have the audacity to do something like this. It has to be someone who knows him, which makes the theft even more brazen and scary. We decide it's not a good idea to stick around, so we hop into a cab and head to the center of town. Kingston is understandably enraged. Everything he owns is gone. It's another Friday night where something disastrous has happened.

The taxi stops at a light. A shoeless kid in filthy rags starts scrubbing the windshield.

Kingston rolls down his window and starts yelling at him. "There's nothing here, *carnal*! Nothing. Get the fuck outta here! *¡Chinga su madre!*"

He turns to me and for the first time since I've known him, I think he's going to cry. "Fuck! Look at me!" he says. "I have no clothes. I'm in a fucking tank top and *chanclas*."

The taxi drops us off in front of a run-down club. The thumping bass from inside gives the impression that the sidewalk has a pulse. "Let's get a beer and figure this shit out," I tell him. We get to the door and the bouncer gives Kingston the once-over.

"Sorry, you can't come in here in sandals," he says. "You have to have shoes on to get in."

I brace for the worst, but Kingston just nods and says, "No problem." As we turn and walk into the night, I'm thankful that our evening is coming to an early end.

Straight Up

There is no shade to protect us from the sun bouncing off the marble tiles of Bellas Artes, Mexico City's most prominent cultural center. A million cars playfully honk at each other as they fight their way down a nearby

Things Fall Apart | 245

boulevard. An organ-grinder mercilessly turns his crank and releases a lilting melody into the afternoon air. *Chilangos* who still appreciate this dying musical art form toss pesos into his upturned cap. Tourists pose for selfies. Couples hold hands on benches while passing vendors hawk cotton candy and balloons. Nearby, teenagers in baggy pants and death metal T-shirts engage in a rap battle. Kingston takes in the ambience in a cool and resigned way. He looks exhausted. He wanted to leave the chaos of the safe house in Lechería for someplace calmer and away from the ears of his soldiers. He wants to get some things off his chest. I don't realize it then, but this will be the last time I ever see him.

For weeks, he's been talking to me about getting out of the game. His nephew dying and his house being robbed have added urgency to this idea he has been mulling over for months.

Jason: When did you decide that you were done?

Kingston: It was after the last time I went to prison and no one wanted to bail me out. I was in prison for seven months in Mexico. They wanted to give me five years for smuggling. I called my people in New York and told them to get me out. I told them I needed 30,000 pesos [$1,500] for bail, and they said they would take care of me. They said they would send someone to help me. I waited and waited, but it never happened.

Jason: That doesn't seem like that much money considering how much you make for them.

Kingston: I know! Come on, man, it's not a lot of fucking money, especially after twenty years of doing this shit. That guy was supposed to be my friend, but he let me down.

That "guy" Kingston refers to is the high-ranking gang member who initiated him into the Bloods when he was a kid back in Honduras. This person calls all the shots from New York and has large crews of people working for him across Latin America. Kingston is so afraid of him that he never says his name. He only refers to him as "this person" or "that guy." A monster *sin nombre* who is omnipresent. Everything that Kingston does has to be vetted by "that guy," including his decision to get out of the game.

Like Chino, Kingston understands that leaving the gang comes with major consequences and is not something to be done lightly. He explains his escape plan.

> **Kingston:** I want to go to New York to talk to this guy to tell him that I quit. I need to ask permission.

> **Jason:** What do you think he'll say?

> **Kingston:** I don't know. He might say it's okay or he might say no. But even if he says it's okay, he might not mean it. He might say it's okay and then send people later to kill me. He's got people everywhere: Mexico, Belize, the United States. I have friends who have gone to talk to him about getting out and then they disappeared. They could be hiding or they could be dead. A lot of people go see him and then you never hear from them again. But even if they let you out, others will remember you. Other people are still looking for you and now you have no protection.

For the past several months, Kingston has been lying low and avoiding parts of Mexico where he was previously active. This is because he thinks he is now being hunted.

Things Fall Apart | 247

Kingston: There's a nigga up in San Luis [Potosí] who's been saying he's going to kill me. He thinks I'm running things up there, but I ain't doing that shit no more. I'm retired from that.

Jason: Are you afraid?

Kingston: No, because I'm in my house all day, locked up. But I want to run away from this world. I go back and forth from feeling safe and then not feeling safe. Every day it's something new to worry about. Someone could come for me today or tomorrow.

It's not just the fear of being killed that haunts Kingston. His lifetime of trauma and violent acts is destroying him from the inside. He believes that escape is not just about physically leaving but also finding some peace and mental stability.

Jason: What would make you happy?

Kingston: I just want to leave all this behind, but I don't know how. I don't know how to cleanse myself of all the stuff that has happened. You know how it is—we all do what we have to do to survive and there is nothing you can do about it. But for me, the biggest fucking things are the memories. It's so many fucking memories, Jason. There are moments where I can't stop thinking about them. That's why I smoke my weed and try to relax, because I end up remembering things and that shit gets me down. It puts me in a bad place. It's like you are stuck with this stuff; it's like a tattoo. All that you do in your life is recorded on you like a tattoo. *Carnal*, there have been so many fucked-up things in my life, but I tell myself that the past is the past and I'm just trying to live in the present. I want a life that moves forward because I'm tired after so many years of doing crazy shit for other people. After all I've done, those people aren't even grateful. And now the only person who has problems is me. I just want to retire and find someone who I can talk to, someone who can help me deal with my mind and all my worries. I know you can get help for this kind of stuff. I know it.

Perhaps one of the biggest ironies of Kingston's life is that he has earned so much money helping people escape violence and poverty, yet he himself is perpetually stuck between the two. Right before we met, he unsuccessfully tried to get his family into the United States. Despite that failure, he is committed to trying again, both for their safety and his own.

Jason: What do you want for your family?

Kingston: I want to bring my kids to the United States. I tried before, but shit got fucked up because I didn't have no money. Immigration caught my whole family. My baby mom, my daughter, my son. They sent them all back. I tried to bring them twice, but it didn't work. I can try again, but I need money to get them across. I can't put my family on the train because those motherfuckers there know me, and if they see my family they're gonna do some bad shit to them. So we would have to travel by bus or car. Or maybe if I go to New York, I can earn money and get somebody to bring my family. I could pay someone I know and trust to bring them.

Things Fall Apart | 249

I have to do this because it's getting dangerous. My baby's mom keeps calling me and saying, "Somebody came by the house asking for you." People are now looking for me in Mexico and Honduras. That's why I'm trying to retire from this shit so that I can do better things with my life. I want to start over so that my family can be okay. I just want to get out. Straight up.

CHAPTER SIXTEEN

Liberty without Tricks
or False Promises

For years Flaco has told me he is leaving the world of smuggling. It's a story on repeat. *It's too dangerous, bro. They almost killed me in Coatza. It's too dangerous, bro. They almost killed me in Tierra Blanca.* He says these things with deep conviction but soon afterward sends me videos of him rolling a fat joint in a Guadalajara safe house or roasting an iguana somewhere deep in the jungles of Chiapas.

Mexico is increasingly cracking down on Central American migration while organized crime tightens its choke hold on the smuggling industry. This means more risk and lower profits for Flaco. But still, he can't seem to pull himself away from the train tracks. He can't cut the umbilical cord to a lifestyle he has always known and loved. I can't blame him. It's easy to see the attraction: fast money, the euphoria that accompanies successfully evading danger, the nonstop partying, the thrill of calling the shots and being a boss. These are the things that attract young people to the occupation in the first place. These are the things that keep people coming back. Keep in mind that in practically every other social context, Flaco is a nobody, a poor and uneducated person who lives hand to mouth on the margins. But on the

Liberty without Tricks or False Promises | 251

migrant trail he is an authority figure, an expert, a king. Smuggling people gives him a sense of power and control, even if it's only temporary. But his brushes with death are becoming more frequent: his hands and feet bound with duct tape; a dirty knife to his throat; a pistol to his head; another plea to God to get him out of one more bad situation. The violence at the hands of cartels and gangs is escalating. Like Kingston, he is starting to read the writing on the wall, and the prognosis is not good. He keeps telling himself to get out before it's too late, but it is unclear if he truly wants that to happen or if it is even possible. Then a series of unfortunate events forces his hand.

"Hey, Jason, how you doing, bro?" he says over the phone. "I got no money. I'm broken, foo. Can you send me like twenty bucks? I need to put some credit on my phone, *hermano*." Flaco has just been deported back to Honduras after spending almost a month in a Mexican detention center. It's a relief to hear his weary voice. He was incommunicado for so long that his family and I began to worry that something really bad had happened. His sister called me out of the blue to see if I could help locate him. I began contacting hospitals in Chiapas and Veracruz to see if they had a patient matching his description. I started looking for stories of his death on the internet. This went on for several tense weeks until he surfaced in Honduras penniless and exhausted. "I'm really done," he says. "It's too dangerous now. Immigration took all my money. They took a lot this time. The *mareros* and the mafia are too much. There's too much kidnapping and murder. I have to think about my family here in Honduras. I have to think about my little boy. I'm done."

Losing thousands of dollars to corrupt Mexican immigration agents who robbed him and then locked him up seems to have scared Flaco straight. He doesn't want to talk about what they did to him, but he gives the impression that it was worse than the normal shakedown and beating. Personally, I am relieved that he is walking away from smuggling. Getting out reduces the chances that I will be texted a photo of him with a bullet in his skull.

Smuggling is an unsustainable lifestyle, even for someone as hardened and smart as Flaco. I make plans to visit him and see the new life he is building. He sends pictures of himself working with a truck driver hauling goods across Honduras. We video chat and he has me talk to his children and his wife as he cackles and puffs on a joint. "Say hello to the gringo," he tells his young son. "He's going to come visit for your birthday." Things seem to be going well for him—as well as they can be for someone making only a few dollars a day. The good news is that he isn't in jail or kidnapped or dead in a ditch. "When you come to visit, we will butcher a cow for my son's birthday. There's gonna be a lot a beer and weed too, foo. *¡Mucha lechuga!*" he laughingly tells me in February of 2020.

By May of 2020, the tone and topic of our conversations has drastically changed. "Another one of my neighbors died today from COVID," he says on a video call while standing on the empty road in front of his house. The government-enforced curfew has rendered his *colonia* a ghost town. "It's really bad here, bro. We can't leave, and most of the stores don't have any food. People are charging more for everything. The government isn't doing anything to help us."

Many Americans struggled financially and emotionally during the pandemic, but imagine what it must have been like for those who were already living on the edge of hell in the Third World. Honduras is a country where 60 percent of the population lives in poverty and is dependent on a daily income. Government-imposed lockdowns prevent people from bringing any cash into the household at the end of the day. No cash means no food, no rent, no medicine. COVID is a health risk for Hondurans, but it is no match for the decades of generational starvation that the pandemic only exacerbates. Government health records showed 430,672 infections and 10,912 deaths as of October 2022, but for many analysts the scariest number was the historic 9 percent shrinkage of the country's economy by the end of

Liberty without Tricks or False Promises | 253

2020, caused by work stoppages. Some predict that the Honduran poverty rate will reach 75 percent in the wake of the pandemic.

Flaco tries to find employment during the government shutdown, but pickings are slim for an uneducated thirtysomething street hustler whom everyone suspects of being associated with shady dealings. Still, he cuts cane, clears brush, and digs ditches when there is someone willing to pay him $2 a day, which is not often. Unsurprisingly, he contracts COVID and spends two weeks in bed. "I couldn't taste or smell anything, bro. It was awful. I couldn't even smoke weed, so you know it was bad," he jokes. But the complications created by COVID in Honduras are no joke. Shit was bad before, but the cocktail created by mixing the pandemic with long-standing violence, economic instability, and government corruption astoundingly makes Honduras more unlivable than ever before.

For the first few months of the pandemic, Flaco struggles to put food on the table and make rent. I send him what I can to help out and cancel my plans to visit. We spend the first part of our respective lockdowns exchanging messages on WhatsApp and video chatting about the party he will eventually have when this global nightmare is over. He does his best to maintain a positive attitude while the world is on fire. The periodic odd jobs keep him afloat. His children keep him laughing. But then death comes banging on his door.

There's No Exception to the Rule

Flaco is so overcome with grief that he can barely get the words out. "They killed my brother, *carnal*. They killed him. They strangled him and stabbed him forty times. They left him like he was garbage. They even stole his shoes. I'm so sad, bro. I just want to go to Mexico, Jason. I want to be anywhere but here. I have so many problems, *hermano*. You know how my life is."

Murders in Mexico and Central America are often captured by cell phone cameras and then circulated on WhatsApp to all interested parties. *Look at what they did to my neighbor, my cousin*, mi carnal. Bodies in cheap coffins. Bodies on a medical examiner's steel table. Bodies in odd contortions on the ground, looking at the world with abandoned eyes. *Look at what they did*. I have reached the point now that when I see someone has texted me a photo, I open it expecting the worst.

In the picture Flaco sends me, his brother (who looks like a younger version of him) is laid out on his back in a field of deep green Honduran grass. His eyes are closed. An unbuttoned shirt exposes a chest dirty with dried blood and riddled with puncture wounds. I can't begin to fathom the rage it takes to stab someone forty times. A line of raw, inflamed skin cuts across his throat, demarcating where someone's hands pulled and twisted the garrote until he could no longer draw breath. The crotch of his blue jeans is damp. He soiled himself in his final struggle for life. The outline of a bystander just outside of the camera's frame casts a shadow over the corpse and gives the eerie impression that a ghost is floating away from the body. But that's not how death works, and I've known that fact for a long time. I look at this picture of a dead body and a deeply repressed memory surfaces about a woman I watched die when I was ten years old.

Chubby cheeks, husky pants, crooked front teeth. A Chicago Bears *1985 Super Bowl Champions* T-shirt. My head is buried in a tattered copy of *Beckett Baseball Card Monthly* as I ignore the sounds of clinking weights and the grunts of bodies mid-exertion. I'm too busy gauging the current prices of Nolan Ryan and Fernando Valenzuela cards. I'm probably calculating what it would cost me in trade to get a Pedro Guerrero rookie. Nearby, my mom jogs on a treadmill, lost in the music coming out of her Walkman. In my mind she is listening to the Main Ingredient's "Everybody Plays the Fool."

Liberty without Tricks or False Promises | 255

It's a song that was crucial to my childhood soundtrack as my working-class mother and I leaned on each other to get through a bitter divorce and a traumatizing custody battle. It's a song that makes me smile and cry. *There's no exception to the rule . . . everybody plays the fool.*

My concentration is broken when I hear a crash and look up to see someone lying on the gym floor. The middle-aged woman had been running on the treadmill next to my mom when she collapsed. A small crowd gathers. The woman is unresponsive to a wet towel put to her forehead. I sit paralyzed and watch my mom perform CPR on this stranger. Chest compressions and mouth-to-mouth. How does my mom know what to do? How does anyone know what to do? An ambulance is called. More people arrive. The woman doesn't react when they cut open her shirt and reposition her to keep performing CPR. She doesn't flinch when a paramedic takes a silver scalpel and performs a tracheotomy. My ten-year-old brain can't fathom how she can just lie there as they carve a hole into her throat. I can't make sense of the lifeless body the paramedics try to put breath back into. I've seen a dead person before, but it was my grandmother and she had been a sick old lady for a long time. I remember her in a frilly coffin looking like she was peacefully sleeping. But this woman is not old. She is not peacefully sleeping. She was just here in this room, running on a treadmill, and now she is gone. I stare at her lying on the floor and know that there is nothing left to do. There is no bright shining light from the heavens. I don't see any angels take her away. After the paramedics remove the body, I watch my mom use a towel to soak up a small pool of blood that was left behind in the dead woman's wake.

When I look at the photo of Flaco's brother lying shoeless in a grassy field, I see that woman from so many years ago. I see something familiar but incomprehensible. I feel an emptiness and a sadness, but not because I knew him. I feel empty because I know there is no escaping this. There is no coming back. I know that the reality for many I have come to know on the migrant trail is what I see in that grassy field. Stab wounds. Bullet wounds. A rope around a neck. Desperation and fury and an ending with no trumpets or fanfare. A paramedic comes and unceremoniously takes away what death leaves behind. I look at this image of a dead young man and know that this is what getting out of the game means for many. I wonder what Flaco sees when he looks at the photo.

"I'm going back to Mexico, bro," he says. "It's better there than it is here. There's too much sadness here." He packs his bag and starts heading north once again. How many times does someone have to flee their home before it stops being home?

In 1998, Flaco watched from a rooftop as Hurricane Mitch washed away houses and bodies. He counts himself lucky because he left Honduras just in time to escape Hurricanes Eta and Iota. Those back-to-back category 4 storms ravaged Central America in November 2020, causing billions of dollars of damage and displacing hundreds of thousands of impoverished people already suffering through a pandemic. When the floodwaters recede, Flaco's neighbors begin their own mass exodus from Honduras.

As soon as I exit the plane and walk onto the tarmac, the smell of dense jungle and burning garbage hits me, invoking a thousand memories, dreams, and nightmares of Chiapas. Because of the pandemic, it's been more than two years since I've visited the southern Mexico border. I send Flaco a voice message to let him know I have arrived. "I'll see you soon, *hermano*," he replies. As I wait for my luggage at the Tapachula airport, I read the various anti-smuggling and anti-trafficking signs that the Mexican government has posted in the baggage claim area. One poster carries the inspirational slogan *Liberty without tricks or false promises*, a critique of the chicanery smugglers and traffickers are known for. I can't help being a little cynical and thinking that the notion of liberty for much of the world is itself a false promise.

CHAPTER SEVENTEEN

Suerte

December 24 on the train tracks is not as grim as one might imagine. Santos and a small group of men are in a festive mood this morning because Good Samaritans from nearby Caborca have been visiting the tracks and bringing gifts for migrants. Tamales. Warm tortillas and beans. Someone has even procured a little booze and marijuana. The men fill their stomachs as drinks flow and clouds of rich smoke ascend into the Sonoran sky. They make toasts to better futures and the pending new year. There is optimism in the air. America is only 150 kilometers north. Everyone hopes they will soon see midwestern sunrises through the cracked windshields of work trucks as they drive to American jobs grooming golf courses or hanging drywall for $14 an hour. There are visions of drinking cases of Bud Light after work and listening to *rancheras* from the bed of an F-150. They joke about better futures where there are no train tracks to sleep on or bullets and knives to dodge. The simple dream of the promised land is enough to make one feel hopeful. Whatever happens is God's will. They just hope that God's will includes a roof over their heads and maybe a gringa to come home to. Someone fires up a portable speaker and soon a lazy reggaeton beat has several people dancing. It almost feels like a real Navidad.

Just as their little party is getting under way, a disheveled Mexican approaches. He sizes up the group. Everyone on the tracks is undocumented, and thus he has the legal upper hand. Besides, this is his *tierra* and these men are intruders. He brazenly walks through the party and grabs the speaker.

"What the fuck do you think you're doing?" someone asks.

The man smirks and produces a blade. Santos takes a few steps back. *Fuck this*. He wants nothing to do with this encounter. He's got enough problems and doesn't need to add a knife fight to that list. The owner of the speaker starts to make a move toward the thief. The man with the knife makes it clear he is ready to use it. Someone picks up a rock and hurls it. It hits the thief in the mouth, sending him to the ground. He stands up and lunges. Two men begin to roll around in the gravel while the knife slashes at clothing and flesh. Santos watches it all happen as if it is a movie. It's not his speaker and he barely knows these people. None of this is worth getting involved in, so he looks on as these men kick the shit out of each other. When it's all done, the Mexican hobbles away bleeding and without a speaker. It's a small migrant victory. Santos and his crew think the matter is settled and return to their Christmas party. No one expects the thief to come back with the police half an hour later.

At the station the officers are seemingly sympathetic. They tell Santos they know he is innocent and that they will release him soon. They promise to get him a lawyer. But they don't release him and a lawyer never shows up. He sits handcuffed in the precinct for hours. "I kept telling the cops I had nothing to do with it," he remembers. "I told them I wasn't involved. Even the Mexican guy who came back said I had nothing to do with it. But the cops just looked at the Hondurans who were there and decided we were all guilty. The Mexican said that he got jumped by migrants and the police believed him."

Suerte | 259

They begin processing the paperwork so that the Honduran involved in the altercation can go to court. Santos gets worried as he watches them fill out the same paperwork for him. By the time he stands in front of the judge, he has told everyone who comes within earshot that he is innocent, but no one listens. When you're poor, Honduran, and undocumented in Mexico, your voice doesn't carry much weight, but it does often come with stereotypes: *Everyone knows that catrachos are violent. They are thugs. Just look at what is happening in their country.* The court seems to harbor these same prejudices.

> **Santos:** The judge looked at me and said that I was responsible for the fight. He said, "You were watching it happen. Why didn't you call the police?" I told him it wasn't just me. There were like ten *cabrones* on the tracks when this happened. I asked, "Why don't you arrest those other people too and bring them in here?" In the end, the judge said it wasn't my fault but I was going to pay for it anyways. He sentenced me to four years and one month.

SANTOS NARROWS HIS EYES against the desert sun. He takes in a necropolis of scorched earth, concrete, and steel. A sea of hardened men uniformed in khaki pants and bright orange shirts plots and schemes and waits while high above armed guards look for excuses to unload a few rounds. Some of the prisoners quietly count the days until they can see the sky unbounded by walls and metal bars. Others know they will never again breathe free air, so they seek out violent diversions to kill time.

The noise from a heated soccer match taking place a few hundred yards away fills the air. *¡Chinga tu madre, cabrón! That was offside!* It's hard for Santos to watch the game and not think about the kid from his cellblock down on his knees in the dirt, screaming and trying to keep his guts from spilling out of a giant gash in his stomach. That's what happens when you talk shit to the wrong person on the opposing team. Nothing around here is a game.

Santos has never been to prison, but he quickly finds his rhythm. A lifetime on the tracks has taught him to mind his own business, a lesson that serves him well in this new environment. Homies invite him to play cards and smoke weed, but he knows that those friendly engagements can turn sour fast: "One of my friends got into a fight over a game of cards and ended up stabbing someone. He went from having a four-year sentence to a seventeen-year sentence. I just tried to stay busy with work." To make ends meet, Santos crafts jewelry and figurines out of recycled plastic bottles and cans. He sells these items to inmates who give them to relatives on visiting day. Because he has no way to contact his family in Honduras, no one comes to visit him. No one even knows where he is (including me). He quietly paces the prison yard, resigned to serving out his forty-nine-month sentence.

Almost two years into his prison stay, Santos finally makes contact with his mother. He explains his situation and she relays the story to his older brother Marvin, a former soldier who has always been the mature and responsible one in the family. From Honduras, Marvin begins the long and slow process of getting his brother's case reexamined. He is struggling to feed his own family but manages to wire Santos a little money to secure a Mexican lawyer. The lawyer thinks they have a good chance of getting charges dismissed if they can get in front of a judge. Marvin scrambles to get more money together. After months of false starts and small money wires to the attorney, Santos finally gets his day in court. He pleads his innocence to the judge, who calls him "a danger to Mexican society." The judge wants him to sign a document attesting to a crime he didn't commit. Santos reluctantly puts his signature on the paperwork. He will do anything not to sleep another night in hell. "You're getting out of here, but you are leaving with a record," the judge tells him. "You aren't leaving here clean." After twenty-seven months in prison, Santos pays a fine of $600 and finally sees the sky outside prison walls.

Batallando

He looks at me with exhausted eyes and then takes a long drag from a cheap Mexican cigarette. I use the tip of my shoe to kick gravel while I search for words to express how I am feeling. The last time I saw Santos we were dancing and partying on the tracks in Pakal-Ná. He was fresh-faced and optimistic. He told jokes and we laughed our asses off. We made plans to reunite in Michigan, where I was living at the time. But that feels like a lifetime ago. A few months after Santos left Pakal-Ná with Sombra, we lost contact. His phone got disconnected. His Facebook account became inactive. I knew he was either in prison or dead. I was relieved to eventually learn it was the former. I am happy to see him, but sitting on the train tracks on the outskirts of Nogales, Mexico, it is clear he is a changed person. He looks road-worn and sad. He's gained weight and his once youthful face now shows worry lines and new scars. Prison has aged him and life on the streets is grinding him down. We sit on the tracks and talk about his plans for the future while the whistles of passing trains scream in the background.

> **Jason:** When I stopped getting messages from you and saw that your Facebook account went silent, I thought something really bad had happened. I thought you were dead.

Santos: [*Laughing*] You're not the only one who thought that. No one knew where I was, so everyone assumed I was dead. People in my village were lighting candles for me. Even after I was able to talk to my mom from prison, people still thought I was dead. They were asking her, "When are they going to ship his body home?" My mom kept telling people, "My son is not dead! Who told you that he was dead?" You know how it is with rumors. People hear something and then they are convinced it's true.

Jason: I know it was awful, but I was glad that you were in prison and not in the cemetery.

Santos: Prison was traumatic, Jason. I lost a lot of time there, but I told myself I just had to hang on until things got better. It's like right now, I'm just trying to be strong until I can get to the other side [of the border].

Jason: What did you do when you got out?

Santos: I spent two months in Honduras. I really had no interest coming back here to Mexico but you know how bad it is in my country. There is no work in Honduras and it's too dangerous for me to stay in my neighborhood, so I had to leave. I didn't want to come back to Sonora after all the time I had spent here in prison. But my brother Marvin had never been here and he wanted me to bring him. So we left.

Santos now has a criminal record in Mexico, which means that if he is caught by Immigration he can face serious prison time for illegal entry and violation of his agreement to never return to the country. It speaks volumes about how dangerous and uninhabitable Honduras is that he would risk long-term incarceration again in a foreign country rather than stay home. He still hangs out on the tracks, but mostly because he is moving across northern Mexico in search of temporary employment in the many migrant-heavy communities that exploit itinerant and undocumented labor. He is working hard to stay out of trouble and keep a healthy distance from anything related to smuggling.

Jason: Have you moved any people since you got out?

Santos: No. I lost all my contacts while I was in prison. It's like I have to start over in every place. People I knew before either left or got killed. It's dangerous now because no one remembers me. But it was getting difficult even before I went to prison. That's why I had to get out of Pakal-Ná. I was starting to have problems with Bin Laden and the Breadman. You couldn't trust those guys. They were very problematic. That's why you always have to study people. If I meet someone on the tracks, I have to watch them and get to know them well because in this *camino* your own friends can betray you.

Jason: How did you and Chino become friends?

Santos: After I tattooed him, we started hanging out and traveling together for months. He was a funny kid who became like my little brother. We had a lot of adventures on the train bringing people from Pakal-Ná to Coatza. We did that a lot. We were always doing stuff together. Partying on the tracks. Getting tattooed. I did a lot of his tattoos, including the *catracho* one on his arm. The last time I saw him was when I left to go north with Sombra and he stayed behind with Jesmyn. I didn't want him to stay behind, but I knew he wanted to be with her, so all I could do was wish him luck. I went to Celaya and then to Caborca, where I ended up in prison.

Jason: And what happened with Sombra?

Santos: I never saw him again after that trip, although one of the women we traveled with ended up in Mazatlán. She still calls me and wants me to bring her up here to the border, but I keep telling her to stay where she is. It's probably better there. I don't want to bring her here because I don't want to be responsible for bad things that could happen to her.

As we sit on the tracks and catch up, I try to imagine a better future for Santos. I need things to work out for him because I know deep down he is trying hard to make the right decisions (whatever that means). I want everything to be okay for him because I am awed by the optimism he has somehow held on to despite what he has been through. I also think to myself that maybe the two hellish years he spent in prison somehow saved him by giving him distance and perspective on a lifestyle that was potentially going to get him killed.

Jason: Do you miss being a *guía*?

Santos: No, because being a guide always means you can end up dead. I would prefer to battle on the street. I would

Suerte | 265

prefer to ask people for spare change. That's how I got here to Nogales. I've just been riding the train and then getting off and begging for money at stoplights. It's hard moving around, but I'd rather be struggling on the streets than taking orders from people who could end up killing me. I'm about to turn twenty-five and I don't want any of this life anymore. I've been doing this for years . . . and the only break I've ever had was the little bit of time I spent working in Phoenix. My life has been pure suffering with so much pain on these train tracks. So much moving back and forth. I am tired of moving and just want to get out. I just want to live my life. That's why I'm battling to get to the U.S.

Jason: What would you do in the U.S.?

Santos: I'd do whatever comes my way. I just want to work. All I want is a normal life, because there is nothing good here on the train tracks. God willing, I will get out of here and make it north.

After several hours of talking, Santos and I prepare to part ways. He will hop a train to Mexicali, and I will walk across the border back to Arizona. He is physically so close to the place he hopes will change everything for him, yet it is just out of reach. Will he make it to the United States, or die trying? How long can he maintain the stamina to keep fighting for a semblance of a normal life, where he no longer has to beg for money or sleep on the dirt? I am inspired by his tenacity and shamed by my own privilege.

We hug. I give him all the money in my wallet and a bag of beans and tortillas I brought. "I'll share this food with people I see on the train," he tells me. I worry this could be the last time I see him. I don't really know what to say. He is about to walk off into the distance and into the unknown and it scares me. Years later I remember this goodbye being difficult and awkward. When I listen back to the audio recording, I hear my own stupid voice saying to him, "I'll come visit you soon in Mexicali, but I should go because the line to get across the border starts to get long right around this time."

CHAPTER EIGHTEEN

Xibalba

It's a slow march toward something ominous. Despite her intuition, Jesmyn follows the men deeper and deeper into the jungle. The late-afternoon sun paints menacing shadows that cut across the train tracks and the surrounding foliage. Their feet step across geometric designs of light and dark, a metaphor for the divergent paths offered up to those on this long road headed north. The Maya, who settled this landscape thousands of years ago, believe that people pass between two worlds when they die: the realm of the living, and Xibalba, the parallel unseen Otherworld where death gods and their helpers rule. Xibalba is where souls go after death. It is also a place where gods are appeased by human sacrifice.

Chino is arrogant and defiant as he walks. "*No pasa nada, mi amor,*" he tells Jesmyn. "Nothing will happen, my love. Everything is going to be fine." She nervously watches as houses get fewer and farther between. The voices of neighbors and small groups of migrants milling about become faint and then disappear entirely. The only sounds left are the buzzing of insects and the crunching of gravel under their feet. Jesmyn is alone with her thoughts and the uneasy feeling growing inside her. Bin Laden and the

Breadman say they just want to talk to Chino in private. They need privacy so that they can work out a problem that has been brewing among them for weeks. Bin Laden reassures her nothing will happen. He even invites the three Guatemalan migrants who have been hanging around with Chino to accompany them to this meeting. Still, the internal voice that has protected her all her life is telling her that something bad is coming.

We ARE SITTING in a restaurant in coastal Honduras, gazing out at the Atlantic Ocean, when Jesmyn recounts this story. The offshore breeze cools our skin as we sip cold drinks and watch the sun disappear over the horizon. It's a beautiful backdrop that feels far away from any danger. This illusion is shattered when our waiter brings our food and I glimpse the 9mm Glock hanging off his waist. Jesmyn unravels a story of violence in the distant Mexican jungle while we take in an ocean view and wonder what dangers might be waiting just outside.

> Jesmyn: I remember how it all started. Bin Laden and the Breadman had been assaulting migrants on the train tracks and they had gotten mad at Chino because he didn't want to help them. They were robbing people with some Guatemalan guys we knew. They were guys who had been working with Sombra before he left. Bin Laden and the Breadman were robbing their own *paisanos* and they wanted Chino to help. But Chino was changing. He'd been doing bad stuff on the tracks for a long time, but that was usually because his friends pressured him to do it or because he was fucked up on drugs or alcohol. He was starting to change and didn't want to do those things anymore.

Xibalba | 269

By this point, Sombra and Santos have already left Pakal-Ná with the group of female migrants they were moving north. Chino's decision to stay behind is his first major step toward separating himself from gang and smuggling life. His refusal to assist others robbing migrants adds to the impression that he has become soft and potentially vulnerable. Jesmyn has a front-row seat to building tensions.

Jesmyn: Things were getting bad between Chino and the Breadman, especially after Sombra left. One night the two of them got drunk and started fighting about a cell phone. Chino was mad at the Breadman for robbing people, and the Breadman told him to leave the train tracks or he was going to kill him. A few days later, we were at the house and Chino said he was going to buy some marijuana. I got worried and told him, "Don't go outside. Don't go looking for trouble. If you want marijuana, ask someone else to go get it." But he was insistent that he would go, so he grabbed a machete and went out. Suddenly, he came running back to the house. He came back so fast that I got scared. At first, I thought maybe he had done something or killed somebody because of the problems he was having. But nothing had happened. He just said, "Don't go to the train tracks right now because it's dangerous." He said that the Breadman was with some people robbing migrants near where he went to buy marijuana. I now wonder if the Breadman saw him with a machete and thought he was going to attack him.

The next morning the Breadman came looking for Chino at our house, but he was at work. He told me that Chino needed to leave the tracks or he was going to kill him. At this point, there was no one left in Pakal-Ná who would stick up for Chino if something happened, so I knew we had to get out of there. We were both scared, but we didn't have enough money to leave yet. I kept telling Chino we should go, but he wanted us to stay and keep working to save money so that we would have enough to start over someplace else. I think the Breadman heard that we were scared. He knew that no one would protect us if he did something.

The events Jesmyn describes took place a week after I left Pakal-Ná and returned home to teach classes in the fall. I knew the Breadman and Bin Laden, but they had largely been peripheral in my research. I had spent time with the former, hanging out at the Pleasure Palace while he smoked weed and quietly knit handbags that he sold on the streets. I would also chat with him while he hawked pastries he got from the bakery where he and Bin Laden worked and slept. The Breadman was often guarded about his story, and I never pushed him to talk. He was mostly hanging around while I talked to others. Still, he was always friendly with me, and our conversations often revolved around how much he missed his children and his growing knitting business. On a few occasions, he mentioned in passing that he and Bin Laden had just been released from prison in Honduras and that they had fled to Mexico to avoid an issue that had arisen in their neighborhood.

I had no problems with the Breadman but could tell that others were suspicious of him. I watched Santos get openly hostile toward him over his propensity for never sharing his marijuana or food but always asking others for handouts. Bin Laden, on the other hand, was someone I found to be a complete asshole; he was often aggressive and condescending to practically everyone. I watched him bully other migrants a few times, and he seemed especially focused on trying to corner newly arrived women. On several occasions he was openly belligerent toward me and vocally unhappy with my unwillingness to give him money for various problems that he seemed to invent on the spot. Some days he told me he was a desperate migrant trying to bring his wife up from the south. Other days, I would run into him on the streets with a client and he would play the role of cocky smuggler. In general, Bin Laden was exceptionally suspicious and I tried to give him a wide berth.

Many people shared my sentiment, and Jesmyn's descriptions of tensions reaching a boiling point in Pakal-Ná are not surprising.

> **Jesmyn:** Me, Chino, and the Guatemalan guys were hanging out at our house when Bin Laden and the Breadman came by saying they wanted to talk. I knew they just came to make trouble. I told them, "If you want to talk, do it right here in front of all of us." The Breadman got pissed. He said, "No, we need to talk about this in private. Let's go down to the tracks and talk." Chino just sat on the porch and tried to stay calm. I kept saying, "Work it out right here. Problems don't get solved by fighting. They get solved by talking about it, so let's talk here." Finally, the Breadman said to Chino, "Let's go. You can bring your girlfriend and your friends with you if you want." So all of us, including the Guatemalans, started heading down the tracks. I never imagined what we were walking toward.

The group stops at a secluded area just outside Pakal-Ná. It's a blind spot where migrants are known to get robbed. Chino and the Breadman begin to have words. "I told you there was going to be trouble around here if you didn't leave," the Breadman tells him. Chino stands his ground. He is scared but refuses to show it. He has a reputation to protect, especially in front of his girl. Jesmyn and the Guatemalans watch as the two men bark at each

272 | SOLDIERS AND KINGS

other. Bin Laden has his back turned to the group and is digging an object out of his pocket.

"That's when I knew they were getting ready to do something," Jesmyn says. "Bin Laden turned back around and I could see he was holding something in his hand. I got really scared, but at the same time I couldn't believe what was happening. I'd never seen anything like that. I never would have believed they could have done something like that."

Chino doesn't see it coming. But Jesmyn does. "When I saw the knife go in I wanted to cry, but at the same time I couldn't. I was frozen."

Bin Laden's blade enters deep into the right side of Chino's chest. He falls to the ground, yelling, "You son of a bitch!" Bin Laden moves quickly to stab him again.

> Jesmyn: Chino was screaming. I saw his hands try to block the blows. One wound punctured his lung and the other almost went into his heart, but he grabbed Bin Laden's hand and blocked part of it. I started to cry. I couldn't stand it, Jason. I wanted to jump in to help him, but I knew that if I got in the middle of that, I would have been fucked too."

Jesmyn is rendered immobile with terror. She turns and pleads for the Guatemalans to help, but by now they are halfway down the tracks. She finds herself alone and crying as she watches someone she loves scream for help. Is this what it looked like when her father was stabbed on a street corner in San Pedro Sula fourteen years ago? Have her past and present somehow merged? Bin Laden and the Breadman are enraged, and she worries she may be next.

> Jesmyn: I wanted to stay with him, but there was nothing I could do, so I ran. Bin Laden yelled at me as I ran away. He

said he would kill me if I called the police, so I went home and hid behind the front door. I strongly believe in God, so I started praying. I said, "Chino is in your hands, God. No one can do anything to him unless you want it to happen." I prayed for twenty minutes and then I got the courage to leave the house and go back to where they had attacked him. There was no one there when I went back, but I saw one of Chino's shoes lying on the tracks. When I didn't see anyone, that gave me hope that he was okay. I thought to myself, "God, please protect him."

BIN LADEN and the Breadman barge through the apartment door excited and out of breath. With eyes running wild, they pace and gesticulate. They smile and laugh.

"We killed him! We killed him! We killed that fucking *culero*!" Bin Laden yells.

"What are you talking about?" Papo asks.

"We killed Chino!" responds the Breadman.

"I thought they were lying," Papo recalls. "They came into the house happy and joking and saying that they killed him. I didn't believe it."

Alma remembers the moment with anger. "These fucking killers showed up and I couldn't believe how they were acting. They were smiling and excited, but I could also tell that they were scared at the same time. They were fucked up on something. 'How could you do that to Chino?' I asked them. 'We are all migrants here. We are all from the same country.'"

JESMYN CAUTIOUSLY WALKS down the train tracks back toward Pakal-Ná. She wonders if she will find Chino lying dead in the bushes. Are

274 | SOLDIERS AND KINGS

Bin Laden and the Breadman now looking for her? She turns a corner and sees a group of people forming several hundred meters away. A police siren starts to get closer. She is too scared to approach.

Jesmyn: I've never felt fear like that, so I stayed away from the crowd and watched from a distance. I didn't want to get close if the police were there. I was worried that Bin Laden would think I called them and then he would try to kill me. As I was standing there watching the crowd, a girl I knew saw me and came running. She said, "Your boyfriend is down there. Go to him. He is asking the police where you are." In that moment I knew that if he was talking he might be okay, so I was relieved. Then I heard an ambulance and I was sure that he was alive, so I ran home and grabbed some of our stuff and went back outside. But as soon as I left the house, I got a bad feeling. I felt something and got worried and then didn't want to walk on the tracks again. Something felt really off, so I took the long way to get to the center of Pakal-Ná where all the taxis are. I ran into one of the Guatemalans that was there when Chino got attacked and I told him I needed to get a taxi to the hospital. I told him we should avoid the tracks. We started walking and I could tell he was scared. We turned a corner and that's when we saw Bin Laden and the Breadman coming towards us.

I was so angry. I really wanted to do something to them. I was so pissed, and at that point I had no fear anymore. I was so angry that I had to do everything I could to control myself. It was in that moment that I wished I had the power to destroy them. The Guatemalan guy got scared when we saw

Xibalba | 275

them coming and he crossed the street. I whispered to him to not be afraid and I just kept walking toward them. I showed no fear.

The Breadman stops her. "What's up?" he asks.

"Nothing," she coldly responds.

The two men eye the backpack and bag of clothes she is carrying.

"Is that son of a bitch dead?" the Breadman asks.

"I don't know. I don't know anything," she replies.

"Well, if he is not dead and is in the hospital, we are going to go there and finish the job."

Jesmyn: I wasn't sure if I was mad at them or happy that Chino was alive.

I just looked at them and they could see that I wasn't afraid. They started asking me where everyone else was. I said that I had no idea. At this point, the Guatemalan guy was on the other side of the street and they said to him, "We don't want to see you around here anymore. If we do, we will kill you." Then the two of them started giving me hard looks like they hated me. I think it made them mad that I wasn't acting afraid. I wouldn't show them any fear and they hated that. So then they started trying to sweet-talk me, especially the Breadman, who always liked me. He started talking to me like nothing had happened. He was saying stuff like, "You have such pretty eyes. You are going to have beautiful kids. Why would you be with someone as ugly as Chino? That guy is garbage. You know he has AIDS, right?" They were trying to get a rise out of me and I just kept brushing them off. I said, "I have no idea what you are talking about. I have to go."

They wanted me to take them back to my house, but I knew I had to get out of there. There aren't a lot of streets in Pakal-Ná that you can use to escape. I thought that they might catch me on one of those small streets and stab me and leave me to die. My mind was running crazy thinking about those things, about what had happened to Chino and what could happen to me next. In that moment I couldn't say anything. I felt like the most voiceless woman in the entire world. I finally just walked away from them and headed to the center of Pakal-Ná where the taxi stand is. I thought that they were going to follow me. I was scared, but I couldn't wait there. I had no choice but to go. Whatever was going to happen was God's will. I just knew I needed to find Chino.

Jesmyn flags down a taxi and heads toward downtown Palenque. By now, darkness has settled over the town as she walks around the central plaza clutching her bags. The place is full of people waiting for a nearby concert to start. She approaches a police officer and tells him she is looking for a friend who has just been hospitalized.

"Which hospital is he in?" the cop asks.

"I'm not sure. How many are there?" she replies.

"Palenque has three. If you want, I can give you a ride to each one until we find your friend."

Once again, Jesmyn gets a bad vibe. It's dark and she's a Honduran woman in a small town in Mexico with no papers. The officer gets visibly annoyed when she politely declines his offer. She quickly heads down the street and hails a taxi. "How many hospitals are there in Palenque?" she asks the driver.

"There's only one," he tells her. "Do you want me to take you there?"

As she drives toward Chino, she wonders what would have happened to her had she accepted that free ride.

Escape

As soon as Jesmyn confirms with the front desk that Chino has been admitted to the hospital, she approaches the security guard at the entrance. "There is a Honduran guy with a stab wound that they just brought in," she tells him. "If someone comes looking for him or his girlfriend, please don't let them in. He has no family around here and should have no visitors. Please don't tell anyone where we are." The guard assures her that they will be safe.

When she enters his room, she sees Chino laid out on a bed with numerous bandages, tubes, and sensors attached to his half-naked body.

> **Jesmyn:** When I saw him, his eyes were closed. I thought that maybe he was in a coma. But then I got closer and I think he could sense I was there. I got close and he opened his eyes. He looked at me and said, "I didn't think you were going to come." That's when I started crying. I couldn't hold it in anymore. I was so happy that he was alive, but I was also sad at the same time. I kept telling him he needed to rest and not talk. He was on a lot of painkillers, but he wouldn't stop talking to me. He just wanted to talk.

278 | SOLDIERS AND KINGS

For nine days, Chino and Jesmyn sit in his hospital room making plans for the future. The nurses pump him full of saline and donated blood. They feed him oxygen to help with his labored breathing while they drain fluids from his punctured lung. They kindly let Jesmyn sleep in his room as long as the two of them promise not to screw around. When the nurse says this, it makes her blush. For all of her toughness, Jesmyn is a churchgoing young woman who would never think to act inappropriately in such a place. Chino keeps the mood light with his incessant joking about having to wear a diaper and use a catheter. He makes all the nurses laugh with his potty humor. By his second day in the hospital, he is feeling better. He calls me and texts photos of his injuries. "Jason, look what the Breadman and others did to me," he says. "They tried to kill me."

I ask him how I can help and he reassures me that Grupos Beta, the wing of the Mexican government charged with assisting migrants, is going to cover his medical bills and his bus ride home.

"Can I call you back on this number to check in with you later?" I ask.

"Don't call me. I'll call you," he says. "I stole this phone from a security guard, so I keep the ringer off so that he doesn't figure out I have it."

"*Pinche Chino,*" I say as we both laugh over the phone.

As his condition improves, he and Jesmyn get more serious about the next steps. They call their families to discuss their plans to leave Chiapas and start over someplace else. Maybe Chino can go back to building houses. Maybe he can even build a little house of their own. They hold hands and pray. Chino talks to Jesmyn about love and God and new beginnings. He speaks to her with a kindness that she finds rare. "In Honduras, a lot of men speak roughly to women," she tells me. "There are a lot of *machistas* who yell and beat women and then don't expect them to fight back. Chino never yelled at me. He never treated me poorly. Even when he would get mad at me, he would just stay quiet and then later apologize. He said that I reminded him of his sister Marina."

Xibalba | 279

At one point Chino thought he was the one saving Jesmyn from Sombra and whatever was waiting for her at the end of the train tracks. As he ponders a new future from his hospital bed, he begins to rethink who is saving whom. He tells Jesmyn, "I thank God for putting you in my life and putting me on a different path."

A few days before Chino is discharged from the hospital, Jesmyn strikes up a conversation in the hallway with a Honduran patient who has been brought in handcuffed by the police. She explains what has happened and why she is there. The prisoner listens to her story and then hands her 500 lempiras [$20]. "I saw this act of kindness as a sign from God that he wanted us to go home," Jesmyn recalls. Forty-eight hours later Chino is bandaged up and holding a bottle of ibuprofen as he stares at the passing Mexican countryside through the window of a bus headed south.

He is banged up and frail but feeling happy. The photos Chino sends me from his journey home show him smiling and wearing new clothes. He has lost some weight in the hospital and is looking forward to fattening up on some home-cooked meals at his grandmother's house. At a bus terminal in Puerto Barrios, Guatemala, Jesmyn and Chino strike up a conversation with a Honduran woman and her child who are headed north. "Once you get into Mexico, take a *combi* if you can," Chino tells her. "The roads are very dangerous. It's ugly out there. It's not like it used to be. Please be careful." As he says these words, he gently touches the woman's son on his shoulder and tries to reassure the child that everything will be okay.

When the bus pulls away, Chino remarks to Jesmyn, "After all this, I just want to start over. I want to erase everything and begin again. I know where the Breadman lives in Honduras. I could go to where his family is and pay him back, but his family doesn't deserve revenge and I don't want to retaliate. I don't even want to talk about it anymore." The two of them fall asleep as they make their way back to Honduras and new beginnings.

CHAPTER NINETEEN

"We Aren't Playing"

I 've been back in the States only a few weeks and I can already tell something is wrong with Kingston. We have parted ways so that I can return to teaching classes at my university. It is difficult to leave him, especially knowing the economic problems he has and the looming danger he is in. We part on good terms, but I can tell he feels like I am abandoning him. I am leaving him behind like practically everyone else he has ever known. But I have to return to work, and being with Kingston has proven expensive for me. Over the many months we were together, I found myself paying for a whole range of things. I covered the cost of transporting his murdered nephew's body from northern Mexico all the way back to Honduras. I bankrolled his failed attempt to start a food stand out of his apartment. I also occasionally paid for some of his day-to-day expenses, including food and his phone bill.

It is standard practice for anthropologists to compensate the people they work with in various ways, including cash, gifts, and the formation of social bonds (e.g., becoming a godparent to someone's child). After more than a decade of doing ethnographic fieldwork on migration, I have developed my own set of rules on how to dispense money and resources so that people feel adequately compensated for the time and information they share with me and so that I don't feel like I am being taken advantage of. In general, I try to pay more than a fair wage if I am taking up someone's time that they could be using to work a regular job. This was often not the case with smugglers, whom I tended to interview when they were on the clock and hence were already making money. In these instances, my contribution was usually in the form of things like food and phone credit.

Working with migrants, I have found that people are hesitant to ask for money, and I often have to insist that they let me pay them for their time. Smugglers, on the other hand, have no trouble constantly asking for cash. This makes sense given that a key part of their job is fostering relationships of negative reciprocity with their clients. In other words, get as much money out of someone today because you don't know if you will see them tomorrow. That being said, I created a lot of boundaries with smugglers regarding how much I would give and when I would compensate them for working with me. I wanted to be viewed not as a client but rather as someone who was invested in maintaining a long-term relationship with them. I made it clear that I could be relied on in emergencies, but I didn't want to be viewed as an endless supply of cash. These boundaries seem to have worked well with everyone except Kingston.

With Kingston, things are different and it's partially my fault. With him, it's like I've completely forgotten all of my own rules. I've become a pushover and practically open my wallet whenever he asks, which is often. For some reason, I find it hard to say no to him even when I know he is using me. But I can't help it. He's charismatic and likable, and when things are good, I love being around him. I've gazed into his difficult past and I feel for him. I also know that he is always on the verge of going back to a lifestyle that can land him in jail or the morgue. I want him to find something better and more peaceful than the violent world he was brought up in. Foolishly, I feel like I can help him stay away from danger. Sometimes I think I am being overly nice to Kingston to make up for my own feelings of guilt for my privileged position. Sometimes I think I'm too afraid of him to say no. I have created a relationship in which he thinks I can solve all his problems, and maybe I do too. This situation is not a good place for me mentally, so I am slightly relieved to get away from him for a little while.

The thousands of miles that now separate us give me some perspective on the relentlessness of his requests for money that begin only a week after we part ways. We exchange text messages almost daily. Our interactions revolve around his paranoia that someone is after him, how broke he is, and a series of catastrophes that may or may not be of his own invention. First, he tells me that he is being chased out of Mexico: "*Mira, mano*, I am at the border and it's really *caliente*. I can't stay here long, brother. I have $200 but need $500 to get across the river. I gotta get out of here." His message comes late at night and I don't see it until the following morning. I call and ask what is happening. He then tells me he is not at the border but is actually in Mexico City and wants to buy a plane ticket to fly north. He just needs me to send him $150 for the ticket and another $300 to get across the river. I suspect he is on a drug bender given the timing of the calls and the sound of his voice. When I tell him I can't send money to pay for his crossing, he stops texting. A week later he calls and says that a family member has been killed in the United States and he wants to send money to help pay for the burial. His call is accompanied by a series of gruesome photos of a young black man in a coffin. I remind him that I previously sent a significant amount of cash to repatriate his nephew's body back to Honduras, and as much as I want to help, I can't keep paying for funerals. Still, against my better judgment, I wire him a little bit of money.

Two days later he calls and says he is getting ready to cross the border by himself to get away from people who are after him. Is he really being chased, or is this drug-fueled paranoia? It's unclear. I wish him luck. Three days later he calls and says he needs help. He is now moving a group of migrants,

"We Aren't Playing" | 283

even though he swore many times that it is too dangerous for him to be on the train tracks.

> **Kingston**: Hey, *hermanito*. Good morning. I'm sending this message to see if you can do me a favor. Listen, man, I need $40 because I'm in trouble. I got people with me, but I can't do nothing because their family is pulling some bullshit and haven't sent no money. I gotta eat and I got babies with me. [*A baby cries on cue in the background.*] I apologize, but please send me money if you can. At least $20 or $30 just to eat. Last night, someone tried to get me. I'm trying to get to Piedras Negras. Even $10 would be great.

I tell him I can't send any money right now. He says he understands. The next day his pleas increase in frequency. He sends a barrage of messages: *I need money to put credit on my phone. I need money to eat. I need money to buy a bus ticket. Someone is after me. I need money to get away. $20. $30. $50. Send what you can, hermano.* I feel my cortisol levels spike every time he texts me. Is he really in trouble? If something bad happens to him, will it be my fault for not helping enough? I start keeping my phone on silent. His unheard messages pile up. I start to think that what I am feeling is potentially similar to how families of his clients must feel when he squeezes them for more and more money to deal with the real and fabricated expenses and calamities that happen on the migrant trail. I remind myself that fleecing clients is something that Kingston does very well. I have become a client. I stop replying to him. A few weeks later, things ramp up when he starts sending voice messages via WhatsApp.

> **Kingston**: Jason, Jason, Jason. Good morning, brother. Look, I'm having a little problem with this guy here. I need

you to call Andy and Snoop. Call all the guys. Tell them they have me. [*Someone mumbles in the background and Kingston speaks to them.*] Give me a chance, *loco*. I'm just trying to talk to my friend. I need to explain to him what is happening so he can call my family. [*Someone grabs the phone and starts yelling at me.*]

Kidnapper: *Oye, güey*, we are from the Mara Salvatrucha and we have been looking for this *cabrón* for a long time! Now we finally have him. We are going to kill him if you don't respond. We are going to send you a video right now to show you what is happening.

If this had occurred early in the course of my fieldwork, I probably would have sent these assholes money without even thinking. But after so many years of documenting the ways that smugglers swindle clients and their families, I have become overly suspicious of everyone, including some of the people I work closely with. I try to imagine what is happening to Kingston at that moment. I then remember a story he told me many times about being kidnapped in northern Mexico.

Kingston: Once, these dudes grabbed me and some people that I was moving. They locked us in a room and tried to get money from my family. All I had to do was make a phone call to my bosses and I was out of there in just a few hours. The people that had me started to apologize once they figured out who I was and who I worked for. That's the only time I've ever been kidnapped.

Kingston trying to sound afraid on the phone is unconvincing and uncharacteristic given all I know about him. It's also strange that he is asking

"We Aren't Playing" | 285

me to call Andy and Snoop, soldiers who are usually more broke than he is. Plus, he has their numbers. Why isn't he calling them? I send a voice message back to his kidnappers telling them that none of Kingston's friends are answering their phones. The kidnappers call back twice. I don't answer, so they start leaving voice messages, which sound like they are reading from a poorly written script.

> **Kidnapper 1**: We have Kingston. We need you to contact all of his family so that they can send 500 pesos, I mean $500. If not, we are going to kill him right now . . . If you want some video proof, we will send it.

Someone else gets on the phone.

> **Kidnapper 2**: *¿Qué pedo, güey?* What's up, *maricón?* I'm gonna send this faggot back to you piece by piece if I don't get my fucking money. I need my fucking money, *puto.*

Then Kingston sends a voice message. "Jason, do me a favor and call Priest and Snoop and tell them these niggas got me."

I hear a voice yell at him, "Hurry up, faggot!"

Kingston's voice is desperate: "Please, man, just call those motherfuckers. Please. Please. Please."

In the background it sounds like someone is hitting him.

> **Kingston**: [*Speaking to a kidnapper*] *Tranquilo*, brother. Jason, listen, man. They got me and they trying to do some dirty shit to me. These niggas is crazy. [*His breathing gets heavy.*] They crazy, but they gave me a chance to call you so that I can try and get what they are asking for. My family

sent like $100 dollars. I just need like $400 more. I gotta pay these niggas because like they said, they gonna kill me! Please talk to my people for me!

Kingston immediately sends another voice message, but now the amount the kidnappers are asking for has changed from $500 to $1,500 and he has miraculously come up with $1,000.

Kingston: Tell Snoop that they want $1,500. I found $1,000. I just need $500 more, brother. That's what they are asking for. [*His voice cracks as if he is crying.*] We are missing $500. Call those niggas. Tell them to sell all my stuff, my plasma TV and whatever else they can to get the money.

I try to remain calm and send a voice message back.

Jason: Kingston, I called Snoop but he didn't answer.

Kingston: Snoop ain't going to do nothing. He is on the street begging for money. I called him but he says he has nothing. Brother, they have me. Please help. They are only giving me like half an hour more and then they are gonna make a video. [*His breathing gets heavy again.*] Oh man, I gotta make things right or they will make a video with me. They already got me fucked up. See if my people can send me another $250.

In a matter of minutes, the amount he owes has gone from $400 to $500 to $1,000, then down to $250. I can't keep track of the evolving debt. I call back to tell him none of his friends are answering their phones. I then receive the video his kidnappers have been threatening to make. It shows

"We Aren't Playing" | 287

Kingston lying on a concrete floor surrounded by dirty clothes and an electric fan. He is barefoot with his hands and feet loosely tied. His pants are falling down, exposing his boxer shorts. Two men in hooded sweatshirts halfheartedly kick him a few times. It is clear that they are not kicking very hard. Kingston asks them to stop, but he can't help but crack a sly grin. He thinks this shit is funny. I wonder how high he must be to make this video and believe it will be convincing. One of the men leans down with a giant kitchen knife as if he is going to stab him in the face. He then suddenly turns to the camera and says, "Turn that shit off." The video lasts eight seconds.

The acting is so bad it's comical. I don't imagine anyone taking it seriously as a threat on a person's life. What makes it even more unconvincing is the fact that despite being hooded, the assailants' hands are visible, making it clear that both men are black. Given the tight-knit Garifuna community in Mexico, it is hard to believe they would be doing this to one of their own, especially someone as notorious as Kingston. I watch the video over and over. Part of me thinks it's ridiculous and laughable. Another part of me is angry that Kingston would resort to these tactics to extract money from me. But I can't really blame him. He is desperate for cash, and in his world this type of extortion is a well-worn strategy. I don't respond to the video, so the "kidnappers" start sending more voice messages.

> **Kidnapper:** All right, *güey*. We have $150, but you still owe us $250. You want to see another fucking video? You want us to cut his dick off? We are going to send you a name to wire the money to. We aren't playing, *culero*.

I send one final voice message.

> **Jason:** I don't have the money, but I will call his friends and see if they can help.

Kidnapper: All right, tell them I'm not playing. If nobody sends the money, we are going to fuck him up.

I put my phone on silent and go for a long walk to clear my head. A few days later Kingston sends a voice message on WhatsApp.

Kingston: Hey, Jason. Holla back.

Jason: What happened?

Kingston: Look, man, those guys grabbed me in Piedras Negras and fucked me up. They tortured me for three days. I'm going to send you some photos. It's a miracle they didn't do more damage. [*He never sends the photos.*] I finally got the money and thank God they let me go. Now I'm trying to get out of here. Can you send me $25 so that I can get a bus ticket?

THINGS SOUR between Kingston and me after the fake kidnapping. We stay in sporadic contact, but it often takes numerous messages from him before I feel too guilty not to respond. I just don't have the energy to keep up with his evolving problems, and most of the time when he calls, it is only to ask for money. I try to be there for him, but it becomes harder to do over the phone. He starts talking more and more about being persecuted. He can't go home to Honduras, and Mexico is growing increasingly dangerous. "I'm done with this gang shit," he says. "But people don't believe that and they are looking for me. I might turn myself in to the Border Patrol to get away from them."

There are long periods of time where I don't hear from Kingston. Then I

"We Aren't Playing" | 289

will receive out-of-the-blue updates from new phone numbers. *¿Qué onda, carnal? What's up, my lost brother? Where are you?* People are still after him. He is still trying to get away. He is running from his violent past but also from himself. He dreams of a reinvention somewhere in the United States, far away from gang life. Maybe Arkansas or Miami or New Orleans. I start to run away from him. I feel guilty as I watch his calls go to voicemail. I return to fieldwork in Mexico, but I keep that fact hidden from him. I avoid places where he might be and I never ask other Garifuna soldiers about his whereabouts. When people find out that he and I were friends, they give me worried or dirty looks. Sometimes they hear his name and spit on the ground. I feel better not knowing where Kingston is. In many ways, it feels like we have reached the end of our relationship. Perhaps we both extracted as much as humanly possible from each other and there is nothing healthy left between us. Maybe I've abandoned him just like everyone else in his life. Maybe I was always just a client. I have dreams sometimes of him dropping me off at a park and saying, "I have to go pick up some money and then I'll get you across." In those dreams he never comes back. I wonder if that's how he feels about me.

CHAPTER TWENTY

Temptation

The words roll off his forked tongue and poison the air. A devil's whisper. "I've got a job for you, Santos," he says. "It's a fucking badass job that I know you can do." This is how the beginning of the end starts. The seduction of desperate young people looking for a way out. Predators peddle hope and prosperity to those who are unsure if they will see the other side of thirty. They offer fast money and power that materializes from flashes of gunpowder and screams for mercy. Profitable violence that becomes addicting and then unsustainable. This new life could be your life. No more sleeping outside. No more feeling like the whole world is shitting on you. No more feeling powerless and unimportant. This could be the real deal. It's only a few months of dirty work until you can save up enough money and then walk away clean. The devil whispers to him, "I know you've got the balls to do this type of work."

Santos thinks about his life up to this point and the continuous cycle of crushing poverty and loss. Hand to mouth and fists to head. Blades inscribing nightmares onto brown bodies. Too many young men like him running for their lives. Too many young men like him no longer drawing breath because they talked out of turn or just had a run of bad luck. He sees his many

Temptation | 291

possible futures through a kaleidoscope: he clings to a screaming freight train, he bangs his head against cell bars, he opens his palms to receive tossed coins from a stranger. All he really wants is to lay his head on a soft pillow and for a little while dream of worlds free of panic and madness. He turns down the offer to join a cartel: "*No, viejo*, I can't do it. I already know too much about the things you are asking me to get into. I've already lived that life. I know what you're offering me and I just can't do it."

THE AIR-CONDITIONING UNIT jammed into the roughly cut window is working overtime to combat the triple-digit heat that makes Mexicali an inferno in June. The room is dark and cool. We only know it's eleven a.m. because we are blinded every time someone opens the front door and lets in the midday sun. Santos sits on a wobbly chair in basketball shorts and a tank top. He has grown his hair out and now has a long black ponytail sticking out the back of a baseball cap. We lazily sip beers fished out of a paint bucket full of ice water as he describes what happened to him after we last parted ways. "I was living here in Mexicali with these guys I knew from Honduras. They got caught up with *la mafia*. They kept trying to convince me to join them, but I knew better. I knew what they were offering, and it wasn't good. Somehow they convinced my brother Marvin to go with them."

Marvin had always been the family's rock. The mature one. The voice of reason. The oldest of six children who became the de facto patriarch after they put Santos's father in the ground.

> **Santos:** Marvin was still in the army when our dad died. I
> remember him coming home for the funeral in his military
> uniform. He was only twenty-three at the time, but he took
> care of everything. In many ways, he became my father. He

292 | SOLDIERS AND KINGS

started taking care of all of us. I remember him always giving me money and buying me toys. We had been close but became even closer when our dad died.

After serving almost ten years of a distinguished military career, Marvin leaves the army and starts a family. He finds work in an American-owned factory in Honduras that helps him provide for his wife and young child while also supporting his mother and siblings when possible. The money Marvin earns while working for the Americans is not much, but at least it's stable and less dangerous and demanding than the military had been. For years, he scrapes by at the factory and tries to look out for Santos even when his baby brother is off riding trains across Mexico. It is Marvin who cobbles together the money to get Santos a Mexican lawyer to reexamine his case. It is Marvin who saves Santos from having to serve forty-nine months in prison. The older brother has come through for him in ways that no one else ever has. So when Santos is deported back to Honduras after his stint in prison, he feels like he owes Marvin for saving his life. This is why, when his brother tells him that his marriage is in ruins and he wants to try his luck in Mexico, Santos agrees to guide him north.

Mexican drug cartels have two types of preferred recruits: impressionable teenagers they can mold into young soldiers, and well-trained ex-military personnel who can be motivated with cash to do dirty work. Marvin had never been involved in gangs or criminal activity in Honduras. He is so straitlaced and serious that the *mareros* in his neighborhood respect him and keep their distance. They leave him alone because he is one of those quiet military men who is committed to protecting his family. He gives the impression that he is not to be messed with, which is close to the truth. But Marvin doesn't have much experience on the streets, nor does he fully comprehend what he is getting into. As Santos remarks, "My brother had been in the army and was well trained, so I think he thought it would be easy. He

Temptation | 293

thought it would be simple to get in and do the things the cartel wanted and then he could get out clean. But it didn't go as planned."

Brotherhood

It is ironic that none of the bullets that shatter the windows or rip through the truck's door kill him. Instead, one of those stray projectiles pierces a flash grenade Marvin is wearing on his tactical vest. It sets off an explosion in the cabin of the vehicle that scorches a significant percentage of his body. Flames run up his arms and back and across his face. His skin peels off like layers of an onion. When he texts Santos images of his heavily bandaged body and head, he is unrecognizable. The brother who had saved his life now seems to be on death's door, another casualty of Mexico's drug war. "I have a feeling that I'm going to die," Marvin tells Santos from an undisclosed location in northern Mexico. "I don't think I am ever going to get out of here. Please come see me," he begs. "Please come say goodbye."

Maybe it's because Marvin has been a loyal soldier, or maybe it's because someone wanted to grant a dying man's last wish to say goodbye to his family, but for whatever reason, the cartel agrees to let Santos see his brother. This sets off a chain of events that could have been pulled from a telenovela.

> **Santos:** The cartel called me and told me to go to a particular train station and they would come for me. I got to the station and waited. A truck picked me up and then we drove for several hours to an airstrip. Then they put me on a little airplane and flew to a small town up in the mountains where my brother was. They had him in a house with a private doctor.

The cartel had their own doctors to take care of their soldiers. That's how I ended up in the mountains working on a farm.

At the time this was all happening, Santos and I were in contact via phone. He began sending me photos of himself working in agricultural fields and corralling horses. The COVID-19 pandemic had just started and I was concerned about his potential exposure to the virus. He kept reassuring me that he was fine and that the community he was in had a low risk of exposure. Little did I know that he was living in one of the many remote villages in northern Mexico that are completely controlled by drug cartels—places where no one comes or goes without permission. Places far beyond the reach of any governmental control. Santos didn't reveal that information until much later, when it was safe to do so.

AT FIRST, NO ONE EXPECTS Marvin to survive. But after a month it becomes clear that he is on the mend. Santos is constantly by his bedside playing the role of nurse as he helps his brother heal and regain movement. Although severely disfigured by the explosion, Marvin is back on his feet in seemingly record time. In just a few months he is well enough to start preparing to go back to work. It is at this point that Santos begins asking about arrangements to return to Mexicali, where he has been renting a room and doing construction work for the last few years.

Jason: How long were you on that farm?

Santos: I was there for like six months. I was trapped up there and they wouldn't let me go. I kept asking them to take

Temptation | 295

me home, but the boss told me I couldn't leave. I said, "Why not? I don't work for you guys. I was just here to visit my brother." They told me that I had seen too much of their business and that if I tried to escape I would have problems. One guy said to me, "If you try to leave, we will kill you."

Jason: What were you doing for those six months?

Santos: After they threatened to kill me, I tried to be nice to them. I tried to do whatever they asked of me. I started working in their fields picking fruits and vegetables. They have their dirty business up there, but they also have their regular business, and so I just got to work doing the regular stuff. Remember when I told you I was working on a *rancho*? That's what I was doing. I was working for them.

Jason: You know, I kept wondering what the hell you were doing on some ranch in the middle of nowhere. I was having a hard time picturing you as a farmer.

Santos: [*Laughing*] I started working for them and didn't complain. I did whatever they asked me to do. I'm not someone who likes to be lazy, so I was always moving around. When they saw that, they started to appreciate me. They said, "This *cabrón* is a real hard worker." They started to like me. I tried to be good and not cause problems, but they still kept telling me I could never leave. My brother started to get better. He began reminding them that I was there to see him and not to work. This is when things started to get tense.

THE EXTENSIVE BURNS across Marvin's face make him look perpetually menacing. But it's not the facial disfigurement that is unsettling. It's the quiet and assured tone of his threats. "You don't want to test me," he says. "You don't want to make problems. You can kill me and my brother, but I promise that I am going to kill a lot of you first. You can kill me, but not before I get at least five or ten of you."

"You seem so sure about what you're saying. How can you be so confident?"

"As long as I have a gun in my hand, you will die too."

"Look, you're going to have to work it out with the boss. I'm going to have to call him."

"I don't care. Get on your radio and call whoever you want. You are the ones who are going to have problems if you don't let Santos leave. My brother didn't come because he wanted to. He is here because I asked him to come. He came here to say goodbye."

"Yeah, but you know the rules. Once you're here, you can never leave. He has seen all of our business and knows our movements."

"Santos is my brother and he won't say anything. He sees this stuff, but he doesn't care. He lives far away from here. He doesn't know anything about this place, nor does he want to. He came to see me and not all the dirty shit you are doing up here."

They call in the *comandante* to deal with Marvin's request. He makes one final plea for Santos's release, coupled with a dark promise.

"Please let my brother leave. He came because I asked him to, not because he wants to work for you. He came to check on me, to see how I am. I will stay here because this is my home. I will die here, but please just let him leave."

A few days later Santos is running along a slow-moving train headed toward Mexicali. He reaches out for something to grab hold of that will take him far away.

Dancing with the Devil

Months after he is released from the farm, Santos and I are in the house in Mexicali that he shares with a rotating cast of migrants who come through on their way to the United States. He cohabitates with a mix of Mexican and Honduran men who might find local work in construction or landscaping for a few months until they can save up enough money to attempt a border crossing. Santos is one of the few in the group who has not tried to migrate to the United States in recent times. Instead, he has chosen to commit himself long-term to backbreaking manual labor in the punishing Sonoran heat. Aside from his six-month stay with the cartel, he has spent the last couple of years trying to make a go of it in Mexicali. He has watched his friends stay in the house for a few weeks or months before entering the desert on foot. Some have made it. Others have found themselves back in Honduras only to start the journey all over again. Santos desperately wants to get to the United States, but he is also fearful of detention and deportation. The thought of being incarcerated again is enough to make him gun-shy.

Still, he makes periodic trips to different parts of the border to scout a potential crossing attempt. In one video he sends me from Los Algodones in Baja California, he pans across the unfinished border wall. In the distance a group of migrants are being chased by the Border Patrol. In another, he strikes up a conversation with an immigration agent through slats in the fence. These videos are painful reminders of just how close he comes to finding that new life he desperately wants. But each time he stares into the desert, he thinks about his previous trips through that hellscape and the young *catracho* on death's door that his fellow drug mules wanted to leave behind. He imagines his mother weeping for a son who disappears and is never heard from again. He remembers the drug mule who told him that he was too soft and not capable of doing the bad things required to make it. Maybe that person was right. But that's okay. He doesn't want to give any more of himself away to the darkness. For now, he is content to move cinder blocks under a fiery sun instead of carrying tightly packed bales of marijuana on his back. The work he does in Mexicali is honest, and he feels good about it. This is home for now.

Santos's phone rings. It's Marvin on the line. "Happy birthday," he says to his older brother. "Did you get the 500 pesos I sent you? Okay, good. Use that money to buy a birthday cake and some sodas. My friend Jason, the gringo, is here. We were just talking about you."

Santos hands me the phone, and Marvin and I exchange pleasantries. I wish him a happy birthday and ask if I can come visit. "Yes, please," he says. "You can come see me whenever you want." Marvin is right; he has plenty of time now. Right after Santos escaped the cartel, his brother jumped back into the fire. Today he is celebrating the first of at least twenty birthdays he will have behind bars while serving time in Mexico for murder. In the end, he kept his promise to the cartel that he would continue to be a good soldier.

The life Santos has carved out in Mexicali is not easy. His situation is perpetually precarious, and work is sporadic because he is undocumented. His movements are all well planned because one stop by a Mexican immigration official can land him right back in prison. But he's currently not begging for change at a streetlight and doesn't worry about someone smashing his head in with a brick while he sleeps on the tracks. He's not living his American dream. But he is also not living the nightmare that characterized almost a decade of being on the streets and locked up. The only fight he is interested in these days is the fight to keep going in hopes that tomorrow brings something better.

He extracts another beer from the paint bucket and begins to shake his ass to Plan B's "Fanática sensual." His roommates and I laugh and cheer him on. It's been many years since I first watched him dance to this song in the jungles of Pakal-Ná. He is older and wiser now but also wearier. However, for a moment it feels like we have time traveled and things are going to be okay. This world still has time left in it to be optimistic and hopeful. There is time to keep dancing in the living room of a dilapidated house on a dusty street less than fifteen kilometers from the United States. This moment reminds me of something Santos once said about working for the *maras* and the cartels: "It's like the devil has a gun and is shooting at your feet to make you dance. You have to keep dancing as long as those bullets are flying, because once you stop, he puts a slug in your chest."

CHAPTER TWENTY-ONE

The Future Belongs
to Those Who Dream

The first explosion scares the shit out of me. I look over just in time to see Flaco lighting off a second firework and tossing it out the car window. "Hahaha!" he screams in delight. I'm driving around with a goddamn oversized Dennis the Menace, but obviously I think it's funny and start laughing. "Play some music," he says. "Play some 2Pac. Play 'Dear Mama.'" A thick bass drum and sharp rim clicks come out of the car's speakers. *If you can make it through the night, there's a brighter day.*

Much has changed since the last time I saw Flaco. He looks a lot rougher around the edges. Bags under his eyes. Deep wrinkles on his face. A few missing teeth. Hardship has sped up the aging process, making him appear much older than he is. He is also the most broke I've ever seen him. "Let's get some beers, foo," he cackles. "I haven't had a beer in like a month because of the new baby. All my money goes to diapers." The last time I saw him in person he was overly concerned about the welfare and future of his then five-year-old son. That child and his mother fled to the United States to seek asylum soon after Hurricanes Eta and Iota battered Central America. Flaco is now in Chiapas with a new teenage Honduran bride and a three-week-old baby girl. "Let's take a ride and I'll show you around," he says.

We begin cruising through Tapachula, a midsize industrial town less than twenty kilometers from the Guatemala border. One of the first things one notices is that the place is populated with thousands of Haitian refugees. In most parts of Mexico, it's rare to see a black person. In Tapachula, they are practically everywhere: selling bottled water and sodas in the central plaza, standing in line at banks waiting for money wires, sitting on street corners and park benches waiting for something to happen. To get here, many of these folks crossed the Caribbean and traveled for months up from South America. They then had to evade immigration checkpoints on the main roads from Guatemala. To capitalize on this, enterprising Mexican smugglers now offer half-hour rides through the jungle on the back of motorcycles for $100. Where there is desperation, there is a profit to be made.

On our way out of town, we pass a soccer stadium with a parking lot crowded with hundreds of migrants waiting in an enormous line for bus tickets. The Mexican government has offered to transfer them for free to another part of the country where they can attempt to fix their immigration papers. It's unclear exactly where they go. Over the last several months, thousands of Haitians have slept in this parking lot for days and weeks at a time, and it shows. Plastic water bottles and soiled clothes are scattered everywhere. The ground is littered with the remnants of makeshift cardboard mattresses and tents made from plastic sheeting. The smell of overflowing porta-johns is thick in the air. Driving by, it feels like I am looking into a crystal ball. Masses of displaced people fleeing earthquakes, hurricanes, viruses, corruption, violence, and of course, poverty. No disrespect to my Mexican family and friends, but shit has to be pretty unbearable in one's home country if you're seeking refuge in Chiapas, the poorest state in Mexico. All this parking lot is missing is a neon sign that reads *Welcome to our global future.*

WE LEAVE TAPACHULA and head to the nearby coastal town of Puerto Chiapas to grab some beers and seafood. Flaco tells me we don't have to worry about any checkpoints because he can now legally travel across Mexico. He previously lost his humanitarian visa after being arrested on suspicion of smuggling. He proudly shows me his new Mexican residency card that an immigration agent sold him for $1,500. He is officially documented and can now come and go as he pleases. We sit down to lunch at an oceanfront *palapa*. Flaco starts slamming Modelos and talking about his current situation.

He's been holed up in Tapachula for over a year after surviving COVID and narrowly escaping back-to-back hurricanes. Mexico City and Guadalajara, once places of refuge, have become too dangerous for him. Heading to the United States is also an impossibility given his criminal record there. He would face several years in federal prison if arrested for unauthorized entry. At least in Mexico he can work legally. He might be destitute in Tapachula, but the city is relatively safe compared with his other geographic options. Even though he is largely out of the smuggling game, his reputation precedes him. If he shows up in a place like Lechería or Pakal-Ná, the assumption is that he is moving people. That assumption, even if it's incorrect, makes him a target of scrutiny for the *maras* and the cartels.

It's better to lie low in Tapachula, where he can make ends meet by doing odd jobs and occasionally transporting people from Honduras to southern Chiapas. There is also currently no *cuota* here, so for the time being he can bring migrants with little risk. "I'm not moving people like I was before," he says. "Now I just do little jobs for friends who need help getting here. It's easy because I know the routes and have a visa. I have lots of friends between Honduras and Tapachula." He has just returned this morning with a young man from his old neighborhood who had recently been shot by gang

The Future Belongs to Those Who Dream | 303

members and needed to escape. It took Flaco three days to go back and forth from San Pedro Sula. These short trips are few and far between, and he usually makes no more than a hundred dollars at a time. Still, it brings in much-needed income, and he doesn't have to be away from his family for weeks or months like before.

A lot has changed about the smuggling game in the seven years that I have known Flaco. For one, more people are migrating across Mexico and headed to the United States than ever before. For Central Americans this increase is the result of unwavering levels of violence and poverty augmented by the impacts of COVID and the displacement caused by hurricanes. Added to this mix now is a steady stream of people coming from places like Brazil, Venezuela, Cuba, and Haiti. In response, cartels have increased the price of head taxes and frequency of kidnappings. Crossing Mexico is more deadly and costly than ever before. Flaco reflects on these changes when I ask him about the old days.

Jason: Do you miss the life?

Flaco: Well, the truth is that I miss being on the streets like before. Like when you saw me in Mexicali. There was always weed, beer, women! You know how it is. It was always like, "Let's fucking do this!" [*He mimics snorting cocaine off an invisible key.*] I miss all that. Before I used to have *billete*. I was moving a lot of people. Sometimes I had like forty to sixty people on the train and was taking them all the way north. I had money then. In those days the *mareros* were only charging $100 in Palenque and the Zetas were only charging $100 in Coatza. Then it was another $100 for the *maras* in Tierra Blanca and another $100 in Orizaba to the mafia. It only cost $400 and then you could get all the way to the northern border. Those guys that you paid the *cuota* to even took care of you, but now it's different. If you don't have money, they kidnap you. Even if you do have money, they still might kidnap you. It's a lot uglier now and there's more costs. Places that used to not have *cuotas* now have them. You have to pay $100 in Huixtla and $100 in Villahermosa. You used to be able to go through those places for free. Now the mafia is even making the guides pay. Before, you could go from Honduras to Houston for $7,000. You would pay $1,000 per person to the mafia and they would let the guide pass for free. Now they want $4,000 per person to cross Mexico and they even make the guide pay. The *pollero* has to pay $4,000. Honduras to Houston now costs like $12,000 to $15,000. It's bigger money these days, so if they catch you without paying or with no cash, they will kill you. Now everything is harder and you make less *dinero*. It's more expensive for everyone. I mean, imagine having to pay $4,000 yourself just to smuggle a group. It's not worth it. But people are still willing to pay that money, and guides are still taking them. But not me, I'm done. It's been three years since I took a group all the way north.

As we eat and stare at the crashing waves of the Pacific, the topic of kidnapping comes up, another factor that led to Flaco's decision to essentially retire. He tells a story about a Garifuna guide who was recently assaulted in Veracruz and robbed of several thousand dollars.

Flaco: The *moreno* had a whole bunch of people with him in a hotel. The mafia came and kidnapped him and made him

The Future Belongs to Those Who Dream | 305

pay a shit ton of money. He thought he was all tough because he had the cash to pay them. He tried to pay them off and be on his way, but the mafia didn't care that he could cover the *cuota*. He had a lot of people in his group, so they just decided to torture him and take all his money. They cut off one of his fucking fingers with a cigar cutter, bro. It's not worth it anymore. The kidnapping and torture are too out of control. I'd rather be selling vegetables in the park than be back on the train tracks.

I show Flaco the video that Kingston sent when he tried to convince me that he had been kidnapped. He scoffs at it and then describes a recent run-in that his sister had with the cartels.

Flaco: That video of your friend is *puro show*. When they kidnapped my sister, they sent me videos where they had a knife up to her neck. It scared the hell out of me. I thought it was a joke, but then I saw it and man it was fucked up. They had her two-year-old kid. They sent me a video of my little nephew with a black plastic bag wrapped around his head and a knife to his throat. I thought they were going to kill him. I was shitting my pants. But that video you showed me is a joke. When they send real videos you know it. They send videos where they hit some *vato* in the head or the face with a machete and then blood comes out. Then you know it's real. That video you showed me is *pura mamada*. If that was real, he would have been begging and crying for help. Look, I don't even like my sister. She is an *hija de puta*. But she is still my sister, and her child is my nephew, so when they sent me those videos, I didn't have any choice but to help them get out of there. What the mafia is doing now really scares me. I'm afraid of getting kidnapped and killed.

Jason: But is it hard not to go back to all that money?

Flaco: Yeah, but it's different now because of my baby. I can't do that kind of work anymore now that I have my little daughter. I have seven other children, all of them boys, but they are all okay. It's my daughter that I really worry about. She is so little and I have to take care of her. I have to find safer work so that I can provide for her and my wife.

Flaco often talks about his other children, but it is clear that he has largely abandoned them.

The last time he went missing, I reached out to his previous partner and mother of his youngest son to ask about his whereabouts. Her response was simple: "I don't speak to him anymore. I have no idea where he is or what he is doing."

In the beginning of our relationship, when I would hear Flaco speak about how much he loved his children, I found it endearing. Now when he says things like, "My other kids are okay," I can't help but think about him repeating the cycle of parental abandonment that often leads to life on the street. It's the road that Kingston and Chino followed early in their youth that led them directly to the train tracks. Will Flaco's children end up on the same path? Will he disappear from his new baby's life in a few years? It's hard to know. I will, however, say that in Tapachula there is something different in his voice and demeanor when he talks about his daughter. Her birth seems to have already slowed his pace and discouraged him from getting back on the migrant trail. Perhaps things are different now. Maybe he is out

The Future Belongs to Those Who Dream | 307

of the game and will see his fortieth birthday. Maybe his love for this little girl will help him break the cycle of walking away from his family.

Hold on Hope

Flaco leads me through the house where he and his wife and daughter are staying. It's a run-down structure on the outskirts of Tapachula, just a few blocks away from the Río Coatán, a body of water that snakes all the way to the Pacific Ocean. There are several rooms in the front portion of the house, followed by a covered concrete patio with an outdoor bathroom and kitchen. Behind the patio is a separate building with a studio apartment currently occupied by a Haitian family. "That's where the baby sleeps," he says, pointing to a hammock hanging outside. "My wife and I sleep on the patio floor. I can't afford to pay the rent on the rooms inside, but the landlord lets us sleep out here for free because of the baby. Whenever the rooms aren't being rented, he lets us use them." I knew Flaco was living rough, but I wasn't expecting to see him this impoverished. Gone are the days of making thousands of dollars per trip and maintaining houses in Pakal-Ná, Guadalajara, and Honduras. The king of the train tracks now sleeps on the ground. There is no plasma TV, no booming stereo, no bags of cocaine. Just a cold concrete floor and a few personal possessions tucked away in a corner.

Flaco introduces me to Salvador, a Nicaraguan man who rents one of the front rooms. He has been in Tapachula for a few months and is planning to start working his way north soon. We sit on the patio as Flaco holds his new daughter and talks about his recent struggles.

> **Flaco:** It's been hard, *hermano*. I couldn't pay the rent on time
> at our last place because I had to use the money to buy stuff

for the baby. The landlord didn't care. He kicked us out the day after my daughter was born. Can you imagine that? We were lucky that the landlord here let us move in.

Jason: So what are you going to do?

Flaco: I just got to keep working. I've been helping clear land for construction projects and sometimes bringing people here from Honduras. It's not easy, but you got to do it.

Salvador: I've been telling Flaco he needs to get out of this house. He needs to get his own place so he doesn't waste money paying rent. He needs to settle down.

Flaco: Let's go to the river. I want to show you something, Jason.

FLACO UNRAVELS the rusty chain that keeps the front gate of the shanty closed. "This is my friend's place," he says as we enter the one-room shack made from salvaged scraps of wood, sheets of corrugated metal, and black plastic tarps. A fence made of chicken wire surrounds the tiny property. Two mangy dogs are tied to a pole out front. Flaco rounds up a few buckets and tree stumps for people to sit on. His wife, Susana, a quiet nineteen-year-old, gets settled in the corner and rocks the baby to sleep. Flaco seems to be on his best behavior around her. He is still loud and occasionally inappropriate when talking to others, but he speaks to her in soft tones and constantly checks to make sure she and the baby are comfortable. Earlier, at lunch, I watched him chug six beers in fifteen minutes, but now he nurses his Modelo. We sit on the patio while Flaco rolls a joint and the sun

The Future Belongs to Those Who Dream | 309

sets over the nearby river. Everything feels momentarily simple and beautiful.

Flaco: No one owns any of this property here. If you clear the land, you can build a little house and no one will bother you. You don't have to pay rent. There's a Mexican family down the way that just built a place. There are some Hondurans I know who also want to move in here.

Salvador: I keep telling Flaco that he needs to build a little house. It's smarter to buy some sheets of plywood and make something. Then you aren't wasting money paying to live in someone else's house.

Jason: Flaco, how much do you think you need to build something here?

Flaco: Maybe like $1,500. That's why I gotta keep working. No money, no honey [*laughs*].

Salvador: Flaco says you are writing a book. What's it about?

Jason: It's about the lives of *guías* and how they end up doing the job. I think most people believe that smugglers make a lot of money and that all that they do is bad stuff. But the story is not that simple. Obviously, a lot of guides do terrible things like steal from people and abuse them. But I also think that some actually try to help people. I also know that a lot of smugglers are struggling themselves. Many of them are living on the streets and have nothing.

Salvador: Well, that's true. Just look at Flaco. He's been doing that work for a long time and he has nothing. He sleeps on the floor.

Flaco nods in agreement. He stands up and tells Salvador and me to follow him to the river. The sun is disappearing over the horizon, but its final rays cast a warmth over Flaco's weary brown face. It's the golden hour, and he looks like street royalty, holding a joint in one hand and a beer in the other. Printed on his shirt is *The future belongs to those who dream*, next to a drawing of a skull. He makes gestures at the surrounding landscape like a real estate developer with grand ambitions. "I would clear this area first," he says, pointing to a patch of dirt and rubble. "Then I'd bring in a bulldozer to flatten the land and put a little house up. There's a well nearby for clean water. Over there I would plant some fruit trees. God willing, I'll build my family a home here. It could be really nice." He's right. This could be a good place to settle down. A refuge away from the train tracks and all the violence and misery and ghosts that haunt that place. Maybe he *can* build something here.

As we are talking, I get a text message from a friend in Mexico City. A tractor trailer with more than one hundred migrants inside has just crashed in Chiapas a few hours north from where we are. Fifty-four people have died. In the not-so-distant past, Flaco could have been riding shotgun and giving the truck driver directions. Jesmyn, Alma, Papo, and the kids could have been in the back. I tell Flaco the news. He shakes his head and says, "It's only getting worse."

CHAPTER TWENTY-TWO

The Soldier Who Would Be King

Chino slumps into a plastic chair and surveys his surroundings. The room is uncomfortably full, mostly with gray-haired old ladies and small children. Many of the men his age and social class are out on the streets or the train tracks, both groups chasing something elusive and often unfulfilling. He stares at the machete scars running across his arm. They have become a road map guiding him to this moment in time and space. The fingers on his right hand twitch uncontrollably, as if tapping out some secret code, perhaps an SOS. He's been asking for help his entire life. But why ask for help in a world that only abandons and disappoints? The pastor eyes the nervous young man from across the room. He knows the type all too well. Kids like him come here only when they are on the verge of something. This person has been brought to the house of God for a reason.

The pastor calls out, "Brothers and sisters, something powerful has just entered our church. I can feel it. Can you feel it? Is there someone who wants to come forward and confess?" Chino knows that the pastor is talking directly to him. He suddenly feels all of his pain and sorrow welling up inside; it's a lifetime of grief and rage that boil his blood and sometimes turn him into a monster. "Does anyone here want to confess?" the pastor repeats. Chino is suddenly on his feet as if someone or something has picked him up.

"The next thing I knew he was at the front of the church," Marina remembers in awe. "I didn't see him walk. It was as if he flew across the room. It was like he levitated."

The pastor puts his hands on the young man's shoulders and asks, "What is your name, brother?"

Chino pauses for a moment. He knows that in God's presence he must be honest. "My name is Roberto."

"Dear God, please help this young man," the pastor cries. "He has a powerful demon inside of him! Help him, Lord! Help him! Who in here is with Roberto today?" Marina raises her hand and the pastor beckons her to the front of the room. "We need you, *hermana*," he tells her. "Your brother has an evil force working on him. He needs your prayers." Chino begins to weep and tremble. He starts to release something dark from deep inside him. His aching voice fills the room as he begs God for forgiveness.

"Marina, I am burning!" he tells his sister. "I am burning! My feet are on fire!" His words and his writhing scare her, but she reaches out to give him comfort.

"I grabbed his arm and it felt like something powerful was holding on to him," she recalls. "His skin was hot to the touch and he was shaking wildly. He started testifying to all the bad things he had done in his life. He testified in a way that shocked everyone in the room."

"Demons!" the pastor yells. "Demons! He has demons inside that are stronger than him! We must pray them out!"

Tears roll down Chino's face as he pleads to the heavens for forgiveness. He promises God he will change his ways. He repents and repents and cries until he hits the point of exhaustion. He releases the darkness festering inside him. When he has nothing left to give, he quietly returns to his seat. He whispers to Marina, "Thank you for bringing me here. I feel like a burden has been lifted. I feel so much lighter now."

On their way out of church, the pastor pulls Marina aside and says, "It's

The Soldier Who Would Be King | 313

good that you brought your brother here today. The spirit of death is very strong inside of him. Your brother walks with death. It persecutes him." A few weeks after his confession, Chino will walk toward Mexico for the last time.

IT TAKES JESMYN AND CHINO three long days on buses to get from Palenque to Villanueva, Honduras, where his sister lives. Three days of rattling mufflers and ceiling-mounted TVs blasting poorly dubbed American movies. The two of them hold hands and whisper secrets as they take in the changing views outside their window. They are happy to put Pakal-Ná in the rearview mirror. They are happy to finally escape the train tracks. Honduras is still the place of insecurity and uncertainty that the two of them have been running from their entire lives. But at least they will face it together. There is hope in unity.

MARINA WELCOMES CHINO and his new girlfriend with open arms. "When I saw him," she remembers, "I was so surprised. I thanked God for bringing my brother back to me because he was different. He wasn't aggressive anymore. He was talking about having kids and getting a job and having a better future. He wasn't the person who I watched leave before. He had changed."

Chino is exhausted and pale but assures everyone that he is feeling better. He just needs time to recuperate from the knife wounds and the long bus ride. The couple plays house at Marina's for two days. They make plans to find their own place while Jesmyn starts plotting out job prospects. Chino takes restless naps and finishes what is left of the ibuprofen he brought from Mexico. "I'm okay," he keeps telling everyone. "I just need to get some sleep."

On the third day home, he takes a hot shower and then tries to change the bandages on his chest. Finally, he admits to Jesmyn that something is wrong. "I can't take it anymore," he tells her. "The pain is too much. I think I need to go to the hospital."

Being broke and sick in Honduras is often a death sentence. The closest poor people usually get to a doctor is whatever advice they can elicit from a neighbor or a pharmacist. If you are lucky, maybe you can access a free clinic. If the clinic can't treat your ailment, people will reluctantly and begrudgingly go to the public hospital, where they encounter long lines, overworked and often indifferent staff, and the wails of those close to dying. Everyone knows that the quality of care you receive is dependent on how much cash you are carrying in your pocket. This is why poor people don't go. The hospital is usually the last option.

Marina and Jesmyn bring Chino to the neighborhood Red Cross. He can barely walk or breathe. He is ghostly white and dripping with sweat. The staff take one look at him and tell the family that he needs emergency surgery right away. They pile into a taxi and head toward San Pedro Sula. Roberto starts to break down. He hugs and kisses his sister and says, "I'm bad, aren't I, Marina? I'm a bad person."

"Why would you say that?" she asks.

"I'm bad because I'm going to make our mom suffer when I die. My poor mom. Please don't tell her when I'm dead. It will kill her."

Esperando

The Honduran public hospital is the medical nightmare you might expect it to be. It is clear that Chino needs immediate attention, but the family hits a series of frustrating financial and logistical roadblocks. Marina bitterly recalls checking her brother in.

The Soldier Who Would Be King | 315

Marina: In Honduran hospitals they don't treat you like humans. They treat you like an animal. In other countries you walk through the front door and there is someone there to help you. Someone to ask what you need. Not here. When we finally saw a doctor, they just gave Roberto a saline drip. They said they needed to operate on him, but no one explained to us what was going on. They said he needed an operation, but they couldn't do it for four days. It was clear he needed surgery the day we checked him in. He had a punctured lung and couldn't breathe.

Chino struggles to draw breath and can barely move. They are in a hospital, but it feels as if the family is on their own in this living nightmare.

Marina: You wouldn't believe how bad the hospital was. No one would help us. We had to carry Roberto up three flights of stairs to his room because he couldn't walk. We had to rent a machine that cost 2,500 lempiras [$100] because his lungs weren't working. Thank God we found the money. I can't tell you how happy that little kid was once we got him on that machine. It was like God himself was giving him breath. After we got the machine, we then had to go out and buy everything else ourselves, including syringes and cotton balls. I had to find seven pints of blood before they would perform his operation. In that hospital they only cared about money, not the patients.

After securing a ventilator, Chino's condition stabilizes and everyone nervously awaits his surgery. He passes much of this time with Jesmyn and

Marina by his side. Both of them pray and speak to him about the power of God to help him heal and find a new way in life. Jesmyn begins to open up to him about her own religious beliefs.

> **Jesmyn:** In Pakal-Ná I never really talked about religion or prayed in front of him. But in the hospital I prayed so that Roberto could hear me. I was praying for him. I wanted him to hear me because he needed God more than me. I would read Psalm 91 to him.
>
> *"'Because he loves me,' says the Lord, 'I will rescue him; I will protect him, for he acknowledges my name. He will call on me, and I will answer him; I will be with him in trouble, I will deliver him and honor him. With long life I will satisfy him and show him my salvation.'"*
>
> In the hospital we talked a lot about how he was going to change. He said he was going to stop using bad words and start going to church. We had so many plans, Jason. Everything was going to turn out okay. My mom and sister were going to help us find an apartment. We were going to get jobs and live together. Everything was going to work out. He had started changing his ways and how he thought about things [*crying*]. I was happy when he found religion. He said to me, "God put me on this road that I am on. This is my opportunity to repent."

For four days, Jesmyn and Marina keep Chino company. They pray and laugh together and try to keep his spirits up. The women sleep on the floor and refuse to leave his side for longer than it takes to go to the bathroom,

The Soldier Who Would Be King | 317

grab something to eat, or chase down medical supplies. But every time Jesmyn leaves, Chino gets nervous and agitated.

> **Jesmyn:** He would get mad if I was gone too long. He would get jealous if he saw me talking to a security guard and be upset when I came back. It would make me sad, but I thought about it later and I think he always felt abandoned. His birth mother left him, and later on she loved her boyfriends more than him. I think he was suspicious of women because he had been abandoned. I think he was worried that I was going to leave him too. But he was a kind person and we were friends. I really loved him.

The family waits and waits and grows increasingly frustrated. The rotating cast of physicians they encounter are often condescending and dismissive of the family's questions and concerns. One doctor comes to the room and tells them everything is fine. Another comes in and says they need to operate soon. Every day they hear a different story. All the while, Chino writhes in pain as his lungs fill with fluid and his breathing becomes more labored. He starts to lash out at any doctor who comes within earshot. He begs Marina to take him away from this house of horrors.

"Marina, what are the doctors saying?" he asks.

"They say that you will have your surgery very soon and that you will be okay."

"No, Marina, these people are lying. Make them tell you the truth."

"Roberto, what can I do? I am asking every doctor I can for news. Some of them just ignore me. Others keep saying, 'Trust the process. You must be patient.'"

Understandably, Chino is losing patience. It's hard to trust the process

318 | SOLDIERS AND KINGS

while drowning from the inside. Marina agonizes over having to bear witness to her brother's pain and frustration.

> **Marina:** After four days he wanted to get out of that hospital. He kept saying, "Move me! Move me! Get me out of here, Marina! I'm dying in here!" I kept asking him, "What can I do?" He was screaming, "I don't want to die here! Please ask the doctors what is wrong with me. Please help me!" We were so desperate and it hurt so much to see him like that. I started wishing that I had all the money in the world so I could get him to a private clinic or make them operate on him right then. I would have done anything. I wanted to help him so bad, but we just didn't have the money. If we had 20,000 lempiras [$825] they could have operated on him right then.

At this point, it has been a week since I have had any communication with Chino or Jesmyn. Neither one of them has a cell phone, so I can't directly contact them. The last message I received from them was from a stranger's phone they borrowed in a bus station in Guatemala. I am at my house in Michigan and have no idea that at that moment Roberto is dying in a hospital because his family can't raise $825 to expedite his operation.

Four days after being admitted, Chino finally gets his surgery. For three hours, a doctor works to repair the large stab wound in his right lung that has been filling his chest with fluid. They close him up and wheel him back to his room, where his sister is waiting. He is groggy but happy and optimistic. Marina's voice quivers as she remembers this moment.

> **Marina:** At six p.m. they brought him back. *Mira*, Jason, when I saw him he looked like such a tender child lying there.

The Soldier Who Would Be King | 319

He was in his bed and had all these tubes coming out of him. He looked at me and said, "I told you that I was going to make it. I told you I would get out of this." I held his hand and he asked me if everything was going to be okay.

Chino is in a lot of pain but is still lucid enough to become angry at the doctors for their slowness. Jesmyn and Marina recall tense moments with medical staff immediately after he returns to his room.

Jesmyn: After he finally had surgery, Roberto was pissed at the doctors for making us wait so long. He started yelling, "Let's get out of here. These sons of bitches are killing people in this place! Look at how they have abandoned me in this room! They won't even give me any water!" At that point because of the operation and the medication he was on, he couldn't drink any water. He was only getting fluids through a tube. The doctors were bad, though. They kept yelling back at him, "Please stop screaming or you will rip your stitches. If you want to die, then go ahead and drink water."

Marina: By this point he had gone eight days without drinking water. All he could have was a saline drip. He was crying to me, "Marina, please give me water. Please help me! I can't take it anymore." His words hurt so bad. It felt so cruel to not be able to give him anything to drink, but the doctors said that even if we put water on his lips it could kill him.

Chino has a restless night of sleep. He struggles to draw breath while feeling as if he were dying from thirst. In the morning, his condition takes a bad turn.

Marina: He started getting worse after the operation. The next day he couldn't breathe. One of his lungs had stopped working. They did an X-ray and saw that the fluid in his chest had moved to his other lung. After the X-ray he came back to the room and was a lot worse. By that point they had to intubate him because he couldn't breathe. They didn't have a machine available, so a nurse had to manually pump air for him. They said the machine he needed would cost 50,000 lempiras [$2,000]. If I couldn't buy one, the other option was to try and rent one from an NGO, but they didn't have one available. I went to the head of the hospital and begged them, but they said I would have to wait until someone died and then they could give the machine to my brother. They gave me numbers to call to try and rent one, but we had nothing left. We had just enough to cover the small things like medicine. But I kept believing that God was going to help us find the money to rent a machine, but that didn't happen. The doctor told me, "Your brother is very frail, so I am going to be frank with you. If you don't find a machine, he is going to die."

Chino has walked with death his whole life: The sickly baby cradled by his grandmother in the back of a truck lumbering toward a free clinic in hopes that they can save his life. The teenager who dodges a bullet because he is asleep in a nearby hammock when a gunman murders his friend. The young man whose dead heart miraculously comes roaring back to life after losing so much blood on a street corner in San Pedro Sula. But you can cheat death only so many times before your luck runs out, and luck is a lot harder to come by when you are poor.

Juan Roberto Paredes, aka "Chino," is barely twenty years old when he

The Soldier Who Would Be King | 321

says goodbye to a world that has rarely been kind to him. He takes one last walk with death but is surrounded by two people who love him very much.

Marina: The last time I saw Roberto he was intubated and moaning. I kept saying, "Fight, *papito*! Fight! Don't give up. You can beat this!" He tried to hang on. We were there with a pump, manually giving him air by hand. In the end, he was just gasping for breath and the suffering he was going through was hurting me so bad. I was praying hard every day for him to live, but I also didn't want to see him like that. After a while, I couldn't bear it. I had to leave the room. I touched his face and then let go of his hand. His hand just fell to his side. I had to run out of there. I was praying in another room with Jesmyn when a doctor came in to tell us that he was gone. He died on August 21 at nine o'clock at night [*crying*].

Jesmyn: The last time I saw him, he was asking God for help and for strength. I was holding his hand and he was struggling to breathe. By then, the doctors knew he wasn't good. He was in bad shape and was getting worse. We were all praying in another room that he would get better. But at the same time, we didn't want him to suffer anymore. When the doctor came in to tell us the news, I knew what it was right when I looked at her. She told us that he was dead, and it was like a stake in my heart. The doctor said, "We did everything we could. There was nothing more we could do." I wanted to see Roberto because I didn't believe it, especially after all the things we had been through. I went to see him and I thought he was just sleeping, but he wasn't. In that moment I couldn't cry or anything. I didn't believe it. I don't know . . . It's like you're with someone and then you're not. [*She pauses for a long silence and then begins whimpering.*] I never imagined that God would have it turn out like this. I never imagined this happening. Roberto was so strong. He didn't want to die. But God knows what He is doing. I won't deny God, because He is perfect, but it hurts getting used to not seeing Roberto, to not being with him and hearing his voice. I know that I will have a better life than he did, and now I just have to do my part so that I can see him again one day when God comes for me [*Jesmyn and Jason crying*].

Even as he died a slow and painful death, Chino seemed to have found something to ease his pain.

Marina: In the hospital he asked us to pray for him. He asked me to read the Bible and sing hymnals. I even brought a pastor who he told his sins to. Roberto repented for everything. Then the pastor prayed and did the oration for reconciliation. Roberto reconciled with God. Afterward he said, "I feel better, Marina, because now God knows all that I have done, but please don't hate me." I told him that I could never hate him because I understood all the things that he had been through in the past. From then on, Roberto was able to leave all of his suffering behind. Sometimes I wonder why this happened, and other times I thank God that it is all over because in some ways Roberto is not suffering anymore. When he was alive, he suffered. When he was sick, he suffered. When he was in Mexico, he suffered. When he was with us here in Honduras, he suffered. So in some ways he is not

The Soldier Who Would Be King | 323

suffering anymore, because honestly, that was not the life that I wanted for Roberto. That was not a life I wanted for him, because all of my brothers had suffered. Now they are all gone. But in his final moments, God gave Roberto an opportunity to repent, and he went with Him in peace.

Velorio

Chino's body is sent to his parents' house for the wake. They dress him in a white shirt and black slacks and place him in a coffin outfitted with a window that exposes his shoulders and head. His puffy, waxen face is visible through the glass frame, which has a large crack across it that someone has tried to repair with packing tape. Embalming fluid has leaked out of his body, and his white shirt and the pillow under his head have a smattering of red stains. The coffin is flanked by flowers and a photo of him in the hospital smiling. As hard as it is to look at him, he has a slight grin on his face, as if he is laughing in his sleep.

The wake goes on all night. The neighbors bring food and drinks. Soft music plays in the background. Marina holds her mother's arthritic hands while trying to keep her composure. She worries that any display of her own overwhelming grief could kill the frail old woman. Jesmyn hasn't yet allowed herself to grieve but finally loses it when she sees the coffin. The tears she has been holding in for days (maybe years) come out of her at full force. The tears will come for a long time afterward as she tries to make sense of this new reality she finds herself in.

Roberto's grandfather Inocente, who is not one for displays of emotion, will break down crying as he faces the prospect of burying another child. He tells Marina, "I will stay with him as long as I can. I will stay with him until the final moments." The old man sits all night with his little boy until it is time to bury him next to his other sons.

All of Chino's wild friends come to the wake. They bring booze and revelry and shovels to dig his grave. They get shit-faced on *guaro* and scream in the street, "Chino! *¡Mi perro!* Why did you leave us!" They act out a mourning ritual that they seem to have memorized. It's a ritual that Chino himself knew all too well from having to say goodbye to his brother and the many friends he outlived in his twenty years of life. Later the young men from his neighborhood will congregate in the cemetery and cry into the night, just as they have done many times before.

CHINO IS BURIED next to Miguel, the older brother he worshipped and loved. As I sit near his grave, I envision the many nights he spent here drinking and crying and cursing God for taking Miguel away. I find some comfort in the fact that the brothers are now together forever. Chino's young nephew and niece sweep the final resting spots of their father and uncle and then lay down bunches of wildflowers they have picked. "This cemetery is filling up with the youth," Marina tells me. "The old people are getting worried that there will be no space left for them." Her parents have buried all of her brothers and two sisters in this graveyard. I look at the children playing in the grass and hope that they will find a better world than the one those around them inherited. I hope that no one will have to find room here for either one of them for a very long time.

We walk back to Roberto's grandparents' house to have lunch. Before we start eating, I tell them that I forgot something at the cemetery and will be right back. It is an excuse to have a few minutes alone at his grave. As I stare off into the green valley just below the graveyard, I suddenly find myself transported back to my bedroom in Ann Arbor, Michigan. I am looking out the window at my neighbor's perfectly manicured lawn. My bare feet are warming in a patch of August morning sun projected onto the hardwood floor. In that moment I keep hitting Play on a short voice message from Jesmyn. The message is simple and direct. "Chino is dead." She has sent a photo of him on a gurney. His mouth is covered with a ventilator. Tubes and wires radiate off his body like snakes. His *catracho* tattoo is partially visible on his left arm. He is cold and lifeless under fluorescent hospital lights. I am motionless staring at my neighbor's lawn. I have no tears yet because I am in disbelief. I think about a kid on top of a freight train smiling and flashing a peace sign. I think about a kid scared shitless in the back of my car telling me he needs to find a way out or they are going to kill him. I think about me driving away as Chino waves goodbye from the train tracks in Pakal-Ná. It doesn't matter that I know full well that the violence and poverty and murderous desperation on the migrant trail are beyond my control. The only thing that matters to me in this moment is that I left and he stayed behind.

CHAPTER TWENTY-THREE

Epilogue

Thank you for your presentation," he says. "It's obvious you were deeply impacted by Chino's death. I have a question, though, and I don't mean to sound callous, but why should we care? I mean, smugglers do horrible things, and many of them die because of it. There are a lot of Chinos in the world."

I stare back at this person and the mostly academic audience that has just listened to me talk about Chino, Kingston, and others for the past hour. I can see some people nodding their heads in agreement with this person's statement. Behind me on a PowerPoint slide is a picture of Chino lying bare-chested on a hospital gurney. It's been years since the photo was taken, but telling his story always makes me feel as if he died just a few minutes ago. Speaking of his death conjures up a range of emotions inside me. Sorrow for the loss of life. Regret for all that I didn't do. Anger because this nightmare is never-ending. Guilt because I stand here in front of a crowd peddling stories of other people's misery. The harsh lights of this university auditorium shine down on Chino's image, giving the impression that we are conducting an autopsy on him. Maybe we are.

I pause to think about the question posed to me. I have been asked similar versions of it many times before. I think I know the response this person is looking for. They want easy answers. They want me to make something as complex and unsettling as smuggling legible and digestible so that they can feel better and perhaps have something smart and concise to scribble in a notebook. Maybe they want me to say that in the end Chino was a hero for running away with Jesmyn. Maybe they want me to say something about forgiveness and the high price of redemption. But I am not in the business of hero-making. Nor is it my place to speak about someone else's redemption. Like the last page of a Willy Vlautin novel, this story comes to an end, but there is no guarantee of a brighter future or happy resolution. Even after there are no more words on the page, the people you have read about will keep on struggling. They will keep moving from one place to another in search of hope. I'm not sure that I have the answer this person wants. All I know is that the realities of the violent world of undocumented migration are complicated.

Human smuggling is a brutal social process that people around the world experience every single day. Chino was just one person caught up in something much bigger than himself and that thing killed him. But he is not unique. There are many just like him around the world in the same predicament who will eventually end up dead or in prison because of the crucial role they play in our growing global migration crisis.

After my talk, someone will pull me aside and say they didn't like what I had to say about smugglers because it made them feel conflicted. They thought that my presentation might have humanized them too much. I respond that smugglers are in fact always complicated human beings. Don't get me wrong, I completely understand that because of the nature of their work they are unlikable, if not outright detestable. But perhaps it's not just smugglers we should be directing our ire toward. What about the larger forces at play that create the violent system of clandestine movement? Every year millions of people are illegally transported across international borders because they are looking for a better life and increasingly fleeing different forms of death. This process is helped along by the fact that there are many low-paying jobs that need to be filled in the Global North. Unfortunately (and often foolishly), migrants have to rely on criminals to protect them from the dangers created by border enforcement policies in places like the southern Mexican train tracks, the Darién Gap of Panama, and the Mediterranean Sea. Global inequality keeps Chinos of the world in business. His death should inspire empathy, guilt, and rage because in different ways, many of us are implicated in it.

As I write these words, news stories are spreading about fifty-three migrants who died after being cooked to death in the back of a tractor trailer in San Antonio, Texas. This story is shocking to the American public because of the high number of fatalities and the barbarity of the deaths. Blame will be (and should be) placed on the smugglers who loaded the truck with people and then abandoned them in the midday Texas sun to die. This story is horrific, but it is not an anomaly. Migrants die every day along the U.S.-Mexico border and elsewhere, and there is largely no public outcry. Moreover, culpability cannot be exclusively attributed to smugglers. Border crossers die in the Sonoran Desert and the South Texas backwoods because global forces and inhumane border enforcement policies push people to make extreme choices in order to save themselves and their families. The unspoken logic is that if people can survive these various death traps and enter the United States, our government and society will turn a blind eye to their presence as long as they work shit jobs for low wages and don't complain about it. Smuggling is a symptom of border enforcement policies and capitalism itself. As tragic as the deaths of these fifty-three migrants are, there are people lining up right now to try their luck in the back of a semi-truck that will soon be barreling down the highway.

I guess we are at the point in the story where, as an academic, I am supposed to put forth my solutions to the complex issue of smuggling.

Epilogue | 329

Unfortunately, what I have to offer is far from satisfactory. I am an anthropologist, not a policymaker. The types of observations and recommendations that my kind tends to make only frustrate those who are looking for easy answers to incorporate into campaign slogans and white papers.

I want to be clear, though. Human smuggling is exploitative and violent. It also cannot be stopped. But it is not the problem. The monstrous injustices created by capitalism that drive migration are the problem: poverty, political corruption, the drug trade, transnational gang violence, climate change patterns created by the richest countries and disproportionately felt by the poorest. These are the things that make undocumented migration (along with its ugly symbiote, smuggling) a lifesaving necessity. These are the things that help make the Chinos, Jesmyns, Almas, Flacos, and Kingstons of the world. Border walls, anti-smuggling task forces, and heightened security measures are expensive and ineffective tactics to deal with a worldwide crisis that has deep economic, political, and environmental roots. When we blindly ratchet up security, we only fuel the smuggling industry. If we want to eradicate undocumented migration, we have to address the push and pull factors that keep the global poor in perpetual motion. This perspective of course upsets those with the myopic and naive vision that migration is just a security dilemma to be resolved with concrete and steel. Those people can't seem to fathom how horrible things must be at home to make loading your family into the back of a semitruck or trudging through the jungle holding a baby feel like your best available options. Those people are also likely in denial about how much their daily life benefits from the fruits of undocumented labor. Perhaps the best way to start a conversation is to accept the fact that humans will forever seek places where they and their loved ones can thrive and feel safe. This means that wherever there are border walls separating the haves and have-nots, you will always find desperate people and enterprising smugglers working their way over, under, and through those barricades at all costs.

330 | SOLDIERS AND KINGS

SANTOS CALLS from a truck stop in northern Arizona. In the background, engines grumble and jack brakes sputter, creating a rhythm that I imagine him dancing to.

In the photo that Alma texts me, an Alabama sun brightens up their living room as Papo helps Dulce blow out the candles on her birthday cake.

Jesmyn squeezes her two-year-old daughter tightly as she tells me about the nightmares of Hurricanes Eta and Iota. Everything she owns is now gone.

"Chino, stop moving!" I yell. "Hold still so I can take your goddamn photo. I want to take a picture because that shirt you have on is funny."

"What's so funny about it?"

"It's a shirt from a university called Brigham Young. That's where a lot of Mormons go to school. Mormons don't drink or smoke or do drugs, so it's funny that you have that shirt on."

"How do you know I'm not a Mormon in training?"

Twenty minutes later Chino comes running down the street toward me.

"Jason, come quick. Immigration is here. There's gonna be a raid."

I grab my camera and chase after him. We turn the corner at the Pleasure Palace to see a Mexican immigration van blocking the end of the street. Several migrants and smugglers have congregated a few hundred feet down the road where it dead-ends. Some plot their escape, others plan their retaliation. Chino looks at me and flashes a defiant grin that burns into my brain forever. He picks up a rock and goes charging down the street. He screams into the jungle air, "Come get me, motherfuckers!"

Acknowledgments

First and foremost, I want to express my gratitude to the many people who opened up their lives to me and who guided me safely across the train tracks. Jesmyn and Marina taught me about compassion and love. Kingston taught me how to listen and watch. Papo and Alma showed me perseverance. Flaco showed me a good time. Santos gave me hope. Chino taught me about the important things in life.

This project wouldn't exist without my agent Margo Beth Fleming and the folks at Brockman, Inc., in my corner. Margo is an amazing sounding board, life coach, editor, motivational speaker, book recommender, and general badass.

Emily Wunderlich is my editor extraordinaire at Viking, who always had a clear vision of how this book should read and whose critical feedback significantly improved every aspect of the project. Most important, she encouraged me to be the writer I wanted and needed to be.

Paloma Ruiz is the behind-the-scenes editorial ninja at Viking whom I want to thank for treating this battered and coffee-stained manuscript with a lot of care and attention.

Thanks to copy editor Shana Jones for her tireless (yet gentle) red pen that made this manuscript all the more readable.

Shout out to Kate Berner and the many good folks at PRH for helping bring this book to the world.

Thanks and love to my mom, Margaret Andersen, for always encouraging me to follow my dreams and for not being too disappointed when I was living in the garage or when I made the questionable decision to become an anthropologist.

Gina Tan is the best big sister I could ever ask for, despite the fact that she is a Giants fan.

Big hugs to my siblings Joy Marchand and Tommy and Randy Tan.

More big hugs to my long-lost sisters Delilah, Deena, and Ruby De León. I am glad we found each other again.

Fred and Barbara Bigham are the coolest in-laws ever, especially when they put up with my impromptu writing offices in Pittsburgh and Massachusetts. Fred, it's really late. Please turn down the music.

Thanks to Frits Bigham, Erin Manzo Bigham, and Lil Warren G. I can't wait to try to make that baby a Dodgers fan.

The research for this book was partly supported by a New Directions Fellowship from the Mellon Foundation and by grants from the MacArthur Foundation.

I would like to thank Michael Brown and the kind folks at the School for Advanced Research for letting me come back to campus for a second round to write a big chunk of this book. SAR is by far my favorite place to put words to paper. Speaking of Santa Fe, big props to El Chile Toreado for making perhaps the best breakfast burrito in the solar system.

The research for this book was largely carried out while I was teaching at the University of Michigan. I am indebted to my many friends, colleagues, and co-conspirators in Ann Arbor. Thanks to Ruth Behar, Jatin Dua, John Mitani (Go, Lakers!), Tom Fricke, Andrew Shryock, Webb Keane, Dan and Lauren Nemser, Dean Hubbs, Lucy Cahill, Amanda Krugliak, Julie Winningham, Amy Rundquist, Melinda Nelson, Liz Roberts, Matt Hull, Krisztina Fehervary, William Calvo-Quirós, Laura MacLatchy, John Kingston, Bruce Mannheim, Mike McGovern, Yasmin Moll, Erik Mueggler, Damani Partridge, Lisa Young, John Speth, Mary Parsons, and Laura and Mike Kirchner. Special thanks to

Acknowledgments | 333

Michael "Lempy" Lempert for all his sage advice and to Howard "Amigo" Tsai for almost killing me with his jokes.

It feels great to be back at my alma mater, UCLA, and I am thankful to be surrounded by inspiring people in the Departments of Anthropology and Chicana, Chicano, and Central American Studies, including Leisy Abrego, Gena Carpio, Karina Alma, Chris Zepeda-Millán, Maylei Blackwell, Abel Valenzuela, Sandy Garcia, Eleuteria "Ellie" Hernández, Raúl Hinojosa-Ojeda, Aomar Boum, Stephen Acabado, Norma Mendoza-Denton, Greg Schachner, Shannon Speed, Tom Wake, and Erin Debenport. Thanks to Willeke Wendrich, Fonz Lopez, Sumiji Takahashi, and everyone in the Cotsen Institute of Archaeology. Special hugs to Laurie Hart and Philippe Bourgois for always being up for a camping trip, even when there's a monsoon. Props to Justin Dunnavant for Dezembering with me. I am also grateful to Jason Throop and Clark "CB" Barrett for welcoming me into their jazz ensemble and showing me how to explode.

Thanks to Conerly Casey for inspiring me in the classroom when I was an undergraduate at UCLA.

The Institute for Field Research supported my anthropological field school in Chiapas in 2015, which kick-started this project. I want to thank everyone who participated that year, including Polina Hristova, Anna Forringer-Beal, Kayleigh Ristuben, Chelsie Rae Goucher, Jessica Tilton, Emma Hays, Greg Sollish, Arianna Dixon, Jihmmy Sanchez, Lenica Morales, Andrea Galvez, Chloe Bergsma-Safar, Juan Mayorga, Anthony Quail, Cristina Moreno, and Celina Doria. Special thanks to Christian Stosik, who housed students and staff in Palenque while always providing an awesome soundtrack. Thanks to Kirk French and Laurel Pearson, who let us crash at their place for the summer.

Obed "Harry Potter" García helped us pave the way during that first trip to Palenque, and Lalo García tallied all the *crónicas crudas*!

Thanks to Juan and Carolino at Yaxkin and the good folks at Dragon Chino and Flor de Azalea.

334 | *Acknowledgments*

Thanks to Junior for the train track haircuts. Thanks to Kelsi, Chuki, Tequila, and *el mudo*. Saludos to Hugo out there somewhere under a bridge.

Gracias to Ernesto in Mexicali, whose opinions about Sublime I deeply respect. Crucial thanks to Miranda Dahlin, a true Boss DJ.

This book has a soundtrack that gives the reader a sense of what I was listening to in the field and while I wrote. That being said, I still want to thank Jason Isbell and the 400 Unit for always making me giddy about record release days.

I read a lot of Jesmyn Ward during the making of this book and want to thank her for constantly writing words that both inspire and break my heart.

Willy Vlautin was a great sounding board and wise big brother when I needed one.

Thanks to Wendy Ewald and Susan Meiselas for constantly inspiring me visually.

My buddy Brian Stannard gave great feedback on an early draft of this book. His passion for writing and literature was an early inspiration, dating back to when I was living on his couch in Westwood.

María Elena García and Tony Lucero are excellent manuscript reviewers and even better friends. I am constantly humbled by their kindness, generosity, and ME's ability to remember people.

I want to thank my therapist Teresa Locascio for helping me work through (and live with) all the dark things that the making of this book dredged up for me.

I lost way too many people over the course of this project. Sometimes it felt like one period of mourning simply bled into the next. The following people are greatly missed.

Jeff Parsons, who made me feel welcome at Michigan and whose old Leica I still carry around my neck.

Ann Cyphers, *la jefa* of Olmec archaeology, who got me to the dissertation finish line and, more important, showed me how to run a field project with tremendous rigor, humor, and love.

Acknowledgments | 335

Jason Vogel, who brought me back to music when I thought I had lost it forever. I hope wherever you are, brother, there is a turntable, a giant stack of records, and a cold case of PBR.

Anson "Wink" Musselman, who made me a drummer and who showed me it was okay to be a weirdo. Long live Brocktoön!

Aran Bellock, who always had a smile on his face (even when he did a front flip onto his bed and put his feet through his bedroom window).

Paul Infante. Mad cows! Wu-Tang forever!

Jeanne E. Arnold, who opened the first door for me and whose same door I now try to keep open for others.

I can't believe the Undocumented Migration Project has been around for fifteen years. I have been privileged to work with such an amazing rotating cast of characters during that time, and I am proud to see so many of them flourishing while trying to make the world a better place. Thank you all for helping make this research possible in different ways. When is our UMP Arivaca reunion gonna happen?

Thanks to Gabe Canter for helping to make our global exhibition Hostile Terrain 94 a reality and for also keeping my dream alive of making a *Goodfellas* meets *Sharknado* film.

Gabriel Silva Collins and Wanda Quintanilla are wonderful and brilliant graduate students who provided insightful feedback on a draft of this book.

Thanks to Nicole "Hot Dog" Smith for keeping it real and not giving me too much grief when I can't keep up.

Thanks to the 2022 Pirates BH Little League baseball team, whom I helped coach to a 3–12* record. It was one of the best experiences of my life. Thanks to coaches Cesar Barreras and Lou Pizante for being part of our Bad News Bears season. Thanks to Adam Episcopo and the 2023 Rockies BH Little League team, who finished 8–3–1, making me feel better about my coaching skills and, more important, providing a wonderful diversion during the final stages of this book.

336 | *Acknowledgments*

Ulises Espinoza has been a partner in crime for many things, including Little League Baseball, eBay addictions, and helping to bring momentum to our Visual Anthropology and Multimodal Praxis (VAMP) group at UCLA. Sock check, foo. Also, you probably do need that F2 Titanium.

María Inclán has let my students and me spend way too many nights on her couch in Mexico City, and for that I am eternally grateful.

Thanks to John Doering-White for teaching me so much about Central American migration.

Raúl "Springsteen" Mejía always makes me feel welcome in Apizaco. *Bebecito?*

Thanks to Amelia Frank-Vitale for being a great reader and for teaching me so much about how to do ethnography with compassion.

Cameron "C$" Gokee is both an excellent freestyler and a master data wrangler who constantly saves the day.

Haeden "Big Red" Stewart made the map of the migrant trails used for this book. Now I'm just waiting for him to make a map of all our spirit rides.

For those looking to learn more, I highly recommend Raúl Pastrana's 2019 documentary *Border South*, which provides an up-close look at the Central American migrant trail in the wake of Programa Frontera Sur. *¡Viva Pastrami!*

Over the course of writing this book, the Undocumented Migration Project collaborated with the Colibrí Center for Human Rights (https://colibricenter .org), a nonprofit that works tirelessly to help reunite people with their loved ones who have died while migrating. I am incredibly proud to be associated with this organization and am awed every day by the commitment and care that Perla Torres put into advocating for families searching for answers.

Austin Shipman was one of the first UMP students to join the fray in 2010. She is still around, except now she keeps our entire operation afloat while navigating with kindness and determination. Thank you for all you do, and sorry for buying your cats lilies.

Acknowledgments | 337

Big chunks of this book were written during the height of the COVID pandemic. Through a random set of events, I ended up in a school pod with several families from my neighborhood. It was through their friendship (and many nights of '90s karaoke) that my family and I made it through those hard times without completely losing it. Thanks to Claire, May, Pearl, Hazel, Rowan, Lupita, Christian, Michael, and Jodi. I owe a great debt to Aimee Scala and Gerta for all the laughs. Trent Teti showed me how to properly drive a minivan. Denny Sheehan regaled us with his memories of the Battle of Appomattox and constantly explained why we should be watching seven-hour-long documentaries on Romania. I'll meet you on Allison Road.

Thanks to the Los Angeles Lakers and Dodgers, especially Robert Horry, Kirk Gibson, and Rui Hachimura.

Geoff "Jefe" Vasile is my brother from another mother who always keeps me grounded.

Many thanks to my long-suffering partner in crime, Mike Wells, who was with me at different times during the research for this book. Mike never ceases to amaze me with his visual brilliance. I also wouldn't want to be eating iguana or rabbit with anyone else. He and I took thousands of photos of the migrant trail, which we hope to release soon as a follow-up visual companion to *Soldiers and Kings*. Stay tuned.

RIP Santi (2004–2022). I hope wherever you are, there is a couch you can destroy. Miss you, little miffer.

Thanks to The War Pigs for getting me back onstage after so many years.

Iggy and Lolo, you guys make me appreciate every day I have on this planet and inspire me to fight for a better tomorrow.

Abby, you are my world.

Appendix: Soundtrack

When I write, I need complete silence. But whenever I hit a brick wall (which is often), I take long walks with my headphones on. I usually need to fill my brain with music to kick-start or restart whatever it is that allows me to bang words out of a keyboard. Sometimes the music I need to get me going is what was playing in the unforgiving heat of southern Chiapas. Other times, I have to pull a song out of the ether* that reminds me of a moment or puts me in a mood to write about certain people, places, times, or feelings. Those songs are played on repeat for days or weeks or sometimes months (writer's block knows no time limit). I play songs over and over and over again until I feel good enough to trust the words coming off my fingertips or at least not totally hate them. This is the soundtrack that got me through the making of *Soldiers and Kings*.

Your personal information will be processed in accordance with our Privacy Policy located here: prh.com/privacy.

---

* It's clear from this list that my musical ether has an Americana/alt-country bent to it, or what Todd Snider calls "unsuccessful country music."

Introduction

"MY LOVELY MAN" BY THE RED HOT CHILI PEPPERS. This ode to deceased RHCP guitarist Hillel Slovak often played in the background when I was a ninth-grader drinking forties of malt liquor in my buddy's mom's minivan. I had a high school friend whose band used to cover this song. That friend died during the writing of this book. When John Frusciante wails (like a mourning Eddie Hazel*), I can't help thinking about the many ghosts I called out to during this project.

1. Honor y Patria

"SE VA EL CAIMÁN" BY BILLO'S CARACAS BOYS. *El muerto sacó la mano y le preguntó la hora.*

2. In the House of Pakal

"CÓMO ME DUELE" BY VALENTÍN ELIZALDE. I couldn't escape this song during my first season of fieldwork in Chiapas. It was literally coming out of everyone's cell phone. I am not sure what is more fitting, the lyric *"cómo me duele,"* or the fact that Elizalde coincidentally name-drops someone named Chino in the intro.

3. Charismatic and Reckless

"HARLEM RIVER BLUES" BY JUSTIN TOWNES EARLE. Earle died just as I was starting to write this book, and his death struck a chord with me. Maybe it's because I saw him early in his career and thought he had so much potential. Maybe it's because he died alone during a pandemic, when the whole world felt like it was alone. For whatever reason, this song about a young man calmly walking toward his own early death hurts as I sing along.

---

* It is rumored that during the recording of Eddie Hazel's famous guitar solo on the Funkadelic track "Maggot Brain," producer George Clinton told him to play as if his mother had just died.

Appendix: Soundtrack | 341

4. La Reina del Sur

"Caleb Meyer" by Gillian Welch. A song for Jesmyn about a woman who takes no shit from the living or the dead.

5. Foot Soldiers

"Fanática sensual" by Plan B. Santos dances toward a dream.

6. Papo and Alma

"El Hoyo" by Manu Chao. Tepito. Jamaica. Sonora. Manu Chao is singing about poverty in Mexico City on this 2007 track, but he could be talking about La Planeta in San Pedro Sula, Honduras, Buenos Aires in Nogales, Sonora, San Fernando in Buenos Aires, Argentina, or Pakal-Ná. So many *barrios* where young people find themselves born in deep holes that they must claw their way out of if they are to survive.

7. Duke of Earl

"Duke of Earl" by Gene Chandler. *Hey, foo, you like oldies?*

8. Kingston

"Tú no vive así" by Arcángel, Bad Bunny, Mambo Kingz, and DJ Luian. The soundtrack as we try to outrun ourselves.

9. Genesis

"Power" by Young Thug. Kingston works his way up the ladder.

10. Apocalipsis

"El mojado acaudalado" by Los Tigres del Norte. Santos leaves. Chino and Jesmyn stay behind. Los Tigres sing about the irony of the American dream.

11. Dinero, Dinero

"Somos de calle" by Daddy Yankee. If I didn't know better, I would say that Daddy Yankee wrote this song for Flaco.

12. Robin Hood

"Young, Wild & Free" by Snoop Dogg, Wiz Khalifa, and Bruno Mars. It doesn't matter what tomorrow brings, because tonight we are alive.

13. Resurrection

"Ruby and Lou" by Richmond Fontaine.

14. Escape

"The Life You Chose" by Jason Isbell. Isbell has been a core part of my life's soundtrack since I first saw him with the Drive-By Truckers in 2002 at the Darkhorse Tavern in State College, Pennsylvania. This track from his 2015 album *Something More Than Free* was playing on my car stereo when Chino and I drove around Palenque looking for a way out for him.

15. Things Fall Apart

"Bitch, Don't Kill My Vibe" by Kendrick Lamar. A Kingston favorite. "I am a sinner who's probably gonna sin again. Lord, forgive me!"

16. Liberty without Tricks or False Promises

"Everybody Plays the Fool" by the Main Ingredient. A song to help you get through the tough times.

17. Suerte

"King of Pain" by the Police. Santos thinks about a rich man sleeping on a bed of gold while he himself chokes on a crust of bread.

Appendix: Soundtrack | 343

18. Xibalba

"Ratamahatta" by Sepultura. A walk into Xibalba.

19. "We Aren't Playing"

"It Ain't Over 'Til It's Over" by Lenny Kravitz. A breakup song for Kingston and me.

20. Temptation

"Crisis de un MC" by Ana Tijoux. Santos ponders the crossroads.

21. The Future Belongs to Those Who Dream

"Hold on Hope" by Guided by Voices. I laugh when I think about what Flaco's reaction would be if I tried to get him to listen to this sentimental track by GBV. *Turn this mierda off, bro!* This song plays while a half-drunk, bare-chested, and optimistic Flaco cackles and throws firecrackers out the car window in slow motion.

22. The Soldier Who Would Be King

"1952 Vincent Black Lightning" by Richard Thompson. A song for Chino and Jesmyn.

23. Epilogue

"Paper Planes" by M.I.A. The credits roll and Chino tries to conquer the world.

Bonus Tracks

These songs were important, but I couldn't find a home for them in the list above.

"Soul Shakedown Party" by Bob Marley and the Wailers. A song to dance to on the train tracks during those fleeting moments when no one has to look over their shoulder.

344 | *Appendix: Soundtrack*

"EL PANADERO" (THE BREADMAN) BY TIN TAN. This campy song from a Mexican film starring Tin Tan played a few times on someone's cell phone the summer I met the Breadman in Pakal-Ná. It's a song that bread vendors across Mexico play when they drive around selling their foodstuffs. The song later took on a dark meaning for me. Right before I finished this book, I visited the train tracks after a two-year hiatus. As I walked toward a group of Central American migrants headed north, a bread truck drove by blasting this tune, causing me to look over my shoulder.

"CHAMPION" BY BUJU BANTON. Driving through Garifuna country in the dark while your passengers hang out the windows and scream like champions.

"PLAY A TRAIN SONG" BY TODD SNIDER. The 2004 studio version is perfection, but the intro on Snider's 2022 album *Live: Return of the Storyteller* is a beautiful addendum.

Notes

INTRODUCTION

2 many names in English and Spanish: See David Spener, *Clandestine Crossings: Migrants and Coyotes on the Texas-Mexico Border* (Ithaca, NY: Cornell University Press, 2009), 88–120, for a detailed discussion of the term *"coyote."*

2 force, fraud, or coercion: Denise Brennan, *Life Interrupted: Trafficking into Forced Labor in the United States* (Durham, NC: Duke University Press, 2014).

2 The response of the Global North: Clare Lombardo, "U.S. Agents Spray Tear Gas at Migrants, Briefly Close Tijuana Border Entry," NPR, November 25, 2018, https://www.npr.org/2018/11/25/670687806/u-s-agents-spray-tear-gas-at-migrants-briefly-close-tijuana-border-entry; Sophia Jordán Wallace and Chris Zepeda-Millán, *Walls, Cages, and Family Separation: Race and Immigration Policy in the Trump Era* (Cambridge, UK: Cambridge University Press, 2020); Transactional Records Access Clearinghouse, "Asylum Denial Rates Continue to Climb," October 28, 2020, https://trac.syr.edu/immigration/reports/630/; Rebecca Maria Torres et al., "Lockdown and the List: Mexican Refugees, Asylum Denial, and the Feminist Geopolitics of Esperar (Waiting/Hoping)," *Environment and Planning C: Politics and Space*, August 16, 2022, https://doi.org/10.1177/23996544221118906.

3 Sneaking people past border guards: Ruben Andersson, *Illegality, Inc.: Clandestine Migration and the Business of Bordering Europe* (Berkeley: University of California Press, 2014); Audrey Singer and Douglas S. Massey, "The Social Process of Undocumented Border Crossing among Mexican Migrants," *The International Migration Review* 32, no. 3 (1998): 561–92; Gabriella E. Sanchez, *Human Smuggling and Border Crossings* (New York: Routledge, 2015); Mahmoud Keshavarz and Shahram Khosravi, eds., *Seeing Like a Smuggler: Borders from Below* (London: Pluto Press, 2022); Spener, *Clandestine Crossings*; see Rebecca Berke Galemba, *Contraband Corridor: Making a Living at the Mexico-Guatemala Border* (Palo Alto, CA: Stanford University Press, 2018), for a discussion of goods smuggling in Chiapas.

5 I am looking in the rearview mirror: Part of this conversation was previously published in Jason De León, "The Indecisive Moment: Photoethnography on the Migrant Trail," in

Photography and Migration, ed. Tanya Sheehan, 115–30 (Milton Park, UK: Routledge, 2018). At that time, I was using the pseudonym "Wizard" instead of "Flaco."

8 **"deep hanging out":** James Clifford, "Anthropology and/as Travel," *Etnofoor* 9, no. 2 (1996): 5–15.

8 *participant observation***:** See Timothy Pachirat, *Among Wolves: Ethnography and the Immersive Study of Power* (Milton Park, UK: Routledge, 2018), for a discussion of ethnography and participant observation.

8 **some excellent examples:** Óscar Martínez, *The Beast: Riding the Rails and Dodging Narcos on the Migrant Trail* (New York: Verso, 2014); Adrian Nicole LeBlanc, *Random Family: Love, Drugs, Trouble, and Coming of Age in the Bronx* (New York: Scribner, 2004); Katherine Boo, *Behind the Beautiful Forevers: Life, Death, and Hope in a Mumbai Slum* (New York: Random House, 2014).

8 **more concerned about positionality, representation:** Part of this concern stems from the fact that many of us continue to work in the same communities even after we publish a book, which means we have to repeatedly face our interlocutors once their stories are in print and out in the world. We are thus accountable (at least we should be) to individuals and the places where we work long after we get our sound bites and photographs. For black feminist and Indigenous critiques of anthropology and ethnography, see Faye V. Harrison, ed., *Decolonizing Anthropology: Moving Further Toward an Anthropology for Liberation* (Arlington, VA: American Anthropological Association, 1991); Linda Tuhiwai Smith, *Decolonizing Methodologies: Research and Indigenous Peoples* (London: Zed Books, 2021); Irma McClaurin, ed., *Black Feminist Anthropology: Theory, Politics, Praxis, and Poetics* (East Brunswick, NJ: Rutgers University Press, 2001).

8 **describe the lives of others:** Ruth Behar, *The Vulnerable Observer: Anthropology That Breaks Your Heart* (New York: Beacon Press, 1997); Peter Benson, *Stuck Moving: Or, How I learned to Love (and Lament) Anthropology* (Berkeley: University of California Press, 2023).

9 **as others have done:** Ted Conover, *Coyotes: A Journey across Borders with America's Illegal Aliens* (New York: Vintage, 1987); Sonia Nazario, *Enrique's Journey: The Story of a Boy's Dangerous Odyssey to Reunite with His Mother* (New York: Random House Trade Paperbacks, 2007).

9 **those I work with:** See Jason De León, *The Land of Open Graves: Living and Dying on the Migrant Trail*, with photographs by Michael Wells (Berkeley: University of California Press, 2015), 11–14, for discussion of the methodological limitations of working with migrants.

10 **disclosed who I was and what I was doing:** This research was covered under University of Michigan IRB #HUM00060495, as well as under the bounds of oral history.

16 **"hostile terrain":** United States Border Patrol, *Border Patrol Strategic Plan 1994 and Beyond* (1994), Homeland Security Digital Library, hsdl.org (721845.pdf); also see De León, *The Land of Open Graves*.

Notes | 347

CHAPTER 1. HONOR Y PATRIA

17 **After decades of internal political corruption:** Elvia Alvarado and Medea Benjamin, *Don't Be Afraid, Gringo: A Honduran Woman Speaks from the Heart: The Story of Elvia Alvarado* (New York: Harper Perennial, 1989); Adrienne Pine, *Working Hard, Drinking Hard: On Violence and Survival in Honduras* (Berkeley: University of California Press, 2008); Dana Frank, *The Long Honduran Night: Resistance, Terror, and the United States in the Aftermath of the Coup* (Chicago: Haymarket Books, 2018).

18 **the real Anchuria:** O. Henry, *Cabbages and Kings* (New York: Doubleday, Page, 1915).

18 **Grupo de Operaciones Especiales Tácticas (GOET):** Xiomara Danelia Orellana, "GOET, nueva fuerza policial en Honduras para misiones de alto riesgo," *La Prensa*, March 9, 2014, https://www.laprensa.hn/sucesos/policiales/562307-98/goet-nueva-fuerza-policial-en -honduras-para-misiones-de-alto-riesgo.

18 **GOET's stated primary mission:** U.S. Embassy in Honduras, "Minors Leaving Honduras with Immigrant Visas," https://hn.usembassy.gov/visas/immigrant-visas/minors-leaving -honduras-with-immigrant-visas/.

20 **shape the country's history for over a century:** See, for example, Alvarado and Benjamin, *Don't Be Afraid, Gringo*; J. F. Hornbeck, *The Dominican Republic–Central America– United States Free Trade Agreement (CAFTA-DR): Developments in Trade and Investment* (Washington, DC: Congressional Research Service, 2012); John A. Booth, Christine J. Wade, and Thomas W. Walker, *Understanding Central America: Global Forces, Rebellion, and Change* (Boulder, CO: Westview, 2012).

20 **seen across Central America:** Leisy J. Abrego, "Central American Refugees Reveal the Crisis of the State," in *The Oxford Handbook of Migration Crises*, ed. Cecilia Menjívar, Marie Ruiz, and Immanuel Ness (New York: Oxford University Press, 2018), 213–28.

21 **less than $5.50 per day:** World Bank, "The World Bank in Honduras," October 4, 2022, https://www.worldbank.org/en/country/honduras/overview#1.

22 **With origins in East Los Angeles:** Elana Zilberg, *Spaces of Detention: The Making of a Transnational Gang Crisis between Los Angeles and San Salvador* (Durham, NC: Duke University Press, 2011); Thomas Ward, *Gangsters without Borders: An Ethnography of a Salvadoran Street Gang* (Oxford: Oxford University Press, 2012).

22 **join their ranks or face death:** Jon Wolseth, *Jesus and the Gang: Youth Violence and Christianity in Urban Honduras* (Tucson: University of Arizona Press, 2011); Anthony W. Fontes, *Mortal Doubt: Transnational Gangs and Social Order in Guatemala City* (Berkeley: University of California Press, 2018); Juan José Martínez D'Aubuisson, *A Year Inside MS-13: See, Hear, and Shut Up* (New York: OR Books, 2019); Roberto E. Barrios, *Governing Affect: Neoliberalism and Disaster Reconstruction* (Lincoln: University of Nebraska Press, 2017), 99–120.

22 **navigate or run from:** Amelia Frank-Vitale, "Rolling the Windows Up: On (Not)

Researching Violence and Strategic Distance," *Geopolitics* 26, no. 1 (2021): 139–58; Amelia Frank-Vitale, "Leave If You're Able: Migration, Survival, and the Everydayness of Deportation in Honduras" (PhD. diss., University of Michigan, Ann Arbor, 2021); Jon Horne Carter, *Gothic Sovereignty: Street Gangs and Statecraft in Honduras* (Austin: University of Texas Press, 2022).

24 **One of the primary goals:** "Mexico: Evolution of the Mérida Initiative, FY2008–FY2022," Congressional Research Service, updated November 1, 2021, https://crsreports .congress.gov/product/pdf/IF/IF10578/22.

24 **In reality, this binational initiative:** Jason De León et al., "Prevention Through Deterrence: Picturing a U.S. Policy," *Sapiens*, February 16, 2016; John Holman, "Mexico's 'Invisible Wall,' a Migrant Double Standard," Al Jazeera, February 16, 2017.

25 **extension of Prevention Through Deterrence:** Raquel Rubio-Goldsmith, Melissa McCormick, Daniel Martinez, and Inez Duarte, "The 'Funnel Effect' & Recovered Bodies of Unauthorized Migrants Processed by the Pima County Office of the Medical Examiner, 1990–2005," October 1, 2006, SSRN electronic journal, DOI:10.2139/ssrn.3040107; De León, *The Land of Open Graves.*

30 **operating at a mom-and-pop level:** Spener, *Clandestine Crossings.*

31 **are now from Central America:** U.S. Customs and Border Protection, "U.S. Border Patrol Southwest Border Apprehensions by Sector," June 10, 2021, https://www .cbp.gov/newsroom/stats/southwest-land-border-encounters/usbp-sw-border -apprehensions.

32 **made this route harder to access:** John Doering-White, "Evidencing Violence and Care along the Central American Migrant Trail through Mexico," *Social Service Review* 92, no. 3 (2018): 432–69; John Doering-White, "In the Shadow of the Beast: Violence and Dignity along the Central American Trail" (PhD diss., University of Michigan, Ann Arbor, 2019).

32 **orders of magnitude more difficult:** Nathaniel Parish Flannery, "As Mexico Tightens Its Southern Border, Central American Migrants Find New Routes North," *Fusion*, April 23, 2015.

33 **gangsters on the migrant trail:** Martínez, *The Beast.*

PART 1. SOLDIERS

39 **"In the sudden silence":** Linda Schele and David Freidel, *A Forest of Kings: The Untold Story of the Ancient Maya* (New York: William Morrow, 1990), 233.

CHAPTER 2. IN THE HOUSE OF PAKAL

43 **one of the most famous Maya archaeological sites:** The site was occupied primarily during the Classic Period (250 CE to 900 CE). See Schele and Freidel, *A Forest of Kings.*

Notes | 349

43 **"national treasure"**: John Noble et al., *Lonely Planet Mexico*, 14th ed. (2014), 377.

44 **migrants passing through every year**: MND Staff, "Blamed for 'Invasion of Violence' in Chiapas Community, Migrants Told They're Not Welcome," *Mexico News Daily*, September 28, 2021, https://mexiconewsdaily.com/news/blamed-for-invasion-of-violence-in-chiapas -community-migrants-told-theyre-not-welcome/; Enrique Romero, "Otro ejecutado en Palenque: Lo balearon al salir de su casa en Pakal-Ná," *Noticias Palenque*, July 14, 2010, https://noticiaspalenque.wordpress.com/2010/07/14/otro-ejecutado-en-palenque -lo-balearon-al-salir-de-su-casa-en-pakal-na/; Chiapas Support Committee, "The Maya Train Doesn't Respond to the Material and Cultural Needs of the Palenque Population," June 15, 2020, https://chiapas-support.org/2020/06/15/the-maya-train-doesnt-respond-to -the-material-and-cultural-needs-of-the-palenque-population/.

45 **long history of migration**: See Martínez, *The Beast*, 27–48.

45 **Central Americans in their towns**: Cody Copeland, "Chiapas Community Evicts Central American Migrants, Burns Belongings," *Mexico Daily News*, March 3, 2020, https:// mexiconewsdaily.com/news/chiapas-community-expels-central-american-migrants/.

48 **worn by *hondureños* into the present**: Steven Dudley, *MS-13: The Making of America's Most Notorious Gang* (Toronto: Hanover Square Press, 2020), 48.

57 **"Violence and migration produce"**: Noelle Kateri Brigden, *The Migrant Passage: Clandestine Journeys from Central America* (Ithaca, NY: Cornell University Press, 2018), 15.

CHAPTER 4. LA REINA DEL SUR

83 **the migrant trail is an especially difficult place for women**: Olivia T. Ruiz Marrujo, "Women, Migration, and Sexual Violence: Lessons from Mexico's Borders," in *Human Rights along the U.S.-Mexico Border: Gendered Violence and Insecurity*, ed. Kathleen Staudt, Tony Payan, and Z. Anthony Kruszewski (Tucson: University of Arizona Press, 2009), 31; Anjali Fleury, "Fleeing to Mexico for Safety: The Perilous Journey for Migrant Women," United Nations University, March 31, 2016, https://ourworld.unu.edu/en/fleeing-to -mexico-for-safety-the-perilous-journey-for-migrant-women; Sylvanna Falcón, "Rape as a Weapon of War: Advancing Human Rights for Women at the U.S.-Mexico Border," *Social Justice* 28, no. 2 (2001): 31–50; Shannon Speed, "States of Violence: Indigenous Women Migrants in the Era of Neoliberal Multicriminalism," *Critique of Anthropology* 36, no. 3 (2016): 280–301; Shannon Speed, *Incarcerated Stories: Indigenous Women Migrants and Violence in the Settler-Capitalist State* (Chapel Hill: University of North Carolina Press, 2019).

83 **Rape at the hands of bandits**: Gabriela Diaz and Gretchen Kuhner, "Women Migrants in Transit and Detention in Mexico," Migration Information Source, Migration Policy Institute, March 1, 2007, https://www.migrationpolicy.org/article/women-migrants-transit -and-detention-mexico.

83 **gendered strategies for mitigating danger**: Brigden, *The Migrant Passage*, 127–29; also

350 | *Notes*

see Anna Forringer-Beal, "(In)Visible Genders: How Central American Women Navigate Agency and Control during Undocumented Migration" (undergraduate honors thesis, University of Michigan, Ann Arbor, 2016), for discussion of makeup use among women migrants.

84 **"The lines that separate smuggler":** Wendy A. Vogt, *Lives in Transit: Violence and Intimacy on the Migrant Journey* (Berkeley: University of California Press, 2018), 154.

86 **Growing up in poverty often enculturates:** Carol Stack, *All Our Kin: Strategies for Survival in a Black Community* (New York: Basic Books, 1974).

87 **norm for much of the world:** Jessaca Leinaweaver, "Informal Kinship-Based Fostering around the World: Anthropological Findings," *Child Development Perspectives* 8, no. 3 (2014): 131–36.

CHAPTER 5. FOOT SOLDIERS

103 *Crisis of men. Crisis of those*: Ana Tijoux, "Crisis de un MC," BMG Rights Management, Universal Music Publishing Group, 2010.

CHAPTER 6. PAPO AND ALMA

110 **"to carry his anger":** Renato Rosaldo, *Culture and Truth: The Remaking of Social Analysis* (Boston: Beacon Press, 1993).

119 **and languishing migrants:** See Amelia Frank-Vitale, "Stuck in Motion: Inhabiting the Space of Transit in Central American Migration," *The Journal of Latin American and Caribbean Anthropology* 25, no. 1 (2020), for a discussion of how migrants can get delayed on the trail and spend weeks to years trying to make forward progress.

CHAPTER 7. DUKE OF EARL

133 **1,517 unidentified migrant bodies in its database:** Humane Borders, "Arizona Open-GIS Initiative for Deceased Migrants," https://humaneborders.info.

139 **working-class Mexican humor called** *chingaderas*: *Chingaderas* are also called *albures*. José E. Limón, "*Carne, Carnales*, and the Carnivalesque: Bakhtinian *Batos*, Disorder, and Narrative Discourses," *American Ethnologist* 16 (1989): 471–86.

140 **escape homophobia in Latin America:** María Inés Taracena, "La Caravana de la Resistencia: For Central Americans Fleeing Homophobic and Transphobic Violence, Heading North Is an Act of Resistance," *NACLA Report on the Americas* 50, no. 4 (2018): 386–91; Héctor Carrillo, *Pathways of Desire: The Sexual Migration of Mexican Gay Men* (Chicago: University of Chicago Press, 2018).

141 *As I walk through this world*: Gene Chandler, "Duke of Earl," Vee-Jay Records, 1961.

141 *Well, I'm an alley cat*: Cypress Hill, "Hand on the Pump," Ruffhouse Records, 1991.

Notes | 351

CHAPTER 8. KINGSTON

154 *I've been a son of bitch since I was born*: Arcángel and Bad Bunny, "Tú no vive así."

157 *I don't like how the government abuses us*: Kafu Banton, "Discriminación," 2004.

158 **sometimes pass for Mexican:** Jason De León, "'Como Me Duele': Undocumented Central American Bodies in Motion," in *The Border and Its Bodies: The Embodiment of Risk along the U.S.-México Line*, ed. Thomas E. Sheridan and Randall H. McGuire (Tucson: University of Arizona Press, 2019).

166 **If you have the money to contract a smuggler:** Spener, *Clandestine Crossings*; De León, "The Efficacy and Impact of the Alien Transfer Exit Program"; Daniel E. Martínez, "Coyote Use in an Era of Heightened Border Enforcement: New Evidence from the Arizona-Sonora Border," *Journal of Ethnic and Migration Studies* 42, no. 1 (2016): 103–19; Sarah Dolfin and Garance Genicot, "What Do Networks Do? The Role of Networks on Migration and 'Coyote' Use," *Review of Development Economics* 14 (2010): 343–59.

CHAPTER 9. GENESIS

176 **help Ronald Reagan fight his growing Cold War:** For an excellent and unique perspective on the relationship between the Cold War, colonialism, and the U.S.-Mexico border, see Michael Wilson and José Antonio Lucero, *What Side Are You On? A Tohono O'odham Life across Borders* (Chapel Hill: University of North Carolina Press, in press).

176 **military service was obligatory for unmarried males:** Samuel Cameron, Grail Dorling, and Andy Thorpe, "It Could Be You! Military Conscription and Selection Bias in Rural Honduras," *European Review of Latin American and Caribbean Studies* 68 (2000): 47–63.

176 **the army periodically carried out "manhunts":** Andy Thorpe and Sam Cameron, "Your Country Needs You! Forced Recruitment in Honduras," *Defense and Peace Economics* 11, no. 1 (2000): 185–95.

176 **"two years of often brutal training at almost no pay":** J. Mark Ruhl, "Redefining Civil-Military Relations in Honduras," *Journal of Interamerican Studies and World Affairs* 38, no. 1 (1996): 48.

177 **"Becoming a fighter may seem an attractive possibility":** Elisabeth Schauer and Thomas Elbert, "The Psychological Impact of Child Soldiering," in *Trauma Rehabilitation after War and Conflict*, ed. Erin Martz (New York: Springer, 2010), 311–12.

CHAPTER 10. APOCALIPSIS

188 **I encountered thousands of empty containers of Electrolit:** De León, *The Land of Open Graves*, 205–19.

190 *"When he opened the Abyss"*: Revelation 9:2–6.

352 | *Notes*

CHAPTER 11. DINERO, DINERO

202 *With effort and work I achieved my status*: Fidel Rueda, "Ya no soy el mandadero," 2015.

203 *"Dinero, dinero. Es lo que todo el mundo quiere"*: Daddy Yankee, "Somos de calle," 2008.

CHAPTER 12. ROBIN HOOD

212 *Roll one, smoke one*: Snoop Dogg and Wiz Khalifa, "Young, Wild & Free" (featuring Bruno Mars), 2011.

CHAPTER 13. RESURRECTION

224 **a town where thousands of Americans have migrated:** Ignacio de los Reyes, "American 'Illegals' in Mexico," BBC Mundo, February 23, 2012, https://www.bbc.com/news/world-radio-and-tv-17098719; Erin Siegal McIntyre, "America's Renegade Retirees," *U.S. News & World Report*, May 3, 2017, https://www.usnews.com/news/best-countries/articles/2017-05-03/more-american-retirees-head-to-mexico-some-illegally, Staff Writer, "Mexico Dealing with Undocumented Americans by Offering Amnesty," *Vallarta Daily News*, February 5, 2015, https://www.vallartadaily.com/mexico-dealing-undocumented-americans-offering-amnesty/; Mary Beth Sheridan, "The Little-Noticed Surge across the U.S.-Mexico Border: It's Americans, Heading South," *Washington Post*, May 18, 2019, https://www.washingtonpost.com/world/the_americas/the-little-noticed-surge-across-the-us-mexico-border-its-americans-heading-south/2019/05/18/7988421e-6c28-11e9-bbe7-1c798fb80536_story.html.

CHAPTER 14. ESCAPE

228 **documentary film we are making:** *Border South*, directed by Raúl Paz Pastrana, Andar Films, 2019.

229 *Soy el mojado acaudalado pero en mi tierra quiero morir*: Los Tigres del Norte, "El mojado acaudalado," 2008.

CHAPTER 15. THINGS FALL APART

242 **world where these skills have been utilized largely in illicit economies:** Philippe Bourgois, *In Search of Respect: Selling Crack in El Barrio* (Cambridge, UK: Cambridge University Press, 2003); Randol Contreras, *The Stickup Kids: Race, Drugs, Violence, and the American Dream* (Berkeley: University of California Press, 2013).

Notes | 353

CHAPTER 16. LIBERTY WITHOUT TRICKS OR FALSE PROMISES

252 **60 percent of the population lives in poverty and is dependent on a daily income:** KfW Development Bank, "Honduras: COVID19 in One of the Most Vulnerable Countries to Climate Change," July 7, 2020.

252 **Government health records showed 430,672 infections and 10,912 deaths:** Reuters COVID-19 Tracker, July 15, 2022, https://graphics.reuters.com/world-coronavirus-tracker-and-maps/countries-and-territories/honduras/.

252 **historic 9 percent shrinkage of the country's economy:** Reuters Staff, "Honduras Central Bank Says Economy Could Grow 5.2% in 2021 after Pandemic, Hurricanes," *Reuters Market News*, March 26, 2021, https://www.reuters.com/article/honduras-economy/honduras-central-bank-says-economy-could-grow-5-2-in-2021-after-pandemic-hurricanes-idUSL1N2LO2VM.

253 **Some predict that the Honduran poverty rate:** KfW Development Bank, "Honduras: COVID19 in One of the Most Vulnerable Countries to Climate Change," July 7, 2020.

CHAPTER 18. XIBALBA

267 **where gods are appeased by human sacrifice:** Allen J. Christenson, trans., *Popol Vuh: The Sacred Book of the Maya* (Norman: University of Oklahoma Press, 2007).

CHAPTER 19. "WE AREN'T PLAYING"

280 **standard practice for anthropologists to compensate the people they work with:** Juan Cajas and Yolinliztli Pérez, "Anthropologists, Economic Retribution, and Informants: Notes about Ethics in Social Research," *AGATHOS* 8, no. 1 (2017): 143–54.

CHAPTER 21. THE FUTURE BELONGS TO THOSE WHO DREAM

301 **rare to see a black person:** In a 2020 survey, 2.5 million people in Mexico identified as Afro-Mexican, representing approximately 2 percent of the entire country's population. Jazmin Aguilar Rangel, "Infographic: Afrodescendants in Mexico," Wilson Center, *Infographics by the Mexico Institute*, July 29, 2022, https://www.wilsoncenter.org/article/infographic-afrodescendants-mexico.

301 **It's unclear exactly where they go:** Lexie Harrison-Cripps, "'No Way Out': Haitian Asylum Seekers Reel in Southern Mexico," Al Jazeera, December 21, 2021, https://www.aljazeera.com/news/2021/12/20/no-way-out-haitian-asylum-seekers-reel-in-southern-mexico.

354 | *Notes*

310 **Fifty-four people have died:** Oscar Lopez, "Mexico Migrant Truck Crash in Mexico: Disaster 'in the Blink of an Eye,'" *New York Times*, December 9, 2021, https://www.nytimes.com/2021/12/10/world/americas/mexico-truck-crash.html.

CHAPTER 23. EPILOGUE

328 **news stories are spreading about fifty-three migrants:** See Andrés R. Martínez and Daniel Victor, "What We Know about the Migrant Deaths in San Antonio," *New York Times*, June 28, 2022, https://www.nytimes.com/2022/06/28/us/san-antonio-migrant-deaths-texas.html; and Amanda Holpuch, "2 Are Indicted in Human Smuggling Case That Left 53 Dead in Texas," *New York Times*, July 21, 2022, https://www.nytimes.com/2022/07/21/us/migrant-death-indictment-san-antonio.html.

328 **Smuggling is a symptom:** Harsha Walia, *Border & Rule: Global Migration, Capitalism, and the Rise of Racist Nationalism* (Chicago: Haymarket Books, 2021), 3.

Index

Note: Italicized page numbers indicate material in tables or illustrations.

Acid
    called *caquero*, 134
    drug use and partying of, 148, 201, 202, 205
    Flaco on sexual orientation of, 139, 140
    Flaco's reliance on, 140–41
    on smuggling run with Flaco, 149
Alma
    author's first meeting with, 46
    and Breadman and Bin Laden's attempt to kill Chino, 273
    business targeted by gangs, 116–17
    childhood of, 114–15
    children of, 115, 116, 117, 125, 224
    and children in Pakal-Ná, 42–43
    and Chino, 48, 117–18, 120, 121
    and going-away party for author, 230
    humanitarian visa application, 123–25
    leaving Chiapas, 225–26
    life in Celaya, 224
    life after leaving Mexico, 330
    living conditions of, 123
    as mole for gang, 118–19
    and Papo's death (alleged), 132, 222, 223
    and Payaso, 55
    safe house operated by, 224
    sense of abandonment, 114–15
    and violence in Honduras, 116
    as witness to killings, 179

American dream
    of Alma's mother, 114–15
    GOET agent on migrants' pursuit of, 20
    of Jesmyn, 94
    lifelong pursuits of, 199
    of Santos, 102
    simple pleasures of, 257
Andy
    and *charol* (begging), 156
    drug use and partying of, 212
    on exploitation of black migrants, 159
    humanitarian visa application, 156
    in Lechería apartment, 155
    military service of, 176
    safe house operated by, 157
    on smuggling Garinuga, 159
anthropologists, 7–8
    and author's background, 12–16
    author's fieldwork, 10, 153–54, 229, 289
    compensation practices of, 280–81
    and cultural relativism, 10
    and ethnography, 14, 15, 229, 280–81
    participant observation by, 8–9
Apizaco, Mexico, *xxix*
Arizona, 102
Arriaga, Mexico, *xxix*, 62
As I Lay Dying (Faulkner), 60

bar fight involving Kingston, 151–53, 153*n*
Barrio 18 (gang), 21, 22

356 | *Index*

begging for spare change (*charol*), 156–57, 166, 265

bestia, la (the beast), 32, 45, 54, 79, 107, 122, 143, 200–201. *See also* trains and train tracks

Bin Laden
aggressive personality of, 270–71
author's interactions with, 270–71
Chino attacked by, 267–75
and Chino's tattoo, 48
distrusted by others, 49, 227, 263, 270
Jesmyn threatened by, 273–75
poor treatment of women, 270
prison time of, 270
and Santos, 49, 263

black migrants and smugglers, 158*n*. *See also* Andy; Garifuna/Garinagu; Kingston; Snoop

Bloods (gang)
as guides for Garinagu, 159, 213
international reach of, 161
involvement in smuggling, 159, 170, 213
and Kingston, 161, 181, 246
in prison, 182
recruitment activities of, 175

border walls, 329

Bourgois, Philippe, 242

Brazil, migrants from, 303

Breadman
author's interactions with, 270
Chino attacked by, 267–75
and Chino's tattoo, 48
distrusted by others, 49, 227, 263, 270
and going-away party for author, 229–30
Jesmyn threatened by, 274–75
knitting of, 49, 270
prison time of, 270
and Santos, 49, 263

Brigden, Noelle, 57

brothels, women sold to, 232

caminadores (walkers), 167–68

capitalism, 329

cartels/mafia
battles for control in Veracruz, 239–40
and *caminadores* at border, 168

control of route through Veracruz, 195
control of smuggling industry, 250
and *cuotas* (fees) paid by migrants, 28, 31*n*, 204*n*, 303, 304, 305
endangering migrants, 56, 169–70
Flaco on violence/threat of, 195, 251, 305–6
and kidnappings, 303, 304–6
recruitment activities of, 292
Santos on dangers of, 299
Santos's brother's involvement with, 291–97
Santos's encounters with, 100, 292–97
smugglers' liaisons with, 32
violence of, 100, 239–40, 251

Casey, Conerly, 14, 15

Casper (Chino's homie), 69

catrachos (Hondurans), 47–48, 74

Celaya, Mexico, *xxix*
and fatigue of migrants, 225
safe house in, 221, 223–24
Santos as guide to, 101, 103, 190

Celia (Chino's birth mother), 64, 68

Central America and Central Americans
colonization efforts in, 48
and demand for smugglers, 32
and demographics of migrants, 31
difficulties of migrating from, 31–32
and drug trade, 17
and expenses associated with migration, 32
gangs in, 21–22, 32*n*
Garifuna migrants, 158, 158*n*
hurricanes' devastation of, 143–44, 256, 300
immigration crisis of 2014, 24
and Mexico's humanitarian visas for, 123–26
motives for migration from, 20, 69–72, 303
poverty in, 303
violence in, 303
See also specific countries

charol (begging for spare change), 156–57, 166, 265

Cheng Chui Ping, 33, 33*n*

Index | 357

Chiapas, Mexico, *xi, xv, xxi*
corrupt federal agents in, 29
as hub of migrants from Central
America, 27
migrant encounters with immigration
officers in, 25–26
Papo and Alma's move from, 225–26
children/minors
arriving unaccompanied at U.S.-Mexico
border, 18
attempting to escape violence, 22
dangers faced by, 213
as drug mules, 95–98
and expenses associated with migration, 210
in extreme poverty, 41–42
and gangs of Southern California, 144
and immigration crisis of 2014, 24
killing people on migrant trail, 170
migration attempts of, 95–98, 102
in Pakal-Ná, 41–43
in safe houses and on train tracks, 196
as soldiers in military, 175–78, 177*n*, 179*n*
and stereotypes of migrants, 157
Chino (Juan Roberto Paredes)
and accommodations on migrant trail, 157
and Alma, 117–18, 120, 121
ambitions of, 4–5
anger of, 76–77
antics on train, 58–60
author's attempt to help, 235–36
author's first meeting with, 46
author's relationship with, 60, 318, 320,
324–25
background of, 4, 63–69
Bin Laden and Breadman's attempt to kill,
267–75
borrowing money from author, 120–21
in BYU shirt, *xxvii*, 330
and "*catracho*" tattoo, 47, 48, 74, 230,
264, 325
and children in Pakal-Ná, 42, 43
criminal behavior of, 68–69
death of, 1–2, 5, 320–25, 326
defiance in face of immigration raid, 330
deportations of, 62
desire for change, 187, 267–68, 279

on difficulties of leaving gang life, 234
on difficulties of migrant life, 62–63
and documentary film, 228–29
erratic behavior of, 117–18, 121
on evading immigration officials, 61–62
gang affiliation of, 69, 108
on gangs in Honduras, 72–73, 79
and going-away party for author, 230, 235
grave of, 4, 5, 324–25
guide work of, 3, 50, 103, 170
hospitalizations of, 277–79, 314–20
humiliation suffered by, 78
injuries and infections of, 186–89, 272–73,
277–78, 313–20
and Jesmyn, 80, 82, 84, 187, 189, 192, 264
and machete attack, 73–74
in Mexico, 74–76
in Pakal-Ná, 108
and Papo, 48, 121–22
plans to leave Mexico, 233–34
precarious life of, 238
religious belief of, 229, 234
repentance of, 311–13, 321–22, 323
return to family in Honduras, 76, 279,
313–14
and Santos, 103, 191–92, 263–64
sense of abandonment, 65, 68, 103, 191,
311, 317
separation from family, 76
in Texas, 61–62
threats of suicide, 117, 120–21, 187
trip to Palenque, 235–36
and trouble with Sombra, 230–35
violence of, 69
as witness to killings, 179
Chuy
drug use and partying of, 239
and Kingston's bar fight, 153
Ciudad de México (Mexico City), *xxix. See
also* Mexico City
Ciudad Hidalgo, Chiapas, Mexico, *xxix*
Ciudad Juárez, Mexico, *xxix*
climate change, 329
Coatzacoalcos, Mexico, *xxix*, 107, 143,
149, 195
"Cómo me duele" (Elizalde), 46–47

358 | Index

Contreras, Randol, 242
Corozal, Mexico, *xxix*, 50, 51
COVID-19 and pandemic, 252–53, 294, 302
coyotes (human smugglers), 32, 32*n*. *See also*
guides (*guías*; human smugglers)
Crips (gang), 213
Cuba, migrants from, 303
cultural relativism, 10
cuotas (fees) paid by migrants
and Alma's work for gang, 119
and cartels/mafia, 28, 31*n*, 204*n*, 303,
304, 305
and economics of smuggling, 55, 204,
204*n*
FEDCCI agent's comments on, 28
to guides, 30–31, 50–51, 56, 108, 304
increases in, 303
and risks faced by guides/migrants,
108, 304

dangers faced by migrants
and arrests of smugglers, 28, 28*n*
attacks by gang members, 213
from cartels, 56
crossing desert, 15, 188–89
extortion and abuse, 170
immigration initiatives' impact on, 29, 169
on path to Pakal-Ná, 45
robberies and assaults, 170
smugglers' mitigation of, 3, 28, 28*n*
women sold to brothels, 232
See also deaths on migrant trail;
kidnappings
deaths on migrant trail
blamed on smugglers, 16
Chino's death, 1–2, 5, 320–25, 326
crossing desert, 15–16, 188–89, 328
in hot tractor trailer in Texas, 328
and immigration policies of U.S., 16
incidence of, 133–34
in tractor trailer wreck in Mexico, 310
and unidentified bodies of border crossers,
222, 223
deportations
avoiding, with language tactics, 75
of Chino, 62

as danger faced by migrants, 3
and Fiscalía, 29
of Flaco, 146, 251
Global North's investment in, 2
and humanitarian visas, 156
lower risk of, on road to Pakal-Ná, 45
and origins of MS-13, 175
of Papo, 111, 112, 113–14, 122
and Programa Frontera Sur, 24
of Santos, 101, 102, 104, 105–7, 292
desert crossings
dangers faced by migrants on, 15, 188–89
deaths of migrants on, 15–16, 188–89, 328
difficulty of, 95–98
and drug mules, 102
and expenses associated with migration,
31*n*, 167, 204, 204*n*
of Garinagu, 160
and immigration policies, 15–16, 29
and Santos, 95–98, 99, 102, 297–98
and stereotypes of migrants, 157
on trains, 201
deviant behavior, concepts of, 14–15
disappearance of people on migrant trail, 222
"Discriminación" (Banton), 157
documentary film on migrant trail, 228–29
drugs and drug trade
as driver of migration, 329
and drug mules, 95–98, 102
and Flaco's partying, 147, 150
and gang life, 145
and going-away party for author, 230
and Honduran criminals, 17
Dulce (Alma's child)
absent father of, 116
Alma's reassurances to, 115, 117
Alma's travels with, 124
birthday of, 330
and Breadman, 229–30
and education, 123, 224
life after leaving Mexico, 330

East Los Angeles, 22
economics of smuggling, 203–4, 210–11.
See also expenses associated with
migration

Index | 359

El Salvador, 19, 19n, 24, 175
Elbert, Thomas, 177, 177–78n
Electrolit, 188–89
Elizalde, Valentín, 46–47, 47n, 58
employment opportunities in Global
    North, 328
environmental crises, 2, 329
Escobar, arrest and deportation of, 25–26
ethnography, 14, 15, 229, 280–81
expenses associated with migration
    cartel taxes/fees, 28, 31n, 204n, 303
    cash to pay for bribes and rides, 210
    debts incurred to cover, 113
    and dishonest smugglers, 168
    drug mule work to cover, 95
    and economics of smuggling, 203–4,
        210–11
    and fees of guides, 30–31, 50–51, 56,
        108, 304
    and process of migrating, 50–51, 55–56
    rising costs, 166, 303–4
    and stages of migration, 167
    See also cuotas (fees) paid by migrants
exploitative nature of smuggling, 329

family structures, 86–87
Faulkner, William, 60
fieldwork of author, 10, 153–54, 229, 289
Fiscalía Especializada en Delitos Cometidos
    en Contra Inmigrantes (FEDCCI),
    27–30
Flaco
    on Acid's demeanor, 134–35, 139, 140–41
    author's relationship with, 5–7, 8, 199–200
    California dreams of, 142, 144
    cartel encounter of, 195
    on changes in guide work, 303–5
    childhood of, 142–43
    children and family life of, 193–97,
        300–301, 306–8
    concern for author's safety, 198
    COVID-19 infection of, 302
    criminal activities of, 141–42, 144, 145
    death of brother, 253–54, 255
    deportations of, 146, 251
    desire to leave smuggling, 195–96, 250

destitution of, 302, 307–8
drug use and partying of, 147–48, 150,
    202, 205
earnings of, 138
on economics of smuggling, 203–4
employment of, 253
in fear for his life, 250, 251
and gang life, 144–45, 195
gang tattoos of, 5
guide work of, 147, 148, 194–97, 199,
    200–201, 302–3, 304
hardships suffered by, 300, 302
hopes to build a house, 309–10
and hurricanes hitting Honduras, 256
and Papo's death (alleged), 131–32, 133,
    134, 136, 221, 222–23
and Payaso, 136
personality of, 132–33
precarious life of, 238
premature aging of, 300
prison time of, 145–46
religious belief of, 200, 204–5
residency card purchased by, 302
return to family in Honduras, 146
return to Mexico, 256
and trains (*la bestia*), 143, 146, 200–201
as witness to killings, 179
work ethic of, 196–97
Forest of Kings, A (Schele and Freidel), 39

Gaby (Alma's child), 116, 117, 124, 224
gangs and gang members
    and Alma, 116–17, 118–19
    author's interactions with, 226–27
    in Central America/Honduras, 21–22, 31,
        32n, 71–73, 101, 102, 233
    and child refugees, 144
    and Chino's background, 69
    and Chino's disobedience to Sombra, 232
    and *cuotas* (fees) paid by migrants, 28, 55,
        119, 303
    difficulty of leaving, 72
    difficulty of recognizing members of, 226
    as driver of migration, 329
    and drug trade, 145
    extortion tactics of, 70, 169–70

360 | *Index*

gangs and gang members (*cont.*)
  Flaco's involvement with, 144–45
  and fluidity in roles on migratory paths, 57
  and Garinagu, 159, 213
  information supplied by locals to, 119
  involvement in smuggling, 29, 170
  and Kingston, 174, 182–83, 245–46
  lure of youth to, 71
  origins of international organizations, 175
  in Pakal-Ná, 226
  in prison, 182–83
  Santos on dangers of, 299
  smugglers' affiliations with, 28, 32–33,
    108, 213
  in Southern California, 144–45
  train tracks controlled by, 213
  violence associated with, 22, 70, 71–72,
    226, 251, 329
  See also specific gangs
Garifuna/Garinagu
  attacked by gang members, 213–14
  and black transnational gangs, 159
  different needs of, 159–60
  discrimination faced by, 158–59
  gang affiliations of, 213
  guide assaulted and robbed, 304
  as soldiers in military, 176–77
  strategies specific to, 158–60
  terms, 158*n*
  See also Kingston
Global North, 2, 328
Goodwin, 194, 195, 199
Grupo de Operaciones Especiales Tácticas
  (GOET), 18–24
Grupos Beta, 278
Guadalajara, Mexico, *xxix*, 195, 201, 302
Guatemala, *xxix*
  attempts to stop migration from, 24
  entering Mexico from, 45
  expenses associated with migration, 211
  process of migrating from, 50
  and U.S. foreign policy, 19
guides (*guías*; human smugglers)
  and accommodations on migrant trail, 157
  accountability of, 166
  arrests of, 33

author's access to, 6–7, 9–12, 11*n*, 59–60
author's boundaries with, 281
bad experiences with, 165
black, 156. *See also* Andy; Kingston; Snoop
Central Americans' need for, 32
and claims of doing God's work, 227
consequences of arresting, 28, 28*n*
coyotes versus, 32, 32*n*
dangers/challenges faced by, 169, 212–13,
  250, 303, 304–5
deaths of migrants blamed on, 16
demand for, 3, 29, 32, 107–8, 329
drug use and partying of, 148
and economics of smuggling, 203–4,
  210–11
entry into smuggling life, 32
and exploitative nature of smuggling, 329
extracting money from migrants, 197
fees and payments made to, 30–31, 50–51,
  56, 108, 304. *See also cuotas* (fees)
  paid by migrants
and fluidity in roles on migratory paths, 57
gang affiliations of, 28, 32–33, 108, 213
gangs' involvement in smuggling, 29, 170
and Garifuna migrants, 159
and GOET agents, 23
harshness required of, 98
human traffickers versus, 2
and humanitarian visas, 156
identities of, protected, 11*n*
importance of looking hard as, 212
kidnapping of guides, 304–5
lives of, 209–11, 238–39
low-budget options, 32
lying of, 50
media portrayals of, 3–4
migrants abandoned by, 3, 188, 328
migrants' social contracts with, 3
money made by, 210
money requested from author, 281
money sent to families, 203
nicknames associated with, 5
nomadic lifestyles of, 104
on-call for other smugglers, 190
process of smuggling, 49–56
and Programa Frontera Sur, 107–8

racialized practices of, 159–60
recommendations for, 165, 166
recruitment of young soldiers, 170
and sexual exploitation, 83, 140
and stages of migration, 166
stereotypes associated with, 7
terms for, 2, 32n
torture of, 305
unethical smugglers, 3, 10
unsustainable lifestyle of, 252
violence mitigated by, 28
women as, 11n
See also Bin Laden; Breadman; Chino
(Juan Roberto Paredes); Flaco;
Kingston; Santos

Haitian migrants, 157n, 301, 303
Henry, O., 20
Hernández, Juan Orlando, 17
homophobia, 139–40
Honduras and Hondurans, xxix, 37
Alma on dangers of living in, 125
attempts to stop migration from, 24
and charol (begging), 156–57, 166
and Chino's issues with Sombra, 233
colonization efforts in, 48
COVID-19 pandemic's impact in, 252–53
as dangerous/violent, 1, 1n, 20, 22–23, 31,
71–73, 111, 112, 185, 214, 262, 263
economy of, 252–53
extreme poverty in, 20, 21, 23, 214, 252
gangs in, 21–22, 31, 71–73, 101, 102, 233
and Grupo de Operaciones Especiales
Tácticas (GOET), 18–24
hardships suffered by families in, 63–67,
71–73
hospitals in, 314–20
humiliation of returning to, 78
hurricanes' devastation of, 143–44,
256, 330
lack of opportunity in, 107, 262
mass exodus from, 256
Mexicans' sympathies for, 75
military service in, 175–78
and origins of international gangs, 175
Papo's return to, 114

political instability in, 17–18, 21
process of migrating from, 50
and racialized smuggling industry, 159–60
risks faced by Jesmyn in, 84–85, 89–94
and Santos, 100–101
stereotypes associated with, 259
and Temporary Protected Status in
U.S., 144
and term "banana republic," 20
and term catrachos, 48
treatment of women in, 278
violence in, 259
human rights
Fiscalía's claims to protect, 29
and U.S. support for Programa Frontera
Sur, 25
human traffickers versus human smugglers, 2
humanitarian visas, 123–26, 156
hunger, 86, 252
hurricanes, devastation from, 143–44, 256,
300, 330

immigration agents
author's encounters with, 25–26
and charol (begging), 157
Chino's defiance of, in face of raid, 330
corruption of, 29, 30, 251
and fluidity in roles on migratory
paths, 57
and Garifuna migrants, 159
implicated in kidnappings, 227
residency card sold to Flaco by, 302
searching for crime kingpins, 33
immigration policies
Prevention Through Deterrence, 15,
16, 24
and Programa Frontera Sur, 24–25, 27,
29, 169
rise in smuggling as result of, 3, 29, 32
smuggling as symptom of, 328
support for GOET agents, 23–24
and Temporary Protected Status in
U.S., 144
inequality, global, 2, 328–29
Inocente, 65, 67, 323–24
Ixtepec, Mexico, xxix

Index

Jesmyn
and American dream, 94
on Bin Laden and Breadman's attempt to
kill Chino, 267–75
and Chino's hospitalization, 277–79,
315–20
and Chino's issues with Sombra, 231
Chino's relationship with, 80, 84, 187, 189,
192, 264
death of Chino, 321–22, 325
death of father, 85–86, 88–89
family structure of, 86, 87–88
and going-away party for author, 230
and hurricanes hitting Honduras, 330
plans to leave Mexico, 233–34
and Pleasure Palace crew in Pakal-Ná,
80–83
religious belief of, 273, 279, 316
return to Honduras with Chino, 279,
313–14
risks faced by, in Honduras, 84–85,
89–94
search for Chino, 276–77
street smarts of, 81, 85
trip to Palenque, 235–36
as witness to killings, 179
Jorge, 148–49, 201, 205
journalists, 8, 83

kidnappings
faked by Kingston, 283–88, 305
Flaco on, 251
immigration agents implicated in, 227
increase in rates/risk of, 303, 304
Kingston on, 168
Kingston
assisting roadside migrants, 207–8
attempts to get family to U.S., 248
authority of, 181
author's first and last meetings with,
162–64, 245–49
and author's return to U.S., 280
bar fight of, 151–53, 153n
on best practices of soldiers, 170–71
and cartel violence, 240
charisma/charm of, 161, 162, 281

and *charol* (begging), 166
childhood and youth of, 172–82
children of, 240, 240n, 248
on dangers/challenges faced by guides,
169–70
death of nephew, 237–38, 239, 245,
280, 282
defense against *mareros*, 213–14
desire to leave guide/gang life, 239,
240–42, 246, 249, 289
desire to start a business, 241, 242
discipline of, 161, 170, 183, 184
drug use and partying of, 239, 247
entry into smuggling, 166
in fear for his life, 246–47, 249
gang affiliation of, 161, 174, 181, 182–83,
245–46
guide work of, 185
home robbed, 243–44, 245
on importance of recommendations,
165, 166
kidnapping faked by, 283–88, 305
on life as a guide, 209–11
memories plaguing, 247–48
on migrant trail, 180
military service of, 175–78, 179
on murders in Mexico, 214–15
in New York, 181–82
perilous life of, 238–39, 242
on Priest, 212
prison time of, 182–84, 245
religious belief of, 241
requests for money from author,
280–89
return to Honduras, 184–85
sense of abandonment, 280, 289
on stages of migration, 166–68
traumas endured by, 177, 178–79,
181–82, 247
on untrustworthy guides, 168–69
veteran status of, as gang member and
smuggler, 160–61, 208, 211
violent tendencies of, 177, 179, 182, 183,
213–14, 247
visa of, 208–9
kinship, as survival strategy, 86

Index | 363

laborers, undocumented, 329
La Ceiba, Honduras, *xxix*, 111, 185
Lalo, 193, 194, 196
Land of Open Graves, The (De León), 15
Lechería, Mexico, *xix, xxv, xxix*, 154–56
levantadores (escorts to safe houses), 31*n*, 168
Lion Kings (gang), 213
López Obrador, Andrés Manuel, 44*n*
Luz, 64, 65, 66, 67, 76

mafia. *See* cartels/mafia
mareros. See gangs and gang members
Marina
  on Chino getting attacked in Honduras, 73–74
  and Chino's childhood, 64–65
  and Chino's hospitalization and death, 314–20, 321–23
  and Chino's repentance, 311–13
  on Chino's returns to Honduras, 76–77, 313–14
  on Chino's suffering, 63–64, 66–68, 69, 322–23
  on family life, 66–67
Marvin, 291–97, 298
Matamoros, Mexico, *xxix*
Maya, 267
Medias Aguas, Mexico, *xxix*
Mexicali, Mexico, *xxix*, 202, 205, 291, 297–98
Mexico, *xxix*
  anti-smuggling/anti-trafficking signs in, 256
  bandits in, 211–12
  Central Americans settled in, 31
  challenges of living in, 62–63
  Chino's life in, 74–75
  corruption in, 26, 29
  crackdown on Central American migration, 250
  dangers faced by migrants/smugglers in, 212–13
  entry points from Guatemala, 45
  and Fiscalía (FEDCCI), 27–30
  Flaco's return to, 256
  Flaco's youth in, 143
  and Grupos Beta, 278

  humanitarian visas from, 123–26, 156
  immigration agents of, 25–26
  lack of economic opportunity in, 241, 242
  migrants from, 31
  Palenque sites, 43–44, 45–46
  and Programa Frontera Sur, 24–25, 27, 29, 169
  reliance on guides to cross, 107–8
  shelters for migrants in, 29*n*
  sympathy for Hondurans in, 75
  traveling on foot through, 51–52
  treatment of migrants in, 84
  See also specific locations
Mexico City, 45, 56, 79, 123, 143, 154, 155, 162, 165, 167, 193, 198, 204, 244–45, 302
migrants
  and American dream, 199
  bad experiences of, 165
  demographics of, 30–31
  dreams of retirement nests of, 199
  factors driving. *See* motives for migration
  and fluidity in roles on migratory paths, 57
  hiding in Celaya, 224–25
  people's fear of, 6
  stereotypes associated with, 157
  stuck mid-journey, 204, 205
  as undocumented laborers, 329
  See also dangers faced by migrants; deaths on migrant trail
migration and migrant trail
  and *caminadores*, 167–68
  costs associated with. *See* expenses associated with migration
  difficulties of, 108–9. *See also* dangers faced by migrants; deaths on migrant trail
  documentary film on, 228–29
  factors driving, 2, 329
  global crisis surrounding, 2, 327–28, 329
  from Guatemala to Mexico, 45
  humans' reliance on, for survival, 2
  increase in rates of, 303
  and *levantadores*, 168
  as lifesaving necessity, 329

364 | Index

migration and migrant trail (*cont.*)
  made on foot, 51–52
  map, *xxix*
  multiple people required for, 166–67
  and *polleros*, 167–68
  stages of, 166–67
Miguel, 66–67, 68, 324
military service of children, 175–78,
    177*n*, 179*n*
minors. *See* children/minors
misunderstanding of migrant crisis, 329
Monterrey, Mexico, *xxix*, 180
motives for migration, 327–28, 329
  displacement caused by hurricanes, 303
  economic hardships, 62
  poverty, 20, 87, 303
  and suffering/hardships in Central
    America, 69–72
  violence, 20, 303
MS-13 (gang)
  Alma's work for, 119
  authority of, 102
  avoidance of term *ocho*, 146*n*
  and *cuotas* (fees) paid by migrants, 55
  difficulty of identifying members of, 227
  Flaco's involvement with, 144
  and Garifuna guides, 213
  and Goodwin, 194
  guides' affiliations with, 108
  Hondurans' reliance on guides from,
    159–60
  involvement in smuggling, 29, 170
  in Lechería apartment building, 155
  origins of, 22, 144, 175
  in Pakal-Ná, 54, 108
  Papo's connection with, 124
  protection offered by, 29
  Sombra's involvement with, 230

Nicaragua, 175–76
Nogales, Mexico, *xxix*, 261, 265
Nuevo Laredo, Mexico, *xxix*

Obama administration, 18, 24
Orizaba, Mexico, *xxix*
Oscar (Jesmyn's father), 85, 87–89

Pakal-Ná, Mexico, *xvii, xxix*
  author's time in, 45–46, 229
  catrachos in, 48
  children in, 41–43
  Chino's time in, 77
  cost of rides from Corozal to, 210
  crime and violence associated with, 44
  and *cuotas* (fees) paid by migrants, 119
  FEDCCI operations in, 28
  Jesmyn's time in, 80–83
  Papo and Alma's time in, 226
  process of guiding migrants to, 49–56
  security increased around, 105
  violence in, 226
  visibility of migrants in, 225
  See also Palenque, Mexico; Pleasure
    Palace
Palenque, Mexico, *xxix*, 222, 227, 235–36,
    276–77. *See also* Pakal-Ná, Mexico
Papo
  arrests and deportations of, 111, 112,
    113–14, 122
  author's first and last meetings with,
    46, 200
  on *charol* (begging), 156
  and Breadman and Bin Laden's attempt to
    kill Chino, 273
  childhood of, 111
  and children in Pakal-Ná, 41–43
  and Chino, 48, 121–22
  death of (alleged), 131–32, 133, 134,
    136–37, 221–23
  and educational opportunities, 112, 113
  employment of, 224
  gang affiliation of, 124
  and going-away party for author, 230
  humanitarian visa application, 123–26
  leaving Chiapas, 225–26
  on legalization of weed, 122
  life after leaving Mexico, 330
  living conditions of, 123
  motive for leaving Honduras, 125–26
  murder associated with motorcycle of, 110,
    114, 125–26
  and Payaso, 55
  safe house operated by, 224

weed sold by, 120, 124
as witness to killings/violence, 111–12, 113, 179
Paredes, Juan Roberto. *See* Chino (Juan Roberto Paredes)
participant observation, 8–9
pasadores, 2. *See also* guides (*guías*; human smugglers)
Pato (shopkeeper in Pakal-Ná), 55, 226–27
Payaso
  killings committed by, 136–37
  knitting of, 54, 136
  and Papo's death (alleged), 136–37
  as Zero's enforcer in Pakal-Ná, 54–55
Phoenix, Arizona, 102
Piedras Negras, Mexico, *xxix*
Pirate
  desire to leave smuggling, 135–36, 195, 205
  drug use and partying of, 201, 202
  on smuggling run with Flaco, 148
  on working for families, 203
Pleasure Palace, 47, 55, 57, 82, 119, 122, 123, 158, 189
  distrust of Breadman and Bin Laden at, 49, 227, 263, 270
  going-away party for author, 229–30, 235
  and immigration agents, 330
  parties at, 56, 229
  and Santos's tattoo work, 47, 189
  See also Alma; Bin Laden; Breadman; Chino (Juan Roberto Paredes); Jesmyn; Papo; Santos
political corruption, 329
polleros (people who receive migrants at border), 2, 167–68, 304
poverty
  deaths resulting from, 86
  in Honduras, 20, 21, 23, 214, 252
  kinship as survival strategy for, 86
  migration driven by, 20, 87, 303, 329
  and violence, 86, 87, 214
Prevention Through Deterrence, 15, 16, 24
Priest, 212
Programa Frontera Sur
  and demand for guides, 29, 32, 107–8
  FEDCCI program on impact of, 27

and human rights violations, 25
methods of, 24–25
and migration from Guatemala to Mexico, 45
origins of, 24
and Santos's arrest and deportation, 107
and security around train tracks, 32
unintended consequences of, 29, 169
prostitution
  and smuggler lifestyle, 139–40
  women sold into, 232
Puerto Chiapas, Mexico, 302

racialized discrimination, 158–59
rail lines. *See* trains and train tracks
Ramona, 85, 88–89
Ramos, 154–55
Reagan, Ronald, 176
Reynosa, Mexico, *xxix*
Roberto. *See* Chino (Juan Roberto Paredes)
Rueda, Fidel, 202
rumor mill on migrant trail, 222, 262

safe houses
  Andy's management of, 157
  author's time in, 7, 8, 164
  in Celaya, 221, 224
  children in, 196
  demand for, 157
  Flaco in, 250
  Garinagu in, 159
  in Guadalajara, 250
  Kingston in, 245
  in Lechería, 245
  levantadores driving migrants to, 31*n*, 168
  as lucrative opportunity, 157
  and *mareros*, 198
  in Mexicali, 202
  in Mexico City, 155
  offered by Alma and Papo, 224
  in Texas, 56
  women in, 11*n*
Salvador, 307, 308, 310
San Luis Potosí, Mexico, *xxix*
San Pedro Sula, Honduras, *xxix*, 1, 87, 116
Sanchez, Gabriella E., 11*n*

366 | Index

Santos
  and accommodations on migrant trail, 157
  ambitions of, 191–92
  and American dream, 102, 297
  arrests and deportations of, 101, 102, 104,
    105–7, 292
  author's first and last meetings with, 46,
    261–66
  and begging for spare change, 265
  and Breadman and Bin Laden, 270
  and brother's imprisonment, 298
  and cartels, 100, 291–97, 299
  childhood of, 99–100
  and children in Pakal-Ná, 42
  and Chino, 103, 191–92, 263–64
  at Christmas party, 257–58
  crossing U.S.-Mexico border, 102
  death of father, 99–100
  desire for employment, 99, 102, 191, 265
  desire to leave guide/gang life, 265,
    290–91
  distrust of Breadman and Bin Laden, 49, 263
  drug-mule work of, 95–98, 102
  and gang life, 102–3, 299
  guide work of, 50, 101, 103, 190–91,
    264–65
  and Jesmyn, 82
  life after leaving Mexico, 330
  in Mexicali, 291, 297–98
  in Pakal-Ná, 108
  precarious life of, 238
  prison time and criminal record of, 257–63
  religious belief of, 190–91
  sense of abandonment, 103, 191
  and Sombra, 230, 231, 261, 264
  tattoo work of, 47, 48, 189–90, 264
  tenacity of, 265
Schauer, Elisabeth, 177, 177–78n
School of the Americas (Fort Benning,
    Georgia), 19n
sex
  and homophobia, 139–40
  and migrant women sold to brothels, 232
  risks of sexual assaults, 83–84
  sex workers, 139–40
  sexual exploitation, 75, 84

shelters for migrants, 29n
Smiley, 89–93
smugglers, human. See guides (guías; human
    smugglers)
Snoop
  author's first meeting with, 158
  and charol (begging), 156
  drug use and partying of, 212, 239
  and Kingston's bar fight, 153
  in Lechería apartment, 154
  on smuggling Garinuga, 158–59
Sombra
  Chino's trouble with, 230–35
  and Jesmyn, 279
  and Santos, 190, 230, 231, 261, 264
Sonoran Desert, 15, 16, 95–98, 188
Special Prosecutor for Crimes Committed
    Against Immigrants. See Fiscalía
    Especializada en Delitos Cometidos
    en Contra Inmigrantes (FEDCCI)
Spider, 102–3
stereotypes of and prejudices against
    Hondurans, 259

Tapachula, Mexico, xxi, xxix, 45, 301–2
Tegucigalpa, Honduras, xxix, 17, 19
Temporary Protected Status, 144
Tenosique, Mexico, xxix
Texas
  children preparing to enter, 180
  deaths of migrants in tractor trailer in, 328
  deportations of migrants, 111, 112
  migrants' arrivals in, 56
  and process of migrating, 56
Tierra Blanca, Mexico, xxix
Tijoux, Ana, 103
Tijuana, Mexico, xxix, 202–3
torture, 30, 100, 177, 288, 305
tractor trailers carrying migrants
  migrants killed in truck in Texas, 328
  migrants killed in wreck in Mexico, 310
  and misunderstanding of migrant crisis, 329
trains and train tracks, xix, 219
  called la bestia, 32
  Chino's antics on, 58–60
  dangers associated with, 32

and Flaco, 143, 146, 200–201
gangs' control over parts of, 213
hitching rides on, 45
map, *xxix*
security around, 32, 45*n*, 51, 123
violence prevalent around, 214
See also bestia, la (the beast)
trust, 6, 9–12

Undocumented Migration Project (UMP), 15
United States
and American dream, 20, 94, 102, 114–15,
199, 257
challenges faced by migrants in, 61–62
children preparing to enter, 180
humiliation of failing to reach, 78
migration policies of. *See* immigration
policies
role of undocumented laborers in economy
of, 329
U.S. Border Patrol
and deaths of migrants, 16
and immigration policies of U.S., 15–16
and Papo's deportation, 112
and photograph of agents on horseback
chasing migrants, 157*n*
support for GOET agents, 19, 24

Venezuela, migrants from, 303
Veracruz, Mexico, 239–40
vías (train tracks), *xxiii*, 43, 43*n*.
See also trains and train
tracks
violence
and anthropological fieldwork, 10
bodies scarred by, 81
captured/circulated via phones, 254
of cartels, 100, 239–40, 251
in Central America, 303
and child soldiers in military, 177,
177–78*n*, 179*n*
contextualization of, 15
and corrupt federal agents, 30
as driver of migration, 303, 329
escalations of, 29, 169, 251
factors driving, 169–70

fear of deportation versus fear of, 102
frequency and commonality of, 222,
255–56, 329
gang-related, 22, 70, 71–72, 226,
251, 329
in Honduras, 1, 1*n*, 20, 22–23, 31, 71–73,
111, 112, 185, 214, 259
migrants as targets of, 213
murder of Flaco's brother, 253–54
in Pakal-Ná, 44, 226
perpetrated by Chino, 69
and poverty, 86, 87, 214
price for killing people, 215
smugglers' mitigation of, 28
and stereotypes, 259
and unidentified bodies of border crossers,
222, 223
in Veracruz, 239–40
witnessed by Papo, 111–12, 113
witnesses of, 179
Vogt, Wendy, 84

Walker, William, 48
Wells, Michael, 15, 207
Wilson, 68, 69
women
and Bin Laden, 270
as human smugglers, 11*n*
risks faced by, 83–84, 212–13,
232, 264
Santos's reluctance regarding, 264
and sexual assault, 83–84
with Sombra, 230–31, 232
traveling with male companions, 83–84
treatment of, in Honduras, 278
See also Alma; Jesmyn
Women in Migrant Smuggling (Sanchez), 11*n*
World Bank, 20

Xatruch, Florencio, 48
Xatruches, 48
Xibalba, 39, 267

Zero, 49–50, 54, 55, 56
Zetas (gang), 100, 303
Zhagüi Pulla, Carmita Maricela, 188